DIGITAL BADGES IN EDUCATION

In recent years, digital badging systems have become a credible means through which learners can establish portfolios and articulate knowledge and skills for both academic and professional settings. *Digital Badges in Education* provides the first comprehensive overview of this emerging tool. A digital badge is an online-based visual representation that uses detailed metadata to signify learners' specific achievements and credentials in a variety of subjects across K–12 classrooms, higher education, and workplace learning. Focusing on learning design, assessment, and concrete cases in various contexts, this book explores the necessary components of badging systems, their functions and value, and the possible problems they face. These twenty-five chapters illustrate a range of successful applications of digital badges to address a broad spectrum of learning challenges and to help readers formulate solutions during the development of their digital badges learning projects.

Lin Y. Muilenburg is Associate Professor of Educational Studies at St. Mary's College of Maryland, USA.

Zane L. Berge is Professor of the Training Systems, Instructional Systems Development Graduate Program at the University of Maryland, Baltimore County, USA.

DIGITAL BADGES IN EDUCATION

Trends, Issues, and Cases

Edited by Lin Y. Muilenburg and Zane L. Berge

NEW YORK AND LONDON

First published 2016
by Routledge
711 Third Avenue, New York, NY 10017

and by Routledge
2 Park Square, Milton Park, Abingdon, Oxon OX14 4RN

Routledge is an imprint of the Taylor & Francis Group, an informa business

© 2016 Taylor & Francis

Library of Congress Cataloging-in-Publication Data
Names: Muilenburg, Lin Y., editor. | Berge, Zane L., editor.
Title: Digital badges in education : trends, issues, and cases / edited by Lin Y. Muilenburg and Zane L. Berge.
Description: New York, NY : Routledge, 2016. | Includes bibliographical references and index.
Identifiers: LCCN 2015041625| ISBN 9781138857599 (hardback) | ISBN 9781138857605 (pbk.) | ISBN 9781315718569 (ebook)
Subjects: LCSH: Digital badges. | Web-based instruction. | Internet in education.
Classification: LCC LB1028.72 .D55 2016 | DDC 371.33—dc23
LC record available at http://lccn.loc.gov/2015041625

ISBN: 978-1-138-85759-9 (hbk)
ISBN: 978-1-138-85760-5 (pbk)
ISBN: 978-1-315-71856-9 (ebk)

Typeset in Bembo
by diacriTech, Chennai

Printed and bound in the United States of America by Publishers Graphics, LLC on sustainably sourced paper.

TABLE OF CONTENTS

This chapter describes the history and context of digital badges in education. Open digital badges have emerged from the *new culture of learning* made possible by the connected and pervasive digital systems of the twenty-first century. These same highly social systems also present us with a *new culture of reputation*, influencing how we build identities online that others find credible and meaningful. Digital badge systems have pushed designers to think in innovative ways about pedagogy and assessment, and also enjoin us to think carefully about what it means to build reputations online that are grounded in verified, quality judgments.

The growing movement around open digital badges as a new way to recognize and communicate competencies will only take root and be valued within society through a functioning ecosystem. This ecosystem includes stakeholders who exchange badges directly, as well as those who add supplementary information and validation. Ultimately, the success of badges will be about more than the badges themselves, but the interplay of stakeholders around the badges, as well as authentication, verification, and validation of the learning and competencies the badges represent.

One of the biggest challenges facing the badging community is an overall lack of rigor in the quality of badging systems, stemming from a misunderstanding of the basic concepts of assessment, credentialing, and the signaling benefits of a credential. In this chapter we discuss the concept of lightweight versus heavyweight badges and explain the argument for lightweight badges along with our counter argument. We then present proposals for how to strengthen the rigor of the badging systems we all use in an attempt to increase the meaningfulness of open badges to end users.

This chapter examines how a well-defined competency-based curriculum can lead to a robust digital badging system in higher education. It provides an overview of CBE including relevant definitions and ways of measuring competencies, examples of implementation models, and a discussion on critical planning elements. The chapter also focuses on how competency-based education supports digital badging as a contemporary means to indicate achievement of specific competencies and provides current examples of implementing digital badging in competency-based approaches.

This chapter presents an overview of theoretical and research-based design considerations for the study and design of the motivational functions of digital badges with a particular focus on learning game environments. We combine our discussion of relevant theories with a review of the empirical research we conducted on this topic. To guide future research, we present the Educational Badge Typology (EBT) and Badging Player Profile (BPP) we developed. These frameworks are tools for designers seeking to implement digital badges within learning contexts that allow them to consider the role and function of badges within the game environment.

Motivation is a significant predictor of learning outcomes and badges are often described as a tool for increasing motivation. This chapter reviews what is currently known about the impact of digital badges on motivation to learn, providing the fundamentals of what badge designers and researchers should consider when evaluating the impact that badges can have on a learning opportunity. The role of motivation in education and how badges can motivate is reviewed along with current research on badges as a motivational tool.

This chapter discusses achievements and skill trees, the video game equivalents of digital badges and pathways. Video games have a long history of using these mechanics to engage players, but they are not common knowledge among many designers of badging systems. The chapter contains descriptions of design techniques used in video games when creating achievements and skill trees as well as examples from popular games.

This chapter shares instructional design principles from practice and experience to create guidelines for digital badge designs. Typical aspects of instructional design such as needs assessment, design and development, and assessment of badges are examined. Unique systemic considerations such as tasks per badge, badge families and structure, meta-badges, and learning paths are addressed. At the conclusion of this chapter the reader will have a better understanding of the design considerations to use when creating digital badges.

This chapter describes the need for digital badges in both formal and informal educational settings, the roles digital badges can play, and how digital badging can integrate the credentials produced in formal and informal settings to provide a comprehensive picture of what people know and can do. We also discuss how badging in formal and informal environments can be used to encourage communication between providers of learning experiences and employers, can provide comprehensive information that can inform hiring decisions, and how the "endorsement layer" of digital badges can be used to convey external support for serious badges.

This chapter begins with how badges are currently impacting existing practices in higher education, and then explores how badges might intersect and begin to merge with other trends in education, specifically learning at scale and big data. As these three trends mature, it is inevitable that we will see them begin to influence one another. Badges are starting to slowly make an appearance in some MOOCs, and the sheer volume of data produced in environments like this will begin to allow badge data to be used for the purposes of learning analytics and adaptive learning.

The credentials that have historically been used to document and certify a person's competency such as transcripts, certificates, and diplomas lack the flexibility and granularity needed to accurately reflect the accomplishments of contemporary learners. One alternative credential system is digital badges. Assigning value to digital badges is an important part of acceptance and use of this new credentialing system. How digital badges are valued has a lot to do with the particular stakeholder who is making the valuation. This chapter explores the different perspectives stakeholders have regarding badges, juxtaposed with several of the salient purposes for using digital badges.

This chapter describes the use of digital badges in an urban TK-12 school district in southern California. The Corona-Norco Unified School District's (CNUSD) college and career readiness initiative, Passport to Success (P2S), has been in place for the past two years. In that time, over 413,000 badges have been earned by TK-12 grade students at 49 school sites. The social nature of digital badges using Mozilla's Open Badge Infrastructure (OBI) allows students over the age of 13 to share accomplishments through social media, thus rewarding students through their peer networks and simultaneously motivating their peers to explore and achieve badges.

The Design Principles Documentation (DPD) project traced the badge development practices of 29 grantees of the MacArthur Foundation/Digital Media & Learning (DML) Badges for Lifelong Learning competition. The project documented the intended practices as outlined in their DML proposals and enacted practices as implemented in their badge systems. With a K-12 focus, this case study examines three projects, AQUAPONS, PASA, and MOUSE Wins!, which were particularly rich in examples of the nuanced, but ultimately important, interactions between intended badging practices and project contexts, and which illustrated the use of badges in formal, informal, and crowd-sourced settings.

If the afterschool movement is to prosper, programs must be recognized as important places of learning. Awarding digital badges represents an excellent strategy to accomplish this. This chapter offers two case studies detailing the use of badges by pioneering afterschool institutions. Key challenges that emerged stem from the fact that badges are a new concept for the afterschool community. To address this, we must reinforce the value and use of badges to recipients. Additionally, leaders in the field must work together to align our collective work with badges for afterschool, raise awareness of badges, and connect with other badge initiatives.

This chapter outlines a case study at Pacific Science Center in Seattle, Washington. The authors, along with a team of designers, constructed a digital badge system for a youth development program aimed at supporting students' college and career readiness. The project included interviews, focus groups, and usability tests with youth participants and program leaders. Each group shared their attitudes towards badges and offered feedback about the system. Participants responded well to the ownership and personalization of education that badges can afford, but offered skepticism when asked to imagine the practicalities of implementation and large-scale adoption of badges.

Digital Badges in Higher Education

This chapter describes the development and implementation of a set of mandatory and optional health care-related digital badges for undergraduates in Purdue University's School of Nursing program. The badges help students make connections between clinical learning and real-world health care issues.

This chapter describes the use of digital badges in an innovative transdisciplinary competency-based program. Badges were designed to reflect mastery of competencies normally found in engineering, technology, and humanities courses. The transdisciplinary curriculum and focus on mastery supported active engagement and synthesis of topics within and outside of course requirements, resulting in deeper learning. Students particularly enjoyed the ability to explore topics of their own interest while developing diverse skills reflected through badges. However, concerns were raised about the novelty of the model, potential lack of alignment with traditional degree programs, and perception of non-traditional transcripts by employers.

This chapter considers case studies of two categories of digital badging systems. The first case evaluates the scenario in which customized badging systems are developed from scratch by developers. The second case considers pre-designed, commercial badging systems that integrate with existing learning management systems. Screenshots and experiential notes are reported for each case and a table synthesizing the strengths and weaknesses of each category is provided and discussed. After considering these two cases, the authors recommend carefully analyzing learning requirements and institutional support before selecting the type of system to be deployed in badging studies or learning environments.

This chapter describes a digital badge initiative for undergraduate composition courses at Coastal Carolina University. In its inaugural semester, the program, Coastal Composition Commons (CCC), was implemented by 63 different instructors and graduate assistants who taught 122 sections of English 101 and 102 courses, which enrolled more than 2,300 undergraduate students, resulting in over 17,000 badge submissions. The CCC assesses composition skills using a flexible design that promotes instructional consistency. This case study details how the digital badge initiative has changed the landscape of the first-year composition program by serving as a fourth credit hour.

In this chapter we discuss challenges in the design of digital badge architectures based on academic delay of gratification, specific to engineering education, and we identify opportunities for fine-tuning solutions through interviews with students and instructors. We distinguish summative from cumulative badge architectures, and we argue that the former can productively rely on the principle of delayed gratification, although there may be some adverse effects of deferral. We also examine several processes through which badges acquire their local significance and effectiveness. Finally, we argue that their meaning is locally constructed and circulated through shared vocabularies of motive.

Digital Badges for Adult Learning

In this chapter, we share our experiences in developing the Teacher Learning Journeys digital badge system to support the professional development of STEM educators. Key elements of the Teacher Learning Journeys system are highlighted. Development and research observations are presented as considerations for what has already been accomplished and for future work. At the conclusion of this chapter the reader will have a better understanding of collecting feedback from learners using a badging system, providing choices around the badging content, levels of badge assessment, instructions and orientation to badges, and mentorship throughout learning experiences.

This case study provides background and details on the evolution of VIF International Education's online professional development platform and the implementation of an iterative digital badging system to formalize teacher progression toward global competence.

In 2014, a team from Swinburne University of Technology, Australia, designed and ran the Carpe Diem Massive Open Online Course (CD MOOC) that deployed digital badges to encourage participants' mastery of key elements of the Carpe Diem learning design process. Other aims in regards to badges included reward, recognition, and motivation of the CD MOOC participants. In this case study, we discuss the design, development, and implementation of badges, and the opportunities and challenges faced in this process. Participants' perception of badges is also discussed.

This chapter describes the design and development of digital badges, currently in a pilot phase, for teaching-related faculty professional development at Indiana University. Designed with a three-level framework, Learning Technologies (LT) badges are intended to help faculty gain comfort with a learning technology, plan and implement its use in multiple courses, and share results with their colleagues and larger community. Peer review of the advanced level badge by IU's teaching academy makes the badges appealing to all levels of faculty. Several academic programs are considering encouraging their faculty to earn LT badges, which could count towards their promotion and tenure applications.

This case study describes the use of digital badges in non-credit, just-in-time, short courses that target horticulture skills for the home gardener or green industry professional. Learners are able to sign up for individual badges, bundles of badges, or the full program. The badge management suite, CSULogic, was developed through an innovative public/private partnership with RelevanceLogic, Inc. This software allows for automation of badge delivery, integration with existing systems, and is agnostic to learning management systems and student information systems, allowing for deployment across sectors and industries outside of higher education. Approximately one-third of learners are awarded badges by assessment performance.

PART I
Trends and Issues

1

HISTORY AND CONTEXT OF OPEN DIGITAL BADGES

Sheryl L. Grant

Open badges are digital image files that contain metadata, and their origins are inseparable from the ethos of open source code and software protocols. No central authority controls them—they can be created by anyone with access to badge-issuing platforms or technical skills, and like most of the Internet, they follow transfer protocols that in theory allow them to be moved by their owners with relative ease across the Web, from one platform or site to another. By clicking the image file, viewers can access relevant information about the badge: criteria to earn it; evidence, such as a portfolio or testimonials; and other kinds of information that describe who issued the badge, to whom, and when.

Open digital badges emerged from a new culture of learning made possible by the connected and pervasive digital systems of the twenty-first century. These same highly social and interactive systems also presented us with a new culture of *reputation*, influencing how we build identities online that others find credible and meaningful. A combination of social media and mobile technology has created unprecedented potential to broadcast to anyone, anywhere, at any time, and the ensuing flood of information—and learning—has raised a fundamental human question: How can we tell what is good? This is not an inconsequential question, as we know from many of our current online practices to measure and rank everything from food, services, products, entertainment, and even dating. Placing open digital badges in the context of the new culture of reputation is not simply a matter of semantics, however. While it is true that digital badge systems have pushed designers to think in innovative ways about pedagogy, learning outcomes, and assessment, these same systems also enjoin us to think carefully about what it means to build reputations online that are grounded in verified, quality judgments. Indeed, many of the badge systems being built include a suite of features that are common in reputation systems: voting, tagging, ranking, rating, "liking," and commenting, to name a few.

The fusion of these two cultures—learning and reputation—is not strictly a digital phenomenon, although technology has created novel ways of merging the two. In the relatively static infrastructure of twentieth-century education, we are wed to a system of accreditation and endorsement to measure *what* is good. Our traditional institutions of learning also use grades, degrees, diplomas, licenses, and certificates to determine *who* is good. To gauge the quality of this "goodness," a small but influential cottage industry has, for better or for worse, sprung up to measure and rank schools and universities based on a combination of hard data, peer assessment, and intangibles, such as faculty dedication to teaching. While the obvious purview for both students and schools is to teach and learn, the overarching system described above blends different systems of assessment and reputation in order to determine what it means to be good—or competent, or proficient, or even masterful—in the eyes of others.

Open digital badges arise from the same human urge, which is to instill a degree of trust that people are who they say they are and can do what they claim they can do. Badges also reflect a desire to resolve a peculiar and novel problem in the digital age: To whom does reputation belong online? Only on the Internet can reputation be tethered to a proprietary system. For example, eBay, which implemented one of the first peer-to-peer evaluation systems, prevented Amazon from importing customer reputation to its own platform (Resnick, Kuwabara, Zeckhauser, & Friedman, 2000). The idea that our reputations could belong to anyone other than us is a recent phenomenon that applies equally to learning platforms like Khan Academy or massive open online courses (MOOCs) where people earn badges that can only be displayed within the technical system where they were awarded. The badges are thus only visible to those who are logged into the system, which limits the value and portability of the reputation to outside audiences. Open digital badges, however, contain standard technical specifications, and these open standards (not to be confused with academic standards) help foster a digital medium of exchange for credentials that previously did not exist, allowing learners to collect, keep, and share the reputation they have built across different platforms.

Principles of Credibility

Badges also display as interactive image files instead of lines of text, a deceptively simple difference that obscures deeply held beliefs about how we evaluate the reliability and validity of someone's reputation—including his or her learning. In theory, these open standards or metadata (data about the data) contain *evidence* of learning, a type of digital shortcut that makes it possible to verify quality judgments directly. While linking a credential to its evidence is not a novel idea, it does take new meaning online. In an open digital badge, if we wish to assess what is good, we have the option to investigate this claim directly. The implications of this cannot be overstated. Our twentieth-century model of education is based on the "assumption that teaching is necessary for learning to occur" (Thomas & Brown, 2011, p. 34), and yet, in the new culture of learning and reputation, digital technologies have made it possible for us to learn anywhere, anytime, from anyone, on any device, including from reputable, trusted sources. As a result, how we learn in the twenty-first century is shifting from "issues of authoritativeness to issues of credibility" (Davidson & Goldberg, 2009, p. 27). Open digital badges will push us to define in greater detail what this means both in theory and practice. We may be tempted to embrace badge systems that conform to more established systems because they align with recognizable conventions and currency. However, if the goal is to create more relevant systems, we need to ask what it means to ground reputation in verified, quality judgments and build novel systems that do more than replicate the status quo of the twentieth century. Open digital badges present us with a design challenge to advance *principles of credibility* that we have yet to clearly define. These principles are being embraced (if not exactly defined) in different fields like design and software engineering, where employers put less stock in schooled learning and traditional credentials, and reputation and evidence alone can be keys to advancement. Perhaps best known for these practices are Stack Overflow, the popular social Q&A site for programmers, and GitHub, a code repository for developers. In these communities, programmers leave traces of evidence that signal what they can do, both technically and socially. Recruiters looking for talented programmers can find potential job candidates in these spaces, as well as verify communication and collaboration skills that can be hard to gauge from a résumé (Capiluppi, Serebrenik, & Singer, 2013).

This vision of connecting different spheres of learning, both formal and informal, with some type of alternative credential like badges has been around for decades. In 1980, Green wrote,

> [C]ertificates, degrees, transcripts, and the like serve an essential role in establishing the 'medium of exchange' that permits activities performed in one institution of the system to be substituted for the same activities as if they had been performed in another. Perhaps some other devices could serve the same function but not be recognized as degrees, certificates, diplomas, or transcripts. (p. 78)

Nearly three decades later, at the 2007 American Educational Researchers Association (AERA) conference, Eva Baker proposed a similar medium of exchange she referred to as "qualifications" in her presidential address:

> My image of a Qualification is validated accomplishment, obtained inside or outside school. A Qualification means simply that, at various levels of challenge, a student has attained a certified trusted accomplishment.... Some Qualifications, such as securing a certification in cardiopulmonary resuscitation or network management, may demand brief, intense involvement. Qualifications would be aligned with integrated goals, tasks, learning experiences, criteria, and tests. (Baker, 2007, p. 313)

James Gee, professor of literacy studies at Arizona State University, was thinking about a similar system in 2007 when he first pitched the idea of digital badges as alternative credentials based on how video games use them to mark progress and show self-determined pathways (Moodie, 2011). In 2011, the two streams of thought merged when the MacArthur Foundation funded Mozilla to design a massively decentralized infrastructure based on standard technical specification that would connect learning across different spheres through the open badge infrastructure (OBI), much as Baker, Green, Gee, and others envisioned.

Badge-Friendly Policies

It is arguable whether digital badges would have gained the traction they have were it not for economic and policy conditions that make the timing ripe for an innovative system of alternative credentials. Badges dovetail nicely with the elimination of seat-time requirements, for example, and the potential to design more flexible learning pathways or scaffolds has made digital badges particularly relevant to competency-based learning. In 2011, Secretary Arne Duncan of the U.S. Department of Education announced, "Badges can help speed the shift from credentials that simply measure seat time, to ones that more accurately measure competency" (U.S. Department of Education, 2011, n.p.). The U.S. Department of Education (n.d.) defines competency-based learning as "a structure that creates flexibility, and allows students to progress as they demonstrate mastery of academic content, regardless of time, place, or pace of learning" (n.p.). Competency-based learning is further described as a "learning revolution" that upends the traditional paradigm of credit hours or seat-time in favor of the "bundling and unbundling" of skills and knowledge (Voorhees, 2001). The National Postsecondary Education Cooperative (U.S. Department of Education, 2002) has undertaken the job of describing skills, abilities, and knowledge necessary to perform specific tasks. Furthermore, badges fit neatly with the efforts of the National Skills Standards Board, created under the Goals 2000: Educate America Act of 1994, a coalition that seeks to catalyze a national system of skill standards, assessment, and certification. Combined, these policy initiatives could have far-reaching implications if the open badges infrastructure can create a trusted medium of exchange that ties it all together.

The key word is trusted. Competency-based learning brings with it a set of challenges that have no easy solutions. The concept of validity has significant meaning in a competency framework (Voorhees, 2001) and badges that represent validity may succeed or fail on this alone. The measure of a competency must have face validity and reflect the true meaning of that competency, or at least be reasonably associated with that competency within a given context—not a simple task. Competencies are also expected to have predictive validity such as the ability to gain admission to college or the ability to perform specific skills associated with a job. Reputation is built on valid, verified, and quality judgments, not just for badge earners, but also for the badges themselves and the medium of exchange within which they are expected to have currency.

Unbundling Education

For an innovation that is less than five years old, open digital badges have been saddled with steep expectations. Badges caught the imagination of the media even before fully functioning use cases were deployed and evaluated, particularly for their potential role in higher education. For many middle-class American families, college education has become an economic burden in a climate where student loan debt is close to one trillion dollars, surpassing both credit card and auto debt combined (Brown, Haughwout, Lee, Mabutas, & van der Klaauw, 2012). As government revenues for post-secondary education continue to decrease, the cost of attending college has increased 2.6 times since 1980 (National Center for Education Statistics, 2011). For academic years 2005–2006 to 2010–2011, 85 percent of students required some form of financial aid (90 percent for students attending for-profit universities), not including loans made directly to parents (Brown et al., 2012). Over half of all college undergraduate students take six years to complete their degree, and those who drop out lack a degree to help pay down their debt. For those who do graduate, employment is not always guaranteed.

Parallel to this economic reality, anyone with an Internet connection has access to free, open educational content, personalized learning systems, and MOOCs, or what some refer to as the "great unbundling of higher education" (Economist, 2012, n.p.). Economists predict that university business models may adapt to subscription-style revenues and greater acceptance of credits earned elsewhere. Others propose that accredited institutions of higher education could supplement existing systems with alternative credentials that increase the return on investment for all students, improving the economic impact on those who graduate and providing some degree of value to those who do not. Whether open digital badges will provide a degree of cohesion and sense-making to this buffet-style approach to traditional and non-traditional learning is as yet unknown.

Many Goals of Badges

In open digital badge systems where learning is the primary goal, the three main purposes of badge systems are to map progress and foster discovery, signal reputation beyond the community where it was earned, and incentivize learners to engage in pro-social behaviors (Gibson, Ostashewski, Flintoff, Grant, & Knight, 2013). If the early state of research on badges for learning is any indication, a majority of systems are using badges to motivate pro-social behavior, whether it is to encourage students to create and be expressive (Barata, Gama, & Jorge, 2013); recognize time management and carefulness (Haaranen, Ihantola, Hakulinen, & Korhonen, 2014, p. 33); take an exam within a certain timeframe and respond to student work with especially helpful feedback (McDaniel, Lindgren, & Friskics, 2012); solve exercises with only one attempt, returning exercises early, and completing an exercise round with full points (Hakulinen & Auvinen, 2014); or author and answer questions (Denny, 2013). One system awarded positive badges to students who commented on blogs, and negative badges to those who did not (Verbert et al., 2013). In another study, badges were a proxy for rank instead of representations of certain skills, and were displayed along with progress bars and storylines to foster healthy competition and exploration toward more specific goals, such as increased lecture attendance, class participation, content understanding, problem-solving skills, and general engagement (O'Donovan, Gain, & Marais, 2013). Another pilot used badges as an abstraction of learning analytics data through a data visualization dashboard designed to improve collaboration and increase awareness of personal activity (Charleer, Klerkx, Odriozola, Luis, & Duval, 2013). Very few of these pilots issued open digital badges, although those that did seemed to have limited value outside the classroom. In pilots where students could share badges with peers, it was unclear if they felt any reason to do so (Davis & Singh, 2015).

Few of these pilots integrated badges into the course's formal grading system. One of the few systems that linked badges with grades reported negative comments from a handful of students, leading researchers to conclude that badges should be optional (Haaranen et al., 2014). Another study found that badges, along with other game mechanics, had a positive influence on lecture attendance, although this did not significantly improve student grades (Nah, Zeng, Telaprolu, Ayyappa, & Eschenbrenner, 2014). Badge type and learner expertise appear to have an effect, according to one study (Abramovich, Schunn, & Higashi, 2013); another study on computer science undergraduates found statistically significant differences in learners' behavior, but only with some badge types, and responses to the badge system varied across two courses. Learner types have also been characterized according to the way they interact with badges. Badge *hunters, sharers*, and *dodgers* (Botički, Seow, Looi, & Baksa, 2014) resemble gamer types identified in an ethnographic study (Jakobbson, 2011). Hunters care about quantity of badges over quality of contributions, whereas sharers care about displaying badges and quality participation, and dodgers appear to have no interest in badges at all. In each of these typologies, researchers noted that students can be a combination of the different types, and may drift between them depending on the task or context. In a separate study, a different typology describes students as *masterminds* likely to be motivated by badges, whereas *conquerors* were motivated by leaderboards and progress bars, and *seekers* were motivated by storylines (O'Donovan, Gain, & Marais, 2013).

Pedagogy is not often explicitly discussed in these studies, even though one researcher observed that, "Technological design and pedagogy have the potential to co-evolve in this new medium" (Bruckman, 2004, p. 239). Students in one class, for example, were encouraged to learn from failure. Instead of a traditional grading system where students began with a maximum grade and had to maintain it, they earned points for each task they completed and worked their way up throughout the course (Hakulinen & Auvinen, 2014). Badge system designers who want to encourage creativity, innovation, and risk-taking may find that their pedagogical and assessment approaches evolve along with technical features in order to create the optimal conditions to support desired outcomes. With badge system design in its earliest stages, it is no surprise that research is limited; the field is emerging and there is a need for a comprehensive research agenda, including such basics as the definition of what a functional badge system entails (Grant, 2014).

Future of Badges

While it is difficult to gauge how many institutions or organizations may be developing badge systems, open digital badges have gained traction in large part because open standards can exist separate from, but compatible with, proprietary platforms. Each organization or institution can develop its own badge system independent of what others may choose to do, underscoring both the strength and weakness of badges. As a medium of exchange to display reputation, badges hold great potential. However, until there is widespread uptake from those who earn and share badges, as well as a trusted network of employers or schools who value them, open digital badges have a ways to go before they become reputable credentials with real currency. At a summit to spur the growth of badges in 2014, the Mozilla Foundation's executive director compared the spread of badges to the diffusion of email between 1983 and 1996, a 13-year period in which email adoption jumped from 100 thousand to over 25 million accounts (Surman, 2014). Badges, according to Surman's estimates, grew from 3,000 in 2012 to 100,000 in 2014. There is certainly motivation from the instructional technology community to experiment with badges and develop platforms, but we also know from early prototypes that badge system design is a degree more complex than putting together a learning curriculum. If email is the comparable analogy here, we should see rapid diffusion of badges across learners, platforms, and institutions in the next five years. Today, as prototypes are launched and policies begin to thread together the different "bundles" of learning both online and offline, only a percentage of earners claim badges they have earned (Grant, 2014), and even fewer store their badges in a repository where they can be accounted for at a broader ecosystem level. The dual engines of innovation and research will need to correct for this if badges are to become as commonplace as résumés and email in the years to come.

References

Abramovich, S., Schunn, C., & Higashi, R. M. (2013). Are badges useful in education?: It depends upon the type of badge and expertise of learner. *Educational Technology Research and Development, 61*, 217–232.

Baker, E. (2007). 2007 Presidential address the end(s) of testing. *Educational Researcher, 36*(6), 309–317.

Barata, G., Gama, S., & Jorge, J. (2013). Engaging engineering students with gamification: An empirical study. In *Proceedings of 5th International Conference on Games and Virtual Worlds for Serious Applications (VS-GAMES).* Bournemouth University, Bournemouth, England. Sept 11–13.

Botički, I., Seow, P., Looi, C., & Baksa, J. (2014). How can badges be used in seamless mobile learning? In J. Cook, P. Santos, & Y. Mor (Eds.), *Proceedings of Bristol Ideas in Mobile Learning 2014 Conference.* Retrieved February 4, 2016 from http://dx.doi. org/10.6084/m9.figshare.1047193.

Brown, M., Haughwout, A., Lee, D., Mabutas, M., & van der Klaauw, W. (2012). Grading student loans. *Liberty Street Economics.* Retrieved May 31, 2015 from http:// libertystreeteconomics.newyorkfed.org/2012/03/grading-student-loans.html#. U1cD7eZdW88.

Bruckman, A. (2004). Co-evolution of technological design and pedagogy in an online learning community. In S. Barab, R. Kling, & J. Gray (Eds.), *Designing virtual communities in the service of learning* (pp. 239). New York, NY: Cambridge University Press.

Capiluppi, A., Serebrenik, A., & Singer, L. (2013). Assessing technical candidates on the Web. *IEEE Software. 30*(1), 45–51.

Charleer, S., Klerkx, J., Odriozola, S., Luis, J., & Duval, E. (2013). Improving awareness and reflection through collaborative, interactive visualizations of badges. In *ARTEL13: Proceedings of the 3rd Workshop on Awareness and Reflection in Technology-Enhanced Learning,* 1103, 69–81.

Davidson, C., & Goldberg, D. (2009). *The Future of Learning Institutions in a Digital Age.* The John D. and Catherine T. MacArthur Foundation Reports on Digital Media and Learning. Cambridge, MA: MIT Press.

Davis, K., & Singh, S. (2015). Digital badges in after school learning: Documenting the perspectives and experiences of students and educators. *Computers & Education, 88,* 72–83.

Denny, P. (2013, April). The effect of virtual achievements on student engagement. In *Proceedings of the SIGCHI Conference on Human Factors in Computing Systems,* pp. 763–772. ACM.

Economist, The (2012). Higher education: Not what it used to be. *The Economist.* Retrieved May 31, 2015 from www.economist.com/news/united-states/21567373-american-universities-represent-declining-value-money-their-students-not-what-it?spc=scode& spv=xm&ah=9d7f7ab945510a56fa6d37c30b6f1709.

Friesen, N., & Wihak, C. (2013). From OER to PLAR: Credentialing for open education. *PLA Inside Out: An International Journal on Theory, Research and Practice in Prior Learning Assessment, 2*(1).

Gibson, D., Ostashewski, N., Flintoff, K., Grant, S., & Knight, E. (2013). Digital badges in education. *Education and Information Technologies, 20*(2), 403–410.

Grant, S. (2014). *What Counts as Learning: Open Digital Badges for New Opportunities.* Digital Media and Learning Research Hub Publications. Retrieved May 31, 2015 from http:// dmlhub.net/publications/what-counts-learning/.

Green, T. (1980). *Predicting the behavior of the educational system.* Syracuse, NY: Syracuse University Press.

Haaranen, L., Ihantola, P., Hakulinen, L., & Korhonen, A. (2014, March). How (not) to introduce badges to online exercises. In Proceedings of the *45th ACM Technical Symposium on Computer Science Education,* pp. 33–38. ACM.

Hakulinen, L., & Auvinen T. (2014). The effect of gamification on students with different achievement goal orientations. In *Proceedings of the Conference on Learning and Teaching in Computing and Engineering (LaTiCE)*, Kuching, Malaysia, 2014.

Jakobsson, M. (2011). The achievement machine: Understanding Xbox 360 achievements in gaming practices. *Game Studies, 11*(1), 1–22.

McDaniel, R., Lindgren, R., & Friskics, J. (2012, October). Using badges for shaping interactions in online learning environments. In *Professional Communication Conference (IPCC), 2012 IEEE International*, pp. 1–4. IEEE.

Moodie, A. (2011). Digital "badges" proposed as alternative way to assess skills. *EdSource*. Retrieved May 31, 2015 from http://edsource.org/2011/digital-badges-proposed-as-alternative-way-to-assess-skills/2475.

Mozilla Foundation and Peer 2 Peer University, in collaboration with The MacArthur Foundation (2011). *Open badges for lifelong learning*. Retrieved from https://wiki.mozilla.org/images/b/b1/OpenBadges-Working-Paper_092011.pdf.

Nah, F., Zeng, Q., Telaprolu, V., Ayyappa, A., & Eschenbrenner, B. (2014). Gamification of education: A review of literature. In *Proceedings of the HCI in Business: First International Conference, HCIB 2014, Held as Part of HCI International 2014*, Heraklion, Crete, Greece, June 22–27, 2014, pp. 401–409. Springer International Publishing.

National Center for Education Statistics (2011). Digest of Education Statistics, 2010 (NCES 2011-015). National Center for Education Statistics. Retrieved April 23, 2013 from http://nces.ed.gov/fastfacts/display.asp?id=76.

O'Donovan, S., Gain, J., & Marais, P. (2013). A case study in the gamification of a university level games development course. In *Proceedings of the South African Institute for Computer Scientists and Information Technologists Conference* (pp. 242–251). New York, NY: ACM. doi:10.1145/2513456.2513469.

Resnick, P., Kuwabara, K., Zeckhauser, R., & Friedman, E. (2000). Reputation systems. *Communications of the ACM. 43*(12), 45–48.

Surman, M. (2014). *Evolution of Open Badges*. Reconnect Learning Summit. Redmond, CA. Retrieved March 1, 2015 from www.slideshare.net/sproutfund/mark-surman-at-the-2014-open-badges-summit-to-reconnect-learning.

Thomas, D., and Brown, J. S. (2011). *A new culture of learning: Cultivating the imagination for a world of constant change*. CreateSpace Independent Publishing.

U.S. Department of Education (2011, September 15). Digital badges for learning. *Ed.gov*. Retrieved from www.ed.gov/news/speeches/digital-badges-learning.

U.S. Department of Education (n.d.). Competency-based learning or personalized learning. *ED.gov*. Retrieved from www.ed.gov/oii-news/competency-based-learning-or-personalized-learning.

U.S. Department of Education, National Center for Education Statistics (2002). *Defining and Assessing Learning: Exploring Competency-Based Initiatives, NCES 2002-159*. Prepared by Jones, E., Voorhees, R. & Paulson, K. for the Council of the National Postsecondary Education Cooperative Working Group on Competency-Based Initiatives. Washington, DC.

Verbert, K., Govaerts, S., Duval, E., Santos, J., Van Assche, F., Parra, G., & Klerkx, J. (2013). Learning dashboards: An overview and future research opportunities. *Personal and Ubiquitous Computing, 18*(6), 1–16.

Voorhees, R. A. (2001). Competency-based learning models: A necessary future. *New Directions for Institutional Research, 110*, 5–13.

2

BADGES AND COMPETENCIES

New Currency for Professional Credentials

Anne Derryberry, Deborah Everhart, and Erin Knight

Courses, credits, and credentials are already well-understood "currency" in our educational ecosystems, but how do we understand what it takes for badges and competencies to be recognized currency, particularly for learners who become job seekers and the employers who would value their achievements? To build this understanding, we analyze how badges work in ecosystems of interrelated and interdependent stakeholders and processes. How do we define our current ecosystems, including the largely unquestioned structures that may or may not be meeting the needs of stakeholders (Everhart, Seymour, & Yoshino, 2015)? How do the roles of stakeholders change when we innovate with badges and competencies in our ecosystems? Which standards frameworks are applicable? What types of endorsement build dimensions of trust and value?

Open badges provide a framework to start to answer these questions and build a new type of currency that can represent more learning, connecting learners directly to real results like jobs and career advancement (Derryberry, 2014a). Open badges use a common technology standard, the Open Badges Infrastructure, which defines the information stored with each badge (badge issuer, recipient, competency represented, assessment criteria, evidence supporting assertion of competence, etc.) and ensures that each badge is interoperable within a broader ecosystem. Any badges using the standard can be combined, stacked, and easily shared, enabling learners to earn badges from many different contexts and collect those badges to represent their professional competencies (Derryberry, 2014b). Because open badges use common definitions as delineated by the standard specification, information about standards alignments, criteria for competency mastery, and third-party endorsements can be included in the badges and carried across ecosystems to add value.

In developing badges and badge systems that reflect both educational and workplace competencies, one must understand the ecosystem in which these badges will reside and the interests and requirements of the stakeholders of that ecosystem. This chapter presents an open badges ecosystem model together with a conceptual framework for considering the ecosystem of a particular community (Derryberry, Everhart, & Knight, 2013). Drawing from examples presented by participants in the massively open online course, Badges: New Currency for Professional Credentials, as well as others, this chapter provides different views of the model as tailored to fit various educational and work-place contexts.

Open Badges Ecosystem Model

Open badges ecosystems used for competency-based learning can be understood through the perspectives of six principal sets of stakeholders:

- Learning providers;
- Assessors;
- Job seekers;
- Employers;
- Standards organizations; and
- Endorsers.

These principal stakeholders relate and interact through a set of components:

- Badges;
- Competency definitions;
- Verification;
- Authentication; and
- Validation.

When each of these elements is represented graphically, the Open Badges Ecosystem Model is organized as indicated in Figure 2.1.

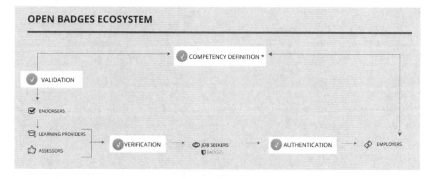

FIGURE 2.1   Open Badges Ecosystem Model (Derryberry et al., 2013).

Analyzing the Open Badges Ecosystem Model

The Current Ecosystem

We begin our analysis by considering the ecosystem of three principal stakeholder categories: learning providers, job seekers, and employers.

Traditionally, we have viewed these three sets of stakeholders as having a fairly simplistic, linear relationship: Secondary and post-secondary education institutions and other types of learning providers (e.g., trade schools) teach students and issue credentials that broadly represent students' achievements. Graduates become job seekers who take their credentials to employers, who, in turn, use job seekers' transcripts and other work/life experience to ascertain whether job seekers are suitable for employment. But we know this sequence of events is not effective in many cases because there are career readiness gaps and employers who are not able to find the skilled workers they need (Manpower Group, 2014).

Facilitating change begins with articulating where we are and what problems need solutions. Are employers getting the information they need, at the right level of specificity, to make good hiring decisions? Do current linear models (learning provider → job seeker → employer) provide good throughput? Are job seekers getting the value they need out of their educational investments? The first challenge is to define a current ecosystem, describing the roles of the primary stakeholders and how value is derived in this ecosystem, including where there are gaps or problems in the value exchange.

Kent State University adopts badges to validate faculty professional development. At Kent State University, like most higher education institutions, faculty hiring and continuation of employment require documented evidence of teaching skills. Kent State lacked a transparent and consistent methodology for documenting teaching skills, for example, capabilities in teaching online courses. The requirements for documenting their own teaching capabilities fell to the faculty, who used many different methodologies and inconsistent references. Even when there was a record of professional development activities, for example, attendance at faculty workshops, the fact of attendance did not provide evidence of what the faculty had learned and could apply. Deans and department chairs had difficulties in reviewing competencies and making decisions about teaching assignments.

To help address this issue, Kent State University's Office of Continuing and Distance Education uses badges to validate faculty professional development activities (Nestor, 2014). Badges provide a way of capturing the competencies gained through workshops and training courses. Rather than simply recording that someone attended training, workshops include assessments verifying participants' ability to apply what they have learned. The leveled-up badges for the workshops document the application of teaching skills such as course design, classroom management, and student collaboration. Learning outcomes for each badge are defined by professional development subject matter experts and evaluated via rubrics. The evidence of learning represented in the badges helps faculty understand and promote their own teaching skills.

The consumers of these badges are deans, department chairs, and department coordinators who need to understand faculty teaching skills and their ability to perform specific duties such as teaching fully online courses. The professional development badges provide documented evidence of teaching skills and indicate the faculty member's ability to learn new skills and evolve as the demands of teaching change. This type of evidence is useful for all stakeholders in tenure and promotion reviews. It is also useful in making practical decisions about which faculty are prepared to teach online, facilitating curriculum planning and new hiring decisions.

Open Badges as Currency

Once the basic ecosystem is understood, the next challenge is to articulate clearly the currency of the ecosystem using badges as artifacts of valid assessments of well-defined competencies, including transparent, portable evidence of a badge holder's achievements. This involves adding a new stakeholder category—assessors—and two new components: badges and competency definitions.

With the inclusion of badges and definitions of competencies in the basic ecosystem model, we can see the decoupling of learning providers and competency/ skill assessment; hence, the addition of "assessors" as another set of stakeholders. Why? Since badges are tied to the assessment of defined competencies, badges are awarded when an individual demonstrates or provides evidence of mastery of competencies. Learning providers can also function as assessors, but these roles can be differentiated, and in some cases separated.

Assessors are responsible for valid and reliable assessments. In other words, assessors must ensure that the assessment activities accurately reflect the targeted competencies, and that they do so consistently, regardless of who the learner *cum* job seeker is or how they attained the competencies (Ary, Jacobs, & Razavich, 1985, p. 213). When an assessment is successfully completed, the assessor issues a badge to the learner in recognition of that individual's competency mastery, and the badge holder adds that badge to his/her professional identity.

The process by which an individual mastered the competencies is not necessarily relevant or important to an employer if a healthy open badges ecosystem reliably assesses the competencies. Further value is provided by the clear definition of competencies represented in the criteria of the badges, as well as demonstrated evidence of competency. More detail about the badge holder's skills and competencies can be communicated than through a traditional diploma or transcript with end-of-course grades. Badges representing competencies become currency when stakeholders in the ecosystem recognize and get use value from them.

New program at the University of California at Davis uses badges to document competency attainment. In 2011, a team within the Agricultural Sustainability Institute (ASI) at the University of California at Davis began to design a new undergraduate major in sustainable agriculture and food systems. The interdisciplinary program, at the nexus of ASI and eight departments in the university's College of Agriculture and Environmental Sciences, is highly hands-on, emphasizing experiential learning through internships and field work.

The curriculum design team knew that traditional approaches to testing and grading would not fully reflect the learning outcomes of the program. They wanted students to be able to present their experiences in ways that were meaningful to themselves and each other, to the faculty, and to employers. Importantly, they needed an approach that was woven through the entire curriculum, not simply on a course-by-course basis.

Ultimately, the curriculum was organized around seven core competencies, which were identified and defined in collaboration with targeted employers. These competencies—understanding values, personal development, interpersonal communications, civic engagement, systems thinking, experimentation and inquiry, and strategic management—are each linked to badges that students can earn through their learning experiences as they gain and demonstrate skills and knowledge (Mozilla Open Badges & HASTAC, 2014). A student can demonstrate systems thinking, for example, by integrating environmental, economic, and societal perspectives into their analysis of complex systems.

Badges can be earned through self-assessment and reflection activities and through portfolio evaluation by faculty and mentors (Open Badges Blog, 2014). Students display their badges in their online profile, together with information the student provides about their learning experience, including evidence (e.g., videos, diagrams, and assessment scores) that demonstrates their competence. The goal is for students to communicate their skills and to learn about what they know through that exercise.

The team at ASI has maintained a rigorous process in designing a badge system that is rooted in the shared values of the institution, faculty, students, and employers. By adhering to these values, ASI has ensured that all constituencies recognize the value of the badges within the ecosystem.

Standards Frameworks for an Open Badges Ecosystem

Existing competency or performance standards frameworks can usefully scaffold the value of badges exchanged among stakeholders in the ecosystem. Often, these frameworks are provided by standards organizations, the next element to examine within the open badges ecosystem.

Employers reference applicable regulations, industry standards, and best practices. Employers need employees whose skills and competencies support and advance business objectives in accordance with these requirements.

Standards organizations get input from academic research, government bodies, and employers about evolving best practices and, in turn, provide guidance, even governance, over business practices. Standards organizations in some cases define which sets of competencies and types of assessment are valid. Collaboration on the design of badge systems between standards organizations, learning providers, assessors, and employers can benefit all stakeholders. When badges are tied to assessments that are themselves aligned to industry standards and best practices, the likelihood of finding the right match between a job seeker (badge holder) and an employer is greatly improved. Further, learning providers can use these alignments to offer programs that better match employer requirements and offer greater value to their learners. If the ecosystem is in balance in this way, the exchange value of badges is high; when the ecosystem is out of alignment, the value of badges is low.

Newport City (Wales) Homes partners with regional employers to develop a set of badges tied to industry standards. Newport City Homes (NCH) provides community services to residents in Newport, Wales. As part of their employee development initiatives, they have created a set of badges that document key competencies (Price, 2014). Employees are required to demonstrate job skills that are valuable not only in their roles at NCH, but also as part of the economic development imperatives in Wales. As such, the definitions of these competencies are tied to industry standards in health and safety, security, government housing guidelines, data management, and other relevant guidelines and regulations. For example, criteria for the housing trainee badge were developed in conjunction with the Community Housing Cymru, the representative body for housing associations across Wales. These criteria include employee requirements aligned to both local and country standards, such as Schedule 1 of the Wales Housing Act, government regulations for rental housing.

Learners participate in a variety of activities to achieve their badges—some topics are learned via online courses, others via face-to-face training and job shadowing. Evidence of learning is captured in compliance training assessments, course activities, recorded observations of relevant work behaviors, and other artifacts that learners can use in multiple contexts.

NCH's badges initiative supports their sustainable communities' goals not only by developing and rewarding applicable skills in their own employees, but also by providing opportunities for learners to broaden their employment options and contribute to the Welsh economy. The badges work alongside traditional certifications to document learning achievements that are practical, valuable, and interoperable in an ecosystem that aligns standards and guidelines with learning outcomes and employment opportunities.

Endorsement of Badges in an Open Badges Ecosystem

For open badges to gain recognition and acceptance within an ecosystem, several elements are needed: endorsers and processes for verification, authentication, and validation. These elements provide the structure that ensures transparency in and confidence about the badging process.

Technically, this includes authenticating that the badge holder is indeed the one who earned the badge, and that the badges displayed by a badge holder are verified as coming from an authorized source. The technology of an open badge system implementation addresses these needs. Basic verification and authentication are handled through the Open Badges Infrastructure, which can verify that a specific badge was in fact issued to a specific learner by a specific issuing organization (Mozilla Project, 2012).

This tells us very little, however, about the value of the badge, a construct that relies on valid and reliable assessment methodologies. How is value derived? What constitutes valid learning and assessment processes? Learning providers have traditionally relied on academic accreditation and/or reputation as substantiation of the value of the credentials they issue. Because badges are agnostic as to the learning processes leading to competency mastery, badge systems open the field for non-traditional learning providers as well as innovative learning methodologies in traditional institutions. While these new providers and approaches may be as effective, if not more so, than traditional strategies, there are legitimate concerns about validating the attainment of competencies these approaches purport to convey to learners. With new approaches comes the need for clear, transparent validation of learning through meaningful, reliable assessment methodologies that reflect the targeted competencies; without such rigor, the value of the badges earned through demonstration and assessment is questionable.

Endorsers provide third-party validation that recognizes the value of badges as assessed and issued by specific badge issuers (Badge Alliance, 2014). Endorsers are organizations with the expertise to analyze the quality of specific badges, including how the badge is defined, the competencies it represents, its standards alignments, the process of assessing the badge earner, and the qualifications of the badge issuer to structure and evaluate the learning achievement represented by the badge. Endorsements can be viewed by job seekers, educators, and employers to better understand the value of specific badges, building dimensions of trust in the ecosystem.

Aurora (Colorado) Public Schools works with postsecondary education institutions and regional employers to gain endorsement and adoption of APS badges. Aurora (Colorado) Public Schools (APS) began the pilot of a district-wide badging program in the spring of 2015 (Aurora Public Schools, 2014). In the first phase of implementation, APS addressed the district's goal to prepare all students to matriculate to postsecondary education or to enter the workforce. APS teachers at all grade levels are awarding badges for achievement of these "twenty-first-century skills," as defined by the State of Colorado.

The badge system was designed by a team within the superintendent's office. All badges are issued by APS teachers through the district's badge platform in order to verify the authenticity of the badges students collect. The district will also be appending badges, together with their associated metadata, to the traditional transcripts in order to verify further that the badges are part of each student's official record.

The rubrics and guidelines established by the district superintendent's office ensure badge awards adhere to state-mandated learning outcomes by grade level, while still providing teachers flexibility to interpret those mandates within the context of their own classrooms and lesson plans. In addition, special attention is paid to district-wide equivalencies so that, for example, the sixth-grade-level "Critical Thinking: Innovation" badge reflects the same competencies, regardless of who receives that badge or which sixth-grade teacher in the district issues it. This multi-pronged approach to validation was deemed critical to transparency and to broad-based recognition of the significance of the badges earned by each student.

APS is working with community colleges in the state to gain endorsement of the community college system for the APS badges, with the goal that APS badges will be accepted as a valid and valued part of a student's application for admission. Ongoing discussions are held with regional employers to seek endorsement of APS badges together with commitments to consider students with particular badge collections as eligible for internships, apprenticeships, job interviews, or other grade-/age-appropriate opportunities.

Each of these factors is seen as essential to long-term adoption and acceptance of the APS badge initiative by students, teachers, parents, employers, and the community-at-large. The stakeholders in this community are working together to establish the value of APS badges in their ecosystem.

Conclusion

Understanding how to value and fully integrate new ways of evaluating and communicating learning, specifically via open badges, into society requires a full ecosystem approach. This ecosystem consists of the expected stakeholders—the badge issuers, earners, and employers, who directly exchange badges for recognition, reputation, and evaluation—in concert with organizations and entities that add standards and endorsements to the badges to influence their valuation. The complexity does not stop there, as the interplay of these stakeholders, perceived value, and usage of the badges involves much more than the badges themselves; also involved are authentication, verification, and validation of the competencies and learning they represent. By enumerating and understanding these ecosystem factors, we can design the right systems to expand the adoption, acceptance, and impact of badges' value.

References

Ary, D., Jacobs, L. C., & Razavich, A. (1985). *Introduction to research in education* (3rd ed.). New York, NY: Holt Rinehart Winston.

Aurora Public Schools (2014). APS Digital Badge Program. Retrieved from http://badge.aurorak12.org/.

Badge Alliance (2014). Badge endorsement: Getting started. Retrieved from www. badgealliance.org/endorsement/.

Derryberry, A. (2014a). Aligning badges with workplace requirements. Retrieved from www.youtube.com/watch?v=uhxWJ6OLn2A.

Derryberry, A. (2014b). The role of badges in alternative credentialing. Retrieved from www.youtube.com/watch?v=Y8-qv1G5DVM.

Derryberry, A., Everhart, D., & Knight, E. (2013). Badges: New currency for professional credentials. Retrieved from www.coursesites.com/s/_BadgeMOOC.

Everhart, D., Sandeen, C., Seymour, D., & Yoshino, K. (2014). Clarifying competency-based education terms: A lexicon. Retrieved from http://bbbb.blackboard.com/ competency-based-education-definitions.

Everhart, D., Seymour, D., & Yoshino, K. (2015). The currency of higher education: Credits and competencies. Retrieved from http://bbbb.blackboard.com/Currencyof HigherEducation.

Manpower Group (2014). The talent shortage continues. Retrieved from www.manpower group.com/wps/wcm/connect/0b882c15-38bf-41f3-8882-44c33d0e2952/2014_ Talent_Shortage_WP_US2.pdf?MOD=AJPERES&ContentCache=NONE.

Mozilla Open Badges & HASTAC (2014). Open badges case study: University of California, Davis, sustainable agriculture & food systems. Retrieved from www.reconnectlearning. org/wp-content/uploads/2014/01/UC-Davis_case_study_final.pdf.

Mozilla Project (2012). Open badges infrastructure. Retrieved from https://wiki.mozilla. org/Badges/About.

Nestor, M. (2014). Kent State University faculty workshop badges. Retrieved from www. kent.edu/onlineteaching/workshops/badges.

Open Badges Blog (2014). Assessment strategies for effective badge systems. Retrieved from http://openbadges.tumblr.com/post/78130197990/openbadgesmooc-session-8-assessment-strategies.

Price, B. (2014). Newport City Homes: Open badges criteria. Retrieved from www. newportcityhomes.com/Downloads/NCH_Criteria.pdf.

3

THE CASE FOR RIGOR IN OPEN BADGES

Richard E. West and Daniel L. Randall

When you first said badges, I had such a bad impression of what that would mean.

This is what one representative of our state's Office of Education told us in a meeting to explain possible applications of open badging for teacher professional development within the state. By the end of our conversation, she was enthusiastic about our proposed ideas. However, she admitted that initially she was hesitant because badging had for her a negative connotation related to gamifying learning. It took a lot of discussion to explain to her that open badges can, in fact, be pieces of rigorous assessment and credentialing systems.

We have been issuing open badges for two years and have had many conversations on the potential value of open badges with university faculty, K–12 administrators, technology coordinators, teachers, and researchers. Often the first step in these conversations is to attempt to rewire misconceptions about open badges and what they can represent in teaching/learning systems. One of the biggest challenges we have seen in the badging community is a flood of badges for things as useless as attendance, creating a login, or simply existing as a learner. We believe these badges represent a misunderstanding of the basic concepts of assessment, credentialing, and the supposed benefit of a credential to learners who want their badges to signal knowledge, skills, or expertise to others. In addition, we believe this flood of "lightweight" badges has given the general public a poor impression of badges, requiring all of us to persuade stakeholders that badging can, in fact, be rigorous.

It is our real concern that if the badging community does not show how open badges and their assessment processes can be rigorous and meaningful, the badging movement will fade away as a fun diversion, but one that ultimately had no real impact on educational reform. In this chapter, we will attempt to do what Joseph (2014) argued the badging community needed: initiate a conversation among badge proponents about how to improve the badging movement. We begin our chapter by overviewing the variety of badges available, and discuss the concept of lightweight versus heavyweight badges (terms already being used to discuss this divide). We will then explain the rationale some have given for lightweight badges, and follow with our counter argument for why this lightweight approach to badging weakens the badging movement, diminishes the signaling power of earned badges, and clutters the ability of people to find meaningful badges. We will then finish with our argument for why badge providers should focus on the rigor of their badging process, and strive to create badges of consequence.

Badge "Weight" and "System"

In the badging community, a distinction has been made between so-called "lightweight" badges and the alternative. While these are the terms typically used, one problem with badging conversations is the practice of using the term "badges" when the intent is to describe a *learning and assessment process*. In the end, badges themselves are merely credentials, and can be awarded at the conclusion of any experience where people have engaged in meaningful learning followed by rigorous assessment. "Lightweight badges" represent learning and assessment processes that reward students for something as basic as participation, with no or little other criteria (Casilli, 2014). An example is the MozFest Reveler badges from Mozilla. These practices issue badges considered by "many in the badge community to be throwaway badges with little to no social meaning" (Casilli, 2014, para. 2).

This is contrasted with more rigorous assessment and learning processes that could make a badge carry "weight" and even "gravity" with potential employers, social networks, and credentialing institutions (Catalano, 2014) because of the quality of the criteria and expected outcomes for learners as well as the strategies for evaluating that learning. For example, Tim Newby at Purdue University awards open badges to preservice teachers for successfully completing projects that require many hours of work in learning about educational technologies and developing lesson plans and units for successfully utilizing the tools in their future teaching.

Another example might be the Supporter to Reporter (S2R) system ("Introducing S2R Medals," 2013). While S2R uses medals instead of badges, their system is unique in that the medals represent real achievement by students developing skills in journalistic writing and production. Because the medals represent true skills and understanding, they serve as gatekeepers for the students' progress: Once students have reached a certain level of expertise and accumulated a number of medals, they are given the opportunity to apply their skills as journalists at real sporting events. Thus, the medals carry real weight for the students' academics and represent authentic achievements. As Tran, Schenke, and Hickey

(2014) explained, this badge system provided substantial motivational power for students, likely because the badges carried strong social capital within the professional community due to the badges being awarded for real achievements.

Besides the contrast between lightweight and heavyweight badging, Joseph (2014) explained that there are differences between local and global badge ecosystems, each with unique advantages and challenges. By local, Joseph meant badges intended only for the person's learning space, such as a class or an educational game. However, global badge ecosystems stretch beyond the immediate learning space to draw connections about learning and competency across institutions and even formal/informal learning. This type of ecosystem is the most powerful, as it gets beyond badging for gamification and allows badges to serve as recognized credentials in learning portfolios to peers, employers, instructors, and other authority figures. As Joseph argued, "Badging systems can be designed to offer both types of values—value within an organization and value to those outside it—but, the required features and networks are different" (para 6). In current conversations about badges, local and global badge ecosystems are discussed together, which undermines much of the conversation because they truly do have different purposes. While a system could conceivably be designed to do both, in reality this is rare. In this chapter, and in our work, we focus on global badge ecosystems—systems where the badges are intended to provide value beyond the immediate learning experience and space, and communicate something about the learner to others. In these kinds of situations, it is critical that the badges be rigorous enough to communicate this learner information correctly.

Argument for Lightweight Badges

Not all in the badging community feel that lightweight badging practices are devoid of value. Casilli (2014) argued that *accretion*, or the layering effect of badges over time, produces value. She posited that badge accretion allows for value to emerge in unexpected ways from the accumulated effect of many different lightweight badges. One example she gave is of a student earning a lightweight badge for attending a class trip to a natural history museum. Alone, this badge may not represent much, but combined with other lightweight badges showing attendance at online webinars or local community classes may "highlight potential pathways and future area(s) of interest" (para. 5). Thus, lightweight badges may not be as meaningful individually, but taken together they paint a fuller picture of the individual's interests and activities (Knight, 2014). This discussion assumes, however, that employers, admissions boards, and other interested parties can understand threads of interests woven by collections of lightweight badges and care about a person's interests and activities as much as they do their competencies, abilities, and performances.

Another important stakeholder for badging systems are the badge earners themselves, and thus a badge that is not valued by anyone else except the earner may still be important, perhaps as a memory of a positive experience or accomplishment (Casilli, 2014). However, if badge earners collect too many lightweight badges along the way, will they continue to hold value, particularly months or years later? Similarly, Knight (2014) argued that if employers or other interested consumers of badges find value in these lightweight offerings, then the badging community should not discredit them. However, it is not yet proven what value these lightweight badges actually provide, and whether employers do, in fact, value them.

Counterargument: How Badging Has Lost Its Way

We do not personally find these arguments for lightweight assessment and badging practices persuasive. First, we believe the argument of accretion, where badges layer and build up value in mass, is tenuous because it relies on employers, educational systems, social networks, and even badge earners themselves digging through the web of badges to understand how they "add up." Like any communication medium, badges benefit when the medium is not cluttered with spam. This is important even if the only consumer of a particular collection of badges is the badge earner him/herself as people often miss good information sent through popular communication mediums when they are overwhelmed by the sea of spam and irrelevant information. For many, email and social media messaging (e.g., overcrowded Facebook/Twitter feeds) have now reached this same tipping point because of the difficulty of sorting the messages of value from amongst the mass of spam. Some may argue that lightweight badges are different because the earner chooses to earn them. However, we also choose to sign up for much of the clutter that comes through our communication channels, and then regret later when it becomes difficult to find or notice what is important.

Badging, while a new phenomenon, still benefits from being largely uncluttered, and thus it is possible to communicate through badges what skills, knowledge, and expertise a person has. However, if every individual earns hundreds, thousands, or hundreds of thousands of badges, then the clutter dilutes the ability of end users to identify the quality badges of value from the rest.

Whereas this problem soon becomes impossible to manage for employers and persons outside of the badge earner, it is also a problem for "badgers" to manage and record their own learning. How many of us have kept every certificate of completion for every course completed? Eventually, the accumulation of all these lightweight credentials becomes burdensome to maintain, and we clean house, discarding these credentials. Too much clutter makes it difficult to derive benefit from the things of real worth, and perhaps badging systems would benefit from the movement towards the "life-changing magic" (Kondo, 2014) of "clutter busting" (Palmer, 2009).

The second challenge with lightweight badging is that it can be demotivating to some learners, particularly when the badges are used to "gamify" an experience without being intrinsically meaningful. The difficulty in motivating learners through extrinsic rewards is supported by many studies in the literature. Deci, Koestner, and Ryan (2001) reviewed decades of research on motivation and found that

> tangible rewards—both material rewards, such as pizza parties for reading books, and symbolic rewards, such as good student awards—are widely advocated by many educators and are used in many classrooms, yet the evidence suggests that these rewards tend to undermine intrinsic motivation for the rewarded activity. (p. 15)

Thus, lightweight badges, often given simply to "encourage" learners to do something the instructor wants, might sometimes have the opposite motivational effect.

The most effective motivation in learning comes from within the learner (intrinsic motivation) or from an emphasis on the learner's ability to choose and direct their learning. We believe for this reason that badging can have a tremendously powerful effect on motivation by allowing learners greater choices in the types of experiences they can participate in and authoritative credit for engaging in these experiences. If future educational systems found ways to marry formal and informal learning experiences together—for example, so that students could earn badges through formal classwork or through informal internship, work, or self-directed experiences—this opportunity to afford greater choice and agency to learners should yield higher motivation. However, for this to work, the badges need to "count"—i.e., the badges would need to represent true learning outcomes and be a credential that matters to others, thus providing the students with a real choice in earning these alternative credentials. If, instead, badges only represent watered-down outcomes of attendance or participation, and not evidence of real learning, they will not be afforded much credibility by authority figures, and thus will not represent a real option for motivated learners.

The third problem with lightweight badging is that it can place undue emphasis on the badge itself—its name and cool graphics—instead of on the assessment that qualified one to receive the badge; it is the focus on micro-assessments and micro-credentials that are so disruptive to current educational models. Earning a badge in and of itself is not necessarily important or worth mentioning—developing a legitimate skill, or acquiring new knowledge and being recognized as having done so successfully, is.

The Disruptive Power of Badges as Legitimate Credentials

While badges can have many uses, we believe the most disruptive and yet perhaps most powerful use is as a micro-credential. Our formal educational system is full of credentials that take many forms, such as degrees, transcripts, certificates, and licenses. However, many of these credentials are only awarded after an extended period of time or a great deal of experience. Additionally, these credentials may not carry as much information as one might suspect. For instance, while a transcript includes lots of information, such as the courses taken and the grades earned, this information is vague and perhaps meaningless to those outside of the issuing institution or even outside a course. What does a course name mean (e.g., is a 400 level course really more challenging than a 200 level course)? What content was covered in the course and to what depth? What content would you expect such a course to cover that was not taught?

In addition, the value of using open badges as micro-credentials is that a person can receive recognition for learning smaller chunks of content and be able to more easily communicate exactly what they know and can do. For instance, an undergraduate introductory web programming course could cover a number of programming topics, such as HTML, CSS, PHP, Javascript, along with an introduction to Ruby. Earning a B in the course does little to show what a student learned as they may have done very well in HTML, CSS, and PHP, but done horribly at Javascript and Ruby. If this were the case, a company looking to hire the student as a summer intern may see this grade and think the student lacks the skills needed for the position, even though the student might never be using Javascript or Ruby in that position.

A worse scenario would be if the company believed the student had the required expertise but planned to have the student work almost exclusively with Javascript. Awarding open badges for each area of expertise the student gained in the course would better communicate the student's skills. Additionally, the metadata contained in the badge can provide deeper insights into the student's abilities with links to the badge requirements the student had to meet and evidence of the work completed. Information about the student's performance is completely open, and the viewer could even re-grade the project themselves to see if it meets the criteria. Many badge providers do not provide this kind of metadata on the badges they issue, and some third-party companies strip out this data in lieu of their own branding. These actions completely miss, in our view, the most powerful and disruptive aspect of badges.

Using open badges as a legitimate credential also provides a way for skills gained in informal (outside of school) settings to be recognized. Since badges can be used by traditional learning institutions as well, open badges provide an exciting opportunity to easily recognize learning that takes place in multiple settings. Returning to our example of the undergraduate web programming course, a student entering the course may already have earned badges for HTML and CSS from an online learning provider. The professor of the course could equate the badges the student has already earned with the HTML and CSS skills the course is meant to teach and excuse the student from doing those assignments, instead giving the student more time and opportunity to learn Javascript and Ruby, two languages the student has little experience with and has been struggling to learn. The end result could be that the student completes the course with a stronger background in all of the course topics.

This scenario is exciting to think about, but is highly dependent on badges having weight and being recognized as legitimate credentials of learning.

Proposed Solutions to Bolster the Badging Movement

In this section, we propose several ideas regarding how to improve the rigor of the badge movement, making it easier for stakeholders to accept and support badging practices.

Badges and Gamification

Badges are often associated with gamification, although many other rewards systems can be used to gamify learning, such as points, levels, ranks, and upgrades. With such a wide range of options for providing rewards within learning systems, we propose reserving badges for achievements and skills that have weight and meaning outside the learning environment. For instance, points or progress towards a level-up can be used as a reward for logging into a learning environment (e.g., attending class), while badges could be reserved for more significant accomplishments, such as learning specific skills or successfully completing challenges.

Another possibility—perhaps a less desirable one since it could be confusing—is to have two types of badges. The first type would only have meaning within the learning environment, while the second type could have meaning outside of the learning environment and would be more rigorous. For example, an educational game or system could use a badging system that awards many lightweight "gamifying" badges within the local ecosystem—badges that mean something to the gamers, but not much to people outside of the system. It would also award weightier badges that recognize significant work and learning, and those badges could be exported as open badges. This kind of approach might be a good compromise, as a gamer might earn dozens of badges in the game, but then only export the most important badges that were meaningful as a credential of real achievement.

Two Components of Badge Rigor

When describing badging systems, we argue for two components of rigor, and the overall rigor of the badge can be compromised if either of the two components is weakened. The first key aspect of a badge's rigor is the criteria required to earn the badge so that, even though the badge is still a micro-credential, earning the badge truly indicates a meaningful accomplishment. The second component of a badge's rigor is in the assessing process. Most of the badges we have created are issued only after a human grader (we call them badge reviewers) has reviewed the learner's submission. This poses natural challenges in maintaining similar practices across all of the badge reviewers, but this can be overcome through training and reviewing of the data analytics to spot abnormal badge issuing practices.

However, the concern over assessment rigor is not unique to human graders, but can also be true of badges issued automatically. Indeed, we first became cognizant of the need for rigor in badging when exploring an early version of Mozilla's Webmaker site. While manipulating some code in an attempt to understand a programming concept, one of the authors managed to unknowingly correct the code. A badge was automatically issued to him even though he did not know what he had done to make the code correct. He is now the owner of a badge that does not accurately reflect his true knowledge and skills. The criteria for earning this badge may have been rigorous, but clearly the process did not maintain rigor when assessing his actual skill.

We recommend being attentive to both components of rigor by first developing quality and defensible criteria for how a person earns a badge and second by being careful that the assessment practices that qualify someone to receive it are valid and reliable.

Collaboration among Badge Providers

One possible method to improve the reputation and rigor of the badging movement could be through developing collaborations among badge providers to create brands of badges that are recognized beyond any one entity. For example, if multiple universities shared and issued badges around the skills required for preservice teachers to teach online effectively, this would likely quickly become adopted as a leading brand of professional development for teachers. Because universities carry prestige, a consortium of universities authorizing, developing, assessing, and issuing badges as a micro-credential would carry substantial weight. Similar consortiums could be organized in other arenas. For example, a consortium of companies providing training on computer science skills, and issuing badges they all endorse, or a professional organization collaborating with community organizations to create and issue badges that validate skills important to the community and the profession.

Final Thoughts

As Moore (2013) argued, for open badges and similar open credentials to be accepted, the assessment practices and criteria they represent need to have "credibility with both educational institutions and employers" (p. 75). It is because we believe in the power of open badges and their flexible evaluation processes to provide a positive disruption to educational practices that we are anxious for the movement to succeed. In order to do so, we believe badge providers need to recognize open badges as more than just points in a gamification system, and more than just glitz to impress learners. We need to consider the power open badges could have as micro-credentials of authentic learning when they are issued following significant, intentional effort and achievement.

To achieve this vision, we offer the following as key principles:

- Badges should be awarded through rigorous assessment processes and thus carry weight and represent real achievement and learning.
- Badges should have value outside of the learning environment and have signaling power to other persons about the learner's skill and knowledge.
- While we believe gamification can be a positive thing in education, badges should do more than be points or check marks.
- Badge providers should use rigorous assessment practices to truly authenticate what a learner knows against clear and measurable criteria.
- Badge providers would likely benefit from collaborating together to build brands that will grow the credibility and acceptance of the badges being issued.

Increasing the rigor of our learning and assessment processes and criteria for open badges is not easy, and will require much thought, design, and attention. However, the payoff could be substantial, and could help open badges achieve the potential many have always thought they could.

References

Casilli, C. (2014, February 26). The myth of the lightweight badge. *Persona*. Retrieved from http://carlacasilli.wordpress.com/2014/02/26/the-myth-of-the-lightweight-badge/.

Catalano, F. (2014, February 25). Digital badges need mass to matter. *edSurge*. Retrieved from www.edsurge.com/n/2014-02-24-digital-badges-need-mass-to-matter.

Deci, E. L., Koestner, R., & Ryan, R. M. (2001). Extrinsic rewards and intrinsic motivation in education: Reconsidered once again. *Review of Educational Research*, 71(1), 1–27.

Introducing S2R Medals (2013, January 22). Retrieved May 14, 2015 from www.makewav.es/story/463170/title/introducings2rmedals.

Joseph, B. (2014, March 13). My beef with badges. *DML Central*. Retrieved from http://dmlcentral.net/blog/barry-joseph/my-beef-badges.

Kleinman, S. (2012, August 27). Taxonomic failure. *Tychoish*. Retrieved from www.tychoish.com/posts/taxonomic-failure/.

Knight, E. (2014, April 8). More beef. *World of E's*. Retrieved from http://erinknight.com/post/82103788980/more-beefs.

Kondo, M. (2014). *The life-changing magic of tidying up: The Japanese art of decluttering and organizing* (First North American edition). (C. Hirano, Trans.). New York, NY: Ten Speed Press.

Moore, M. G. (2013). Independent learning, MOOCs, and the Open Badges Infrastructure. *American Journal of Distance Education*, 27(2), 75–76. doi:10.1080/08923647.2013.786935.

Palmer, B. (2009). *Clutter busting: Letting go of what's holding you back*. Novato, CA: New World Library.

Tran, C., Schenke, K., & Hickey, D. T. (2014). Design principles for motivating learning with digital badges: Consideration of contextual factors of recognition and assessment. In J. L. Polman, E. A. Kyza, D. K. O'Neill, I. Tabak, W. R. Penuel, A. S. Jurow, K. O'Connor, T. Lee, & L. D'Amico (Eds.), *Learning and becoming in practice: The International Conference of the Learning Sciences (ICLS) 2014, Volume 2* (pp. 1027–1031). Boulder, CO: International Society of the Learning Sciences.

4

COMPETENCY-BASED EDUCATION AND THE RELATIONSHIP TO DIGITAL BADGES

Rhonda D. Blackburn, Stella C. S. Porto, and Jacklyn J. Thompson

Competency-based education (CBE) or competency-based training is an offshoot of outcomes-based education, with a prominent difference between the two: In the former, advancement is achieved by visible mastery of specific skills, as opposed to time spent on study considered in the latter. Behaviorism and performance measurement based on observable behaviors are the cornerstones of CBE (Horton, 2002). A significant growth of various competency-based approaches are a result of several factors including: the steady demand for flexible adult education, an expanding open education movement, doubts about the value of traditional U.S. higher education, recent Department of Education (DOE) endorsements of competency projects in higher education, changes to federal student aid policies, and contributions from the Gates and Lumina foundations (Gallagher, 2014).

Online competency-based education is considered by many as a major disruption in higher education with the potential to reconcile the growing skills gap while meeting the needs of an increasing population of post-traditional learners who recognize the value of specific, easily identifiable, and portable skills in the job market (Weise, 2014). The demographics of students looking into secondary education have certainly shifted. Students are more commonly working adults who are looking for opportunities to advance their careers or move into other fields. They need educational options that are purposeful, authentic, and closely connected to the needs of the labor market. These prospective students need to have their knowledge and acquired skills recognized in such a way that they will enter their learning path in a more personalized fashion. Thus, learners' competencies should be easily displayed and understood by employers and educational organizations.

Digital badges are a digital display that acknowledges, recognizes, and validates the achievement of skills and competencies through explicit evidence. At the core of the description of a digital badge is competency. Therefore, to build a robust badging system, a competency-based curriculum should be in place. This concept is especially true in higher education, where the curriculum is, for the most part, described through courses, which may not explicitly specify the students' accomplishments.

In the following sections, we demonstrate how a competency-based curriculum is a good option for implementing a robust badging system in higher education and offer explanations and examples that may aid in the planning of such systems. We start with a conceptual definition of competencies and explain how a solid assessment framework is required to measure the achievement of such competencies. Next, we showcase how institutions are implementing competency-based education on their campuses and conclude with a discussion of the ties between the competency-based curriculum and digital badges.

A Competency-Based Curriculum: Defining and Measuring Competencies

In developing curriculum, the starting point is most commonly describing the learning objectives. How do learning objectives compare to competencies? At its heart, competency is a fundamental concept in the field of curriculum development, especially in adult education. It is based on explicitly defining the applied knowledge and skills necessary for someone to perform successfully certain real-world work activities. Learning objectives speak to instructional outcomes and, therefore, they need to be measurable statements. These measurable statements are then the origin of course assessments, which will verify that the student has in fact learned what the course intended to teach. For the most part, when writing curriculum with clear learning objectives, with a student-centric approach, one is closer to being able to develop a competency-based curriculum (Everhart, 2014). Generally, each competency will be associated to one or a few interrelated learning objectives. Such objectives, which can be directly measured as part of the learning experience, are all required to demonstrate one's competence in a given task. That said, it is possible to develop curriculum that is entirely described through competencies (Everhart, 2014).

The advantage of setting competencies as the base for a new curricular architecture is that learning can be broken into independent modules, which can stand on their own, without being necessarily connected to a course (Weise, 2014). This modularity allows for flexibility in the curriculum such as rearranging, re-combining, stacking, and re-scaling to tailor to the needs of students or to be used by different programs targeting distinct industries in a multidisciplinary fashion. It gives students more choice, both in terms of the size of the credentials as well as subject areas. This potential is a definite driver for lower costs for higher education institutions.

The quality of a CBE program will depend directly on its competency framework, which defines and supports the actual credential. Competency-based credentials require clarity and transparency among academic leaders, faculty, students, and employers (Bushway & Everhart, 2014). Bates (2014) acknowledges that deriving the competencies the right way, such that the needs of students, educators, and employers are met, is key and also the most challenging part of CBE; this is an iterative process that "tries to break down abstract vague goals into specific measurable competencies" (para. 8). Being measurable is of essence, since CBE requires specific evidence that demonstrates achievement of competencies.

When we discuss the development of competencies, we are referring to the entire construction of the instructional structure of the course, meaning the development of learning outcomes and assessments, which will serve as the tool for measuring the mastery of such competencies. As discussed by Johnstone and Soares (2014), "The process for mapping competencies to courses, learning outcomes, and assessments is explicit" (p. 15). Competencies are established first at the program level, and then serve as drivers to topics addressed in different courses, which will have distinct learning outcomes with different levels of mastery aligned to assessments. The latter, which can take a variety of forms, from essays to quizzes to projects, should be "built using the expertise of industry and academic subject-matter experts, thus ensuring content validity" (Johnstone & Soares, 2014, p. 18).

As part of the process of achieving competencies at their own pace, students rely heavily on feedback about their performance. They should know exactly how and when they will get such feedback in order to plan their studies. The richness and timeliness of faculty feedback about students' progress towards demonstrating the assigned competencies are key elements in high-quality, competency-based programs and the feedback should be explicitly aligned with competencies (Bushway & Everhart, 2014).

Implementing a CBE program requires not only these major changes in the curriculum architecture and validation of assessments, but also the development of a comprehensive student support system, which will provide students with the resources (learning materials, assessment instructions, rubrics, personal feedback, etc.) they need to succeed. All these changes have a significant impact on the business models adopted by institutions.

Implementation Models in Higher Education

Competency-based education programs come in many flavors and designs, but they come down to two distinct models, direct assessment and credit equivalency. To implement either, the accreditation agency will be involved, but the adoption of direct assessment requires approval by DOE, in order to be eligible for federal financial aid.

To dig deeper into each model, direct assessment allows an institution to break away from the credit hour and seat time by assessing students on what they know and allowing them to progress depending on their achievements (Book, 2014). In this approach, institutions can create a program that has an open path or a more prescriptive path through competencies. Students are provided with an assessment for each competency to determine their achievement. Depending on the achievement level, students take one of two paths; they either achieve the competency and move to the next one, or they are directed to resources and are subsequently reassessed until competence is reached. As they progress through the program, students have the opportunity to interact with other students, but there should be some form of contact with their mentor/faculty/coach at least once a week to determine how they are progressing. The completion of the competencies provides students with a credential.

The other model, credit equivalency, is more traditional and relies on the credit hour (Book, 2014). This option consists of courses that are mapped back to credit courses and seat time, which contain a group of competencies with assessments and content. Institutions have flexibility on how they set up the courses, which may include but are not limited to:

- assessing students first to guide them in their learning;
- providing resources, formative assessments, and/or activities that students can use before taking their summative assessment;
- separating competencies into distinct units with resources and assessments; and
- combining competencies together to show how they stack or interact with one another.

These options are not exclusive from one another but are decisions that institutions must consider as CBE programs are being developed. In this approach, many institutions take the learning objectives from credit hour courses and align them to competencies. This provides a direct walk-over from the CBE courses back to the credit hour courses. With this alignment, the credit equivalency model may be more cohort based, which has greater potential, as compared to direct assessment, for scheduled or optional collaborative opportunities.

Since both the direct assessment and credit equivalency models are self-paced with the option of rolling start dates and program cohorts, students will be progressing through the program at different paces with the potential of different paths; therefore, they will require more student support than in traditionally paced programs. To accommodate this change and deliver high-quality support and guidance to students, the faculty role will need to be unbundled to have different people take over the many tasks of a faculty member. The unbundled roles can include assessor, mentor, advisor, coach, competency experts, and tutor (Bushway &

Everhart, 2014). Both models can experience distribution of the faculty role, but it may look different depending on the model and institutional expectations.

Throughout both of these models, assessment is key. One decision is between objective and authentic assessments or utilizing both to show mastery (Bushway & Everhart, 2014). Assessments that determine competency achievement need to be robust and aligned to real-world skills and scenarios; therefore, competencies should be defined through explicit learning objectives that demonstrate all dimensions of the competency. The achievement of the competencies within a program rely on these assessments, which in turn are critical to the integrity of the program.

Critical Elements of a CBE Program

As institutions plan for the implementation of a CBE program, there are many areas that are critical to success. In addition to the model used, other decisions include competency structure, student assessment, unbundling of the faculty role, and collaboration opportunities.

One of the primary advantages of a CBE program is the transparency that is inherent in a CBE credential and the close alignment between competencies and assessments (Bushway & Everhart, 2014). As stated earlier, assessments are critical and must be valid, reliable, secure, and linked to a robust and valid competency structure (Johnstone & Soares, 2014). As with traditional models, an assessment can take many forms. Whether it is an objective exam, authentic assessment, or a rubric-based assessment, it needs to show mastery of a competency. One way to do this is to look at various industries and mimic a workplace skill through such assessments (Bushway & Everhart, 2014). While this is a powerful way to show mastery in a competency, this approach may require more time to assess, multiple assessors, and attention to the inter-rater reliability of graders (Johnstone & Soares, 2014).

As stated earlier, unbundling the faculty role may be critical to ensure high-quality student support. As assessments are submitted, the person assessing will need to provide feedback quickly for student progression. An advisor will work with a student on a study plan, which will inform the coach or faculty mentor on student progress and provide guidance to the student working through the course of study. In addition to a faculty mentor, an expert may be assigned to each competency to help students who experience setbacks (Bushway & Everhart, 2014). There are many other roles that can be implemented; therefore, the institution should determine resource allocation and how faculty members are compensated for this work. Helping students at the right time is a significant advantage to this division of labor.

One consideration that may be a challenge is collaboration between students, since students may be at different segments of the program even if they start at the same time. "That said, the social component of traditional higher education can be an integral part of learning, and this dynamic may suffer when students work independently, without consistent cohorts of peers in educational programs" (Educause Learning Initiative, 2014, p. 2). The opportunity for students to collaborate, ask questions, and share insight with each other should be available since a self-paced environment can be quite isolating and sometimes discouraging. Providing collaboration opportunities, which may require different tactics than traditional models, can make students feel like they are part of a community of learners (Hill, 2015). For example, institutions can consider the addition of time-based cohorts within their curriculum to increase collaboration. Allowing the student to partner with someone who is working on the same materials to develop a cohort project increases the opportunity for team-based assessments.

CBE and Digital Badging

The working adult is a pragmatic learner (Leader-Kelley, 2013) juggling work, family, and school demands and acquiring much of their skills and knowledge through their activities and experiences in the workplace. Explicitly recognizing such experiences, providing applicable assessments, and matching them to formal education have long been part of adult learning, including among those working on prior learning assessments, for example. Therefore, adult learning needs should be met by strategies that are targeted, purposeful, and authentic. Digital badges based on competency curriculums are one promising way to address these needs.

As discussed, competencies are a way to describe achievements, skills, and abilities in a way that can be understood by a variety of groups, without any need to determine the exact path of how these were acquired, whether through academic training or on-the-job experience. Using competencies as building blocks, digital badges serve as micro-credentials and give competencies a standardized visual format that can be shared among learners' social and professional networks and/or displayed in e-portfolios using software plug-ins from badging platforms and then recognized by colleagues, educational institutions, and employers. The ability to link badges to artifacts, which are tied to competencies, allows the viewer to verify the knowledge and skill of the person holding the badge. With this deep connection, badges become more than a visual symbol, they are explicit evidence of skills, competencies, and experience.

In addition to supporting academic progress, badges can be developed to support behavioral tendencies, such as when students help each other. For example, in a CBE program, students could earn a badge of "guider" based on helpful interactions in discussion threads and chat sessions. These badges would indicate to other students that this is a person who could help them, which is encouraging in a self-paced program.

In Practice

Higher education institutions can use competency approaches with digital badging to expand degree, certificate, and non-credit extension programs as well as award micro-credentials throughout a program. Badges serve as supplements and alternatives to traditional grading and indicate mastery of skills and achievements to audiences in and outside the class (Kim, 2014). The following examples highlight important aspects of competency-based digital badging programs including: alignment to workplace skills; flexibility and personalization; sequential learning; importance of mentors, frequent assessment, and feedback; and the value of issuing micro-credentials.

Since 2014, Concordia University Wisconsin has offered an online Masters of Educational Technology with achievement of competency-based digital badges such as Digital Literacy and Collaborative Learning embedded throughout the program. The program was built with input from employers on relevant competencies and emphasizes a flexible, individual approach, with each student guided by a mentor, and multiple opportunities for assessment and feedback from instructors and peers (Bull, 2015). The program differentiates its competency-based badges from traditional CBE (Bull, 2014), but it aligns closely with the credit equivalency model by mapping badges to partial credit hours. Badges equate from a quarter credit hour to a full credit hour, with about four to six badges earned per three-credit online course (Bull, 2015).

As another example, in 2015, Brandman University partnered with Credly, an online toolkit for managing digital badges, to offer the first DOE-sponsored direct assessment competency-based Bachelor's degrees that provide "official digital badges to certify discrete skills as students advance through degree-based programs" (Credly, 2015, para. 2). Brandman's approach emphasizes the ability to earn badges throughout a program and share and display them as "professional capital" in real time (Brahm as quoted in Credly, 2015, para. 3).

Institutions can also consider non-credit, skills-based digital badging programs, like the Certified Gardener and Integrated Sustainability Management Programs from Colorado State University. These online programs from CSU are based on a hierarchical system of badges that can be earned individually or grouped together, including Trek Badges, Quest Badges, and finally Mastery Badges (Colorado State University, n.d.), and exemplify scaffolding and sequential learning by encouraging mastery of granular skills first and showcasing advancement.

CBE and Digital Badges in the Future

Lifelong learning encompasses many forms of learning and instructional methodologies, and more importantly, it includes both formal and informal learning and recognizes the achievement of new knowledge and skills through many paths (Leader-Kelley, 2013). Lifelong learning has gained strength given the continuous societal need to retrain workers. In the current crossroads of needs and demands, competency-based education represents a two-fold disruption in the achievement of credentials: The curriculum architecture defines achievements through a well-known and accepted framework of abilities, skills, and knowledge with a direct association to evidence-based assessments, while the learner support system is construed in such a way that allows students to progress at their own pace with personalized and timely feedback to ensure their success aligns to individual needs. As competency-based education continues to broaden its scope within higher education, and the competencies used become accepted by employers, the badges associated with CBE programs will gain importance in the labor market. In the future, employers will begin to look for visual indicators of skills needed for a position and will be looking to digital badges, which offer the visual language to express these credentials.

The relationship between CBE and digital badging has great potential in higher education to provide an ecosystem for lifelong learners where skills, competencies, and levels of mastery are recognized and distinguished. CBE and digital badging also offer modularity for potential reuse and remixing as well as creating new models of paying for credentials, such as by piece or subscription. In the context of higher and continuing education, one solid path to a robust digital badging system is to build a competency-based curriculum that includes a powerful assessment framework.

References

Bates, T. (2014, September 15). The strengths and weaknesses of competency-based learning in a digital age [Blog post]. Retrieved from www.tonybates.ca/2014/09/15/the-strengths-and-weaknesses-of-competency-based-learning-in-a-digital-age/.

Book, P. (2014). *All hands on deck: Ten lessons from early adopters of competency-based education* [White paper]. Retrieved from WICHE Cooperative for Educational Technologies website: http://wcet.wiche.edu/wcet/docs/summit/AllHandsOnDeck-Final.pdf.

Bull, B. (2014, September 7). You can now earn a Master's Degree in #edTech through competency-based digital badges [Blog post]. Retrieved from http://etale.org/main/2014/09/07/you-can-now-earn-a-masters-degree-in-edtech-through-competency-based-digital-badges/.

Bull, B. (2015, April). *Competency based digital badges as curricular building blocks in online degree programs*. Session presented at USDLA 2015 Conference, St. Louis, MO.

Bushway, D., & Everhart, D. (2014, December 8). Investing in quality competency-based education. *Educause Review*. Retrieved from www.educause.edu/ero/article/investing-quality-competency-based-education.

Colorado State University (n.d.). Skills-based digital badges for learning. Retrieved from www.online.colostate.edu/badges/.

Credly (2015, January 7). Brandman University teams up with Credly to issue digital badges as part of competency-based education degrees. Retrieved from http://blog.credly.com/brandman-cbe-badges/.

Educause Learning Initiative (2014, February 11). Seven things you should know about competency-based education [Fact sheet]. Retrieved from www.educause.edu/library/resources/7-things-you-should-know-about-competency-based-education.

Everhart, D. (2014, October 30). Competency based learning key characteristic: Outcomes-based [Blog post]. Retrieved from http://blog.blackboard.com/competency-based-learning-key-characteristic-outcomes-based/.

Gallagher, C. (2014). Disrupting the game-changer: Remembering the history of competency-based education. *Change: The Magazine of Higher Learning, 46*(6), 16–23. Retrieved from http://dx.doi.org/10.1080/00091383.2014.969177.

Hill, P. (2015, February 9). Flat world and CBE: Self-paced does not imply isolation [Blog post]. Retrieved from http://mfeldstein.com/flatworld-cbe-self-paced-does-not-imply-isolation/.

Horton, S. (2002). The competency movement. In S. Horton, A. Hondeghem, and D. Farnham (Eds.), *Competency management in the public sector: European variations on a theme* (pp. 3–15). Retrieved from www.iospress.nl/book/competency-management-in-the-public-sector/.

Johnstone, S., & Soares L. (2014, March). Principles for developing competency-based education programs. *Change: The Magazine of Higher Learning, 46*(2), 12–19. Retrieved from www.tandfonline.com/doi/pdf/10.1080/00091383.2014.896705.

Kim, J. (2014, June 1). A course badging case study. *Inside Higher Ed.* Retrieved from www.insidehighered.com/blogs/technology-and-learning/ course-badging-case-study.

Leader-Kelley, C. (2013, September). Lifelong learning: Luxury or survival? *The evoLLLution.* Retrieved from www.evolllution.com/featured/lifelong-learning-luxury-survival/.

Weise, M. (2014, November 10). Got skills? Why online competency-based education is the disruptive innovation for higher education. *Educause Review.* Retrieved from www.educause.edu/ero/article/got-skills-why-online-competency-based-education-disruptive-innovation-higher-education.

5

GOOD BADGES, EVIL BADGES?

Impact of Badge Design on Learning from Games

Melissa L. Biles and Jan L. Plass

Digital badges are visual indicators of accomplishments or skills within a digital environment that are awarded to the user in recognition of a particular action or series of actions related to the content. These graphic artifacts represent evidence of specific claims about learning recognized via a badge system that identifies the relevant skills and achievements and defines the criteria and assessment guidelines by which the system evaluates whether those criteria have been met (Design Principles Documentation Project, 2014). In the game industry, with the introduction of Microsoft's Xbox Live Gamerscore in 2005, Sony's PlayStation Network trophies in 2008, and Valve's Steam achievements also in 2008, badges gained widespread use representing in-game achievements, providing focused goals, challenges, clear standards, and performance affirmation within an online social context (Dickey, 2005).

Badges used in educational contexts are seen as a way to evaluate learning outside of a formal school environment by providing a symbolic reward for particular knowledge, skills, or achievements (Abramovich, Schunn, & Higashi, 2013). Services like the Mozilla Open Badges Project allow these badges to be shared within a common infrastructure, thereby permitting badges to be collected across different platforms and experiences. While educational badge use is gaining in popularity in online learning contexts, such as Edmodo.com, the Khan Academy, and Mozilla's P2PU, the field of research into the effects of different types of badge design on cognitive, motivational, and learning outcomes is relatively new.

In this chapter, we explore the motivational function of badges and their use as incentives to guide and recognize players' learning-related behaviors. In the first part of the chapter, we outline some of the theoretical underpinnings around the design of incentive systems within learning games, exploring situated learning, individual and situational interest, motivation, and achievement goal theory. In the second part of the chapter, we provide a brief overview of game designers' insights into incentive system design as well as several developing typologies around the uses and functions of badges.

Theory Guiding Design

In order to provide a theoretical foundation for the study and design of badges with a motivational function, we start by exploring the context of our investigation into badges—learning with digital games. Learning is a process that is highly contextual and involves the co-construction of knowledge in a community of practice (Lave & Wenger, 1991). For adult learners, the context in which learning is situated is often their real life, but it has been suggested that for middle school students, video games can provide similarly rich contexts in which meaningful learning can take place (Gee, 2003). As a medium, video games combine rule-based systems with simplified representations of reality that provide students with opportunities to explore aspects of identity, engage in meaning-making through cycles of action and interpretation, and practice perspective-taking (Squire, 2006). Some game worlds, such as *Quest Atlantis*, create immersive environments where learners attempt to solve problems by developing hypotheses, conducting experiments with simulated versions of real-life instruments, and interacting with other players and non-player characters (NPCs) in an interactive narrative (Barab, Thomas, Dodge, Carteaux, & Tuzun, 2005). We are interested in how badges shape this context, what aspects of the learning process are affected by badges, and how this impact depends on the specific designs of badges. Of particular interest here are learners' individual and situational interest in the learning activity and topic, as well as their motivation to learn.

Individual and Situational Interest

Interest and motivation are often described as interdependent (Ainley, 2006; Krapp, 2005; Schiefele, 1991). Interest can directly affect students' motivation, learning strategies, and ability to process information (Schiefele, 1991). In fact, the word *motivation* often appears as part of the definition of interest, such as Hidi's (2006) definition as "a unique motivational variable, as well as a psychological state that occurs during interactions between persons and their objects of interest, and is characterized by increased attention, concentration and affect" (p. 70). Interest is typically described as content-specific for an individual, e.g., a learner may be interested in history but not in math. In addition, interest mediates the relationship between students' overarching goal orientation, their task-related goals, and their motivation to learn (Ainley, 2006).

Situational interest, which is brought about by different circumstances or events, differs from individual interest, which is characterized by an intrinsic desire or predisposition to engage with a particular subject matter or activity repeatedly over a period of time. For example, a person may not be interested in math (low individual interest), but might find a math game with badges situationally interesting. This is important since situational interest can lead to individual interest in the topic that persists over time (Hidi & Renninger, 2006; Krapp, 2007; Schiefele, 1991). One method by which this transition can occur is outlined by Hidi and Renninger's (2006) four-phase model of interest development: triggered situational interest, maintained situational interest, emerging individual interest, and well-developed individual interest. Triggered situational interests are the short-term changes in affective and cognitive processing, which have often been found to be triggered by the environment in which the content is presented (e.g., group work, puzzles, computers, and technology), therefore making a video game context a highly likely vehicle to deliver the targeted learning content in a way that encourages the learner to enter into the first phase of the journey toward well-developed individual interest.

We have found evidence that different learning game design elements (e.g., game mechanics, mode of play, and badge use) can impact the situational interest experienced by the learner (Plass & Kaplan, in press). Using our geometry puzzle game, *Noobs vs. Leets*, we isolated the game mechanic, i.e., the core player interactions with the game state, to create a rule mechanic and an arithmetic mechanic. Results showed that the arithmetic condition was situationally more interesting than the rule condition; with regard to learning outcomes, there were diminishing returns over time. This suggested that while the arithmetic mechanic may promote learning in the short term, in order to sustain the learning gains over time, the conceptual rule-based mechanic was more effective (Plass et al., 2012).

Other research comparing three different modes of play (solo play, two-player competitive play, or two-player cooperative play) in a game on factoring for middle school students showed that competition and collaboration elicited greater situational interest than individual play, suggesting that the social mode of play is able to impact affect (Plass et al., 2013). These studies and their follow-ups into further aspects of learning games (Biles, Plass, & Homer, 2014; Biles & Plass, 2015; Homer et al., 2014; Plass, O'Keefe, Biles, Frye, & Homer, 2014) indicate that different design factors can impact both situational interest and learning outcomes.

Motivation in Games

Although it is accepted that video games, as a medium, exhibit characteristics that increase player interest, there are a number of differing perspectives on player motivation. Sherry, Lucas, Greenberg, and Lachlan (2006) outline six reasons why people play games: competition, fantasy, social interaction, challenge, diversion, and arousal. Other research by Yee (2006) identified three main motivational components for online gamers: achievement, social, and immersion.

Motivation and player types. Within the game industry, attempts to answer the difficult question of why people play video games have been made using methods such as opinion polls, measures of prior experience, and evidence from success of other games, but rarely do they delve into the details surrounding the true core motivations of the player (Klug & Schell, 2006). Game designers have historically approached this topic from a more practical perspective by trying to understand factors like player types, play styles, and reasons for playing (Frye, 2013). For example, Bartle (1996) described four player types based on in-game behavior in Multi-User Dungeon (MUD) games: killers, achievers, socializers, and explorers. Alternatively, Klug and Schell (2006) suggest nine player types: competitor, explorer, collector, achiever, joker, director, storyteller, performer, and craftsman. Frye (2013) combined these and other social science and game industry perspectives within a multi-dimensional framework of seven different player profiles: competitor, explorer, socializer, challenger/achiever, fantasizer, escaper, and stimulation seeker.

Using Frye's (2013) player framework as a guide, our research on badges identified five different player types based on the different motivations that emerged from student interviews (see Figure 5.1). For the students who were not motivated by the badges to begin with, the reasons revolved around a lack of a common platform for sharing across games (*socializer*) and the desire for the badge to be linked to some sort of in-game reward (*achiever*) that has some degree of utility (e.g., power-up or currency).

Notably, within the context of educational games, some students reported that the learning content or the mechanic of the game required more focus and attention; therefore, the badges became a secondary motivation. Overall, the *stimulation seekers* were mainly focused on enjoying the graphics, story, or characters, were more interested in attaining a flow state, and generally wanted easy, manageable levels that didn't require too much effort. The *explorers* wanted to investigate their environments, learn more about what was occurring within the game, and

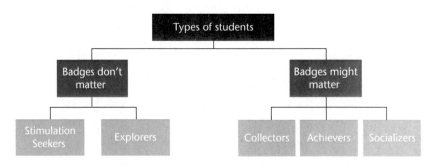

FIGURE 5.1 Badging Player Profile (BPP). Student reactions to badge situations.

focused more on the mechanics of play. The *collectors* focused on challenges and achievements that they could acquire and admire, even admitting that they would play harder levels just to get all of the "things." The *achievers* looked for new, more challenging experiences that made them think or made them feel that they did something the average person could not. Lastly, the *socializers* focused on whether or not they could show off or share with their peers, where rankings created importance and drive to succeed.

Goal orientation. Achievement is inextricably linked to goals, since individuals find it useful to have a clear idea of what they are working towards (Beck, 1983). The academic study of achievement motivation is centered on two types of goal-oriented activity: (1) *mastery goals,* where the focus is on learning and understanding in order to achieve competence; and (2) *performance goals,* where the focus is on achievement relative to peers or avoiding negative views of their competency (Dweck, 1986). Depending on the type of goals the students are aiming towards, they will respond differently to changes in a situation, especially failure (Ames, 1992; Urdan, 1997). Mastery goals have been shown to have a slight advantage over performance goals; however, the range of conflicting outcomes in past research is likely due to the influence of other factors (Utman, 1997). For example, goal orientations, when combined with students' interest in the situation and the topic, can affect their motivation to learn in a given setting (Krapp, 2005; Schiefele, 1991).

Goal orientations can be invoked or reinforced with particular types of feedback (Butler, 2000; O'Keefe, 2013). Because performance-approach goals are generally focused on demonstrating ability relative to others, rather than developing it (Dweck & Leggett, 1988; Elliot, 2005), normative feedback, such as a percentile score, can support a performance-approach goal orientation (Butler, 1993, 1995). In contrast, mastery-approach goals are concerned with developing abilities and improving upon them (Dweck & Leggett, 1988; Elliot, 2005). Therefore, feedback about how one has performed compared to their previous performance, such as their objective score on a game across several trials, can support a mastery-approach goal orientation (Butler, 1993, 1995). Badges can be designed to provide either type of feedback, and we are interested in how such designs impact learning outcomes.

Mastery-approach goals are highly adaptive. They provide a framework that supports an authentic desire for challenges and learning, and resilience in the face of failure (O'Keefe, 2013). Performance-approach goals have also been shown to be beneficial, although they support a motivation for learning that is less authentic. Most notably, they tend to be associated with relatively higher task performance and achievement (Harackiewicz, Barron, Pintrich, Elliot, & Thrash, 2002) due to motivational factors such as anticipated negative social consequences.

In our preliminary study into the relationship between badges and students' mastery goal orientation, middle school students (N = 52) were randomly assigned to play for 25 minutes either the *badges* or *no-badges* version of *Noobs vs. Leets,* a digital game to teach geometry. Our findings from pretest and posttest geometry scores suggested that badges overall did not result in increased learning. However, further analysis using pretest scores on the mastery achievement goal orientation subscale from the *Patterns of Adaptive Learning Scales* (PALS) (Midgley, 2002) suggested that badges can help students with low mastery goal orientation, but may hinder students with high mastery goal orientation. A subsequent study (N = 85) using the same game, assigned students to play a performance, mastery, or no-badges version of the same game. While students in the performance badges condition performed significantly better on the posttest than the mastery badges condition, there was a significant interaction between badges and situational interest. Students with high situational interest performed better with mastery badges and students with low situational interest performed better with performance badges (CREATE, 2015).

Badges in the Context of Digital Games for Learning

Our research has suggested that commercial learning game designers have reservations about the volume of badge implementation projects being created across educational contexts that don't appear to be informed by current game industry heuristics (Biles, Plass, & Homer, 2014). While this criticism has clear relevance within the learning game design field, the frameworks around the use and function of badges within commercial games can also be generalized to multiple badge contexts when we consider how these incentive systems are designed and implemented. Ultimately, we believe that the way that badges are designed, and how they are interpreted by the learner, will determine the motivational and cognitive effects they will have on users (Plass et al., 2014).

Motivation and Badging

There are a number of differing viewpoints about the nature of the relationship between player motivation and badging systems. While some game designers we interviewed believe that badges might stifle students' intrinsic motivation and cause an increased focus on winning new badges, others within the Open Badges community support the use of badges, considering them to be a promising way to evaluate student performance (Grant, 2014). Initial findings by Li, Huang, and Cavusoglu (2012) on badge use in *StackOverflow* found that participants who earned more badges reported increased motivation to contribute in a range of online activities. Preliminary research with cloud-based learning systems found that the increase in number of badges earned was linked to a decrease in performance avoidance goals (Higashi, Abramovich, Shoop, & Schunn, 2012). While altering particular game elements (i.e., goals, choice, and personalization) has been shown to affect the intrinsic motivation of the player (Abramovich et al., 2013), we found a lack of research connecting badges designed for specific goal-related functions with player motivation frameworks.

Incentive System Design

Among the game features that designers use to motivate players are the game narrative, game mechanic, game character design, aesthetic design, the musical score/sounds of the game and the incentive system (Plass, Homer, & Kinzer, 2015). The most commonly used feature in games, or in gamification, is the incentive system, which can include points, stars, power-ups, and the like. Our semi-structured interviews with game designers (N = 5) with a combined 80 years of professional experience in game design and theory have highlighted four high-level concerns around incentive system design (CREATE, 2015). First, they stressed the importance of integrating well thought-out incentive design from the beginning of the game design planning process, rather than design elements being added on at the end as an afterthought. Since incentive design can take many forms, from the more subtle narrative framing to more overt points or rewards, creating an end product that seamlessly combines the appropriate incentivizing structures with the types of game mechanics being used is a necessary part of the iterative development process. Second, the game designers highlighted the need to take into account the characteristics of the target audience, in particular factors such as player type and the target audience's familiarity with the game genre. For example, for a player who is able to speed run *Super Mario Bros*, an incentive for merely completing all the levels is not going to be very motivating to them as they are looking for feedback and recognition of more challenging types of in-game achievements (Biles, Plass, & Homer, 2014).

Third, the designers emphasized that the game's incentive system plays a key role in increasing and maintaining appeal. When the main goal of the incentive system was defined as maintaining and sustaining engagement with the game, usability was emphasized as playing a major role in incentivizing the player (Biles, Plass, & Homer, 2014). On a basic level, if the experience is visually or auditorily pleasing to the player, their affective response has the potential to greatly impact the player's engagement and perseverance. Similar learning benefits were found with affective design research that showed inducing positive emotions in learners via the visual design of learning materials (Plass & Kaplan, in press; Um, Plass, Hayward, & Homer, 2013).

Last, another key strategy mentioned by the designers was to include multiple routes and incentives within a game. Creating clear mechanics and rules that are easy to understand, yet allow players to make their own decisions about what they find interesting and what they want their goal to be, allows for different player types to tailor the game experience toward their own particular preferences and inclinations (Biles, Plass, & Homer, 2014). After all, as one game designer emphasized, a game feature that is extrinsic to one player's gameplay experience is intrinsic to another player's gameplay experience. This ensures that the game has potential appeal to a wider variety of prior experience levels, player types, and individual interest levels within the target population.

Function of Incentive Systems

Our interview research also revealed three main functions of the game's incentive system: signaling, challenging, and affirming. *Signaling* is when the incentive system implicitly provides a tutorial for in-game activities by showing which aspects are either important or not important to focus on in order to be successful within the game. Signaling can also highlight experiences that others are having that might be of interest to the player via methods like social sharing, peer rankings, or alternatively, to highlight in-game actions and modes of play that the game designer thinks are interesting and noteworthy. *Challenging* is when the incentive system presents tasks that require particular levels of skill or persistence to achieve. This sets the bar for receiving that 5-star or 100 percent rating, to push the player out of the comfort zone of their normal level of in-game performance. *Affirming* is when the incentive system acknowledges what the player is doing by providing just-in-time affirmation of in-game actions so that the player feels like the game is paying attention to them (by using appropriate, relevant feedback). This helps the player realize they are improving by giving them a standard to achieve that is considered a normative skill level to move on to the next challenge. When players don't receive this type of feedback, our interviews with students revealed that they can become disheartened or unmotivated because they feel they are not successful at progressing at an appropriate rate within the game.

When designing badge systems, learning game designers need to make conscious decisions about which types of accomplishments or skills to recognize via badges. In our research, game designers emphasized that badges should be used in ways that increase appeal and don't just replicate something the game has already recognized or rewarded via alternate game structures (Biles, Plass, & Homer, 2014). These choices can affect how players perceive the function of those badges relative to the game structure and their own personal goal orientation and other internal characteristics.

Function of Badges

A number of scholars have started to conceptualize different frameworks from which to approach badges. Hickey's (2012) heuristic outlines four badge functions: (1) *recognizing learning*—both formal and informal, often in the form of a credential; (2) *assessing learning*—formative and/or summative assessment, linked to evidence-centered design (ECD); (3) *motivating learning*—extrinsic versus intrinsic debate; and (4) *evaluating learning*—tracking patterns in badge acquisition to illuminate learning pathways. Conversely, from a social psychology perspective, Antin and Churchill (2011) outline five badge functions: (1) *goal setting*—a challenge to achieve; (2) *instruction*—what types of activities are possible within a system; (3) *reputation*—representative of a user's interests, experience, and expertise; (4) *status/affirmation*—status symbol or evidence of past successes; and (5) *group identification*—shared experience around a set of activities.

Other approaches take a more descriptive perspective, categorizing typical badge types (aka trophy and achievement systems) in mainstream video games, such as *Grand Theft Auto, Mass Effect, Spore,* and *World of Warcraft* in 14 different content classifications that occur: tutorial, completion, collection, virtuosity, hard mode, special play style, veteran, loyalty, curiosity, luck, mini-game, multi-player, paragon, and fandom (Montola, Nummenmaa, Lucero, Boberg, & Korhonen, 2009). As badges in these games don't link to any concrete external rewards, they mostly parallel Hickey's (2012) recognition of player performance and achievement. On a more granular level, connections can be drawn with Antin and Churchill's (2011) function by loosely pairing the content classifications according to the following categories: (1) *goal setting*—completion, collection, virtuosity; (2) *instruction*—tutorial, special play style, curiosity; (3) *reputation*—virtuosity, hard mode, veteran, loyalty, multi-player, fandom; (4) *status/affirmation*—hard mode, special play style, veteran, loyalty; and (5) *group identification* (most of the aforementioned classifications). Depending on the player's perception of the badge and their motivational state, these content types can be classified into different functional categories based on the game content and genre.

Combining concepts from achievement goal theory and existing badge frameworks with main themes from student and game designer interviews, we focused in our own work on the types of badges linked to formative, process-based characteristics inherent to in-game activity, resulting in the Educational Badge Typology (EBT) framework (Figure 5.2) that outlines our approach to framing the different functions of badges within learning games. The EBT was further refined during a focus group of educators, industry peers, and academics during a conference convened around the topic of educational badge research and design (CREATE, 2015).

On the top level, we divide badges into two main categories: (1) *formative, process-based* badges that serve to monitor the student's learning and provide continual feedback on their learning progress and engagement with the game's sub-goals; and (2) *summative, credentialing* badges that serve as evidence of a particular learning progression made up of *meta level badges* that outline main learning goals and the multiple *criterion badges* within each meta badge that specify the particular subgoals that constitute evidence of relevant task completion. Within formative, process-based badges, we further subdivide into those badges that are related or unrelated to the overall learning goals. Badges unrelated to learning goals might include tasks like character customization or exploration of narrative components

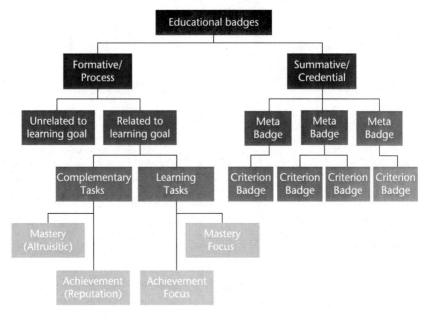

FIGURE 5.2 Educational Badge Typology (EBT). Framework for classifying the functions of educational badges within digital learning environments.

of the game. Badges related to learning goals are divided into complementary tasks and learning tasks. *Complementary* tasks can either be classified as *Mastery* (altruisitic), such as helping other students, or *Achievement* (reputation), such as advancing to a certain social status. Learning tasks are those directly connected to learning goals or common core standards outlining domain-specific knowledge. These tasks can be either *Mastery* focused where the student needs to demonstrate learned competency or *Performance* focused where the student needs to demonstrate excellence in that competency when compared to their peers or a set cut-off level.

In our own research, we compared badges unrelated to learning with badges that were closely aligned with learning goals and employed key functions identified by the earlier qualitative research, such as signaling, challenging, or affirming. Our findings suggested that badges designed with these functions in mind related to the learning goals and were more supportive of increased cognitive outcomes (Biles & Plass, 2015). Subsequent research into badges aligned with learning goals compared badges with an achievement versus a mastery focus, and found that while badges that emphasized performance achievement did better overall, the students with greater situational interest demonstrated stronger learning outcomes when using mastery badges (Plass et al., 2014).

Summary and Conclusion

The goal of this chapter was to provide a theoretical foundation for the motivational formative function of badges, with a specific focus on games for learning. We combined our discussion of relevant motivational theories (situational and individual interest, motivation, goal orientation, and achievement in games), incentive system design, and uses and functions of badges, with a review of the empirical research we conducted on this topic.

Since digital badges are a relatively new phenomenon, only limited research has been conducted on their impact. In order to guide future research, we developed the Educational Badge Typology (EBT), which classifies the different functions of badges. This typology, along with the Badging Player Profile (BPP) and the three main functions of incentive systems outlined by game designers, can be used by designers seeking to implement digital badges within learning contexts by allowing them to consider the role and function of badges within the game environment before designing and implementing badges within their own systems.

Our research findings coupled with insights from theory and practice suggest that badges do not always help support learning from games. The badge type used interacts with students' interest and motivation to affect learning. This is consistent with more general findings on external rewards in learning. Future research should be conducted to generalize our findings to other badge ecosystems, other learner populations, and other subject matters and to further investigate the theoretical foundations of the impact of badges. It seems clear that badges are here to stay; yet our investigation suggests that their impact will depend on the design and function of these badges and how well they are connected to the learning process.

References

Abramovich, S., Schunn, C., & Higashi, R. M. (2013). Are badges useful in education?: It depends upon the type of badge and expertise of learner. *Educational Technology Research and Development, 61,* 217–232.

Ainley, M. (2006). Connecting with learning: Motivation, affect and cognition in interest processes. *Educational Psychology Review, 18*(4), 391–405.

Ames, C. (1992). Classrooms: Goals, structures, and student motivation. *Journal of Educational Psychology, 84*(3), 261.

Antin, J., & Churchill, E. F. (2011, May). *Badges in social media: A social psychological perspective.* Paper presented at Computer-Human Interaction (CHI) 2011 Gamification Workshop Proceedings, Vancouver, Canada.

Barab, S., Thomas, M., Dodge, T., Carteaux, R., & Tuzun, H. (2005). Making learning fun: Quest Atlantis, a game without guns. *Educational Technology Research and Development, 53*(1), 86–107.

Bartle, R. (1996). Hearts, clubs, diamonds, spades: Players who suit MUDs. *Journal of Virtual Environments.* Retrieved from www.mud.co.uk/richard/hcds.htm.

Beck, R. C. (1983). *Motivation: Theories and Principles*. Englewood Cliffs, NJ: Prentice-Hall.

Biles, M. L., & Plass, J. L. (2015, April). *Figuring out the when, where, and why: An educational badge typology and badges impact survey*. Paper presented at the Annual Meeting of the American Educational Research Association (AERA), Chicago, IL.

Biles, M. L., Plass, J. L., & Homer, B. D. (2014, March). *Good badges, evil badges?: An empirical inquiry into the impact of badge design on goal orientation and learning*. Presented at the HASTAC Workshop, What Should We Ask About Badges?: Framing a Research Agenda for the Field, Boston, MA.

Butler, R. (1993). Effects of task- and ego-achievement goals on information seeking during task engagement. *Journal of Personality and Social Psychology, 65*(1), 18.

Butler, R. (1995). Motivational and informational functions and consequences of children's attention to peers' work. *Journal of Educational Psychology, 87*(3), 347.

Butler, R. (2000). What learners want to know: The role of achievement goals in shaping information seeking, learning, and interest. In C. Sansone & J. Harackiewicz (Eds.), *Intrinsic and extrinsic motivation: The search for optimal motivation and performance* (pp. 161–194). San Diego: Academic Press.

CREATE (2012). Noobs vs Leets. [Computer game]. Retrieved from http://create.nyu.edu/dream.

CREATE (2015). HASTAC report: Badges & learning. New York, NY: Consortium for Research and Evaluation of Advanced Technology in Education, New York University. Retrieved from http://create.nyu.edu/wordpress/wp-content/uploads/2015/02/HASTAC-Report-Badges-and-Learning-CREATE.pdf.

Design Principles Documentation Project (2014). Interim report: January 2014 update. Bloomington, IN: Center for Research on Learning and Technology, Indiana University.

Dickey, M. (2005). Engaging by design: How engagement strategies in popular computer and video games can inform instructional design. *Educational Technology Research and Development, 53*(2), 67–83.

Dweck, C. S. (1986). Motivational processes affecting learning. *American Psychologist, 41*(10), 1040.

Dweck, C. S., & Leggett, E. L. (1988). A social-cognitive approach to motivation and personality. *Psychological Review, 95*(2), 256–273.

Elliot, A. J. (2005). A conceptual history of the achievement goal construct. In A. J. Elliot & C. S. Dweck (Eds.), *Handbook of Competence and Motivation* (pp. 52–72). New York, NY: Guilford Press.

Frye, J. M. (2013). *Video game player profiles: Bridging industry, game studies and social science perspectives* (Doctoral dissertation). Retrieved from ProQuest Digital Dissertations (UMI 3599871).

Gee, J. P. (2003). *What video games have to teach us about learning and literacy*. New York, NY: Palgrave Macmillan.

Grant, S. L. (2014). *What counts as learning: Open digital badges for new opportunities*. Irvine, CA: Digital Media and Learning Research Hub.

Harackiewicz, J. M., Barron, K. E., Pintrich, P. R., Elliot, A. J., & Thrash, T. M. (2002). Revision of achievement goal theory: Necessary and illuminating. *Journal of Educational Psychology, 94*, 638–645.

Hickey, D. (2012, September 9). Intended purposes versus actual functions of digital badges. Retrieved February 11, 2015 from http://remediatingassessment.blogspot.com/2012/09/intended-purposes-versus-actual.html.

Hidi, S. (2006). Interest: A unique motivational variable. *Educational Research Review, 1*(2), 69–82.

Hidi, S., & Renninger, K. A. (2006). The four-phase model of interest development. *Educational Psychologist, 41*(2), 111e127. Retrieved from http://dx.doi.org/10.1207/s15326985ep4102_4.

Higashi, R., Abramovich, S. J., Shoop, R., & Schunn, C. D. (2012). *The roles of badges in the computer science student network.* Paper presented at the Games Learning Society, Madison, WI.

Homer, B. D., Kinzer, C., Plass, J. L., Letourneau, S., Hoffman, D., Hayward, E., … Kornak, Y. (2014). Moved to learn: The effects of interactivity in a Kinect-based literacy game for beginning readers. *Computers and Education, 74,* 37–49. Doi: 10.1016/j.compedu.2014.01.007.

Klug, G. C., & Schell, J. (2006). Why people play games: An industry perspective. In P. Vorderer & J. Bryant (Eds.), *Playing video games: Motives, responses, and consequences* (pp. 91–99). Mahwah, NJ: Lawrence Erlbaum.

Krapp, A. (2005). Basic needs and the development of interest and intrinsic motivational orientations. *Learning and Instruction, 15*(5), 381–395.

Krapp, A. (2007). An educational-psychological conceptualisation of interest. *International Journal for Educational and Vocational Guidance, 7*(1), 5–21.

Lave, J., & Wenger, E. (1991). *Situated learning: Legitimate peripheral participation.* New York, NY: Cambridge University Press.

Li, Z., Huang, K. W., & Cavusoglu, H. (2012, December). *Quantifying the impact of badges on user engagement in online Q&A communities.* Paper published in Proceedings of International Conference on Information Systems. Orlando, FL.

Midgley, C. (2002). *Goals, goal structures, and patterns of adaptive learning.* Mahwah, NJ: L. Erlbaum Associates.

Montola, M., Nummenmaa, T., Lucero, A., Boberg, M., & Korhonen, H. (2009, September). Applying game achievement systems to enhance user experience in a photo sharing service. Paper published in *Proceedings of the 13th International MindTrek Conference.* New York, NY.

O'Keefe, P. A. (2013). Mindsets and self-evaluation: How beliefs about intelligence can create a preference for growth over defensiveness. In S. B. Kaufman (Ed.), *The complexity of greatness: Beyond talent or practice* (pp. 119–136). Oxford: Oxford University Press.

Plass, J. L., Homer, B. D., Hayward, E. O., Frye, J., Huang, T. T., Biles, M., … Perlin, K. (2012). The effect of learning mechanics design on learning outcomes in a computer-based geometry game. In S. Göbel, W. Müller, B. Urban, & J. Wiemeyer (Eds.), *E-learning and games for training, education, health and sports: 7th International Conference, Edutainment 2012 and 3rd International Conference, GameDays 2012, Proceedings* (pp. 65–71). Berlin: Springer Berlin Heidelberg.

Plass, J. L., Homer, B. D., & Kinzer, C. K. (2015). *Playful learning: An integrated design framework* [White paper]. Retrieved April 30, 2015, from CREATE Lab: http://create.nyu.edu/wordpress/wp-content/uploads/2015/01/G4LI-White-Paper-02-2014-Playful-Learning.pdf.

Plass, J. L., & Kaplan, U. (in press). Emotional design in digital media for learning. In S. Tettegah & M. Gartmeier (Eds.), *Emotions, design, learning and technology.* New York, NY: Elsevier.

Plass, J. L., O'Keefe, P., Biles, M., Frye, J., & Homer, B. D. (2014). *Motivational and cognitive impact of badges in games for learning.* Poster presented at the Annual Meeting of the American Educational Research Association (AERA), Philadelphia, PA.

Plass, J. L., O'Keefe, P., Homer, B. D., Hayward, E. O., Stein, M., & Perlin, K. (2013). Motivational and cognitive outcomes associated with individual, competitive, and collaborative game play [Special issue]. *Journal of Educational Psychology, 4,* 1050–1066.

Schiefele, U. (1991). Interest, learning, and motivation. *Educational Psychologist, 26*(3–4), 299–323.

Sherry, J. L., Lucas, K., Greenberg, B. S., & Lachlan, K. (2006). Video game uses and gratifications as predicators of use and game preference. In P. Vorderer & J. Bryant (Eds.), *Playing video games: Motives, responses, and consequences.* Mahwah, NJ: Lawrence Erlbaum Associates.

Squire, K. (2006). From content to context: Videogames as designed experience. *Educational Researcher, 35*(8), 19–29.

Um, E., Plass, J. L., Hayward, E. O., & Homer, B. D. (2013). Emotional design in multimedia learning. *Journal of Educational Psychology, 104*(4), 1050–1066.

Urdan, T. C. (1997). Examining the relations among early adolescent students' goals and friends' orientation toward effort and achievement in school. *Contemporary Educational Psychology, 22*(2), 165–191.

Utman, C. H. (1997). Performance effects of motivational state: A meta-analysis. *Personality and Social Psychology Review, 1*(2), 170–182.

Yee, N. (2006). Motivations for play in online games. *CyberPsychology & Behavior, 9*(6), 772–775.

6

IMPACT OF BADGES ON MOTIVATION TO LEARN

Samuel Abramovich and Peter Wardrip

One of the suggested merits of digital badges is their ability to capitalize and build on motivation. Specifically, advocates note that badges could strengthen existing learner motivation or enhance opportunities to increase motivation to learn (Gibson, Ostashewski, Flintoff, Grant, & Knight, 2013). This suggested use of badges, as a pedagogical tool to both support and increase motivation to learn, holds much in common with the perceived benefit and use of badges in non-educational contexts. For example, earning platinum status in a frequent flyer program comes with digital recognition in the form of a symbol that is visible on the flyer's account with that airline (and with a physical badge in the form of a luggage tag). The ubiquity of digital badges in various commercial enterprises provides ample evidence that suggests the use of badges will motivate customers.

However, education and learning are distinctly different constructs than commercial enterprises. Motivation to learn is an intricate concept and is not an implied foundation or automatic result of any educational intervention, including badges. Consequently, commercial badge systems are likely to fail when simply applied to learning opportunities. Instead, armed with knowledge of empirically driven theories of motivation and their nexus with badges, educators can design badge systems that use badges to increase motivational impact while also minimizing potential negative impacts on learning. This chapter details the relationship between badges and motivation theory. We first briefly highlight what current research can tell us about the importance of motivation to learning. We then describe how digital badges can motivate, explaining the connection to some of the originating models for digital badge systems and embedding how learning motivation theories can predict the impact of badges. We conclude with some early research on badge systems that helps us further unpack how badges can increase motivation to learn along with design principles for badges systems.

Role of Motivation in Education

Educational psychologists have firmly established the importance of motivation in learning (e.g., Elliott & Dweck, 2005). Specifically, motivation is an established predictor of educational outcomes (Broussard & Garrison, 2004; Dörnyei & Ushioda, 2013). Positive motivation to learn or constructive motivational goals can reliably forecast student-learning gains at similar levels as improved teacher instruction or pedagogical innovation (Clark, Howard, & Early, 2006). In other words, increasing students' motivation to learn can be as effective as improving the other qualities of their education. This is particularly notable given that the implied positive effects of motivation are independent of other learning predictors such as prior knowledge or socio-economic status (Gottfried, 1990). Further, the importance of motivation for learning is a common anecdote in discussions of education. Individuals who have achieved mastery in a content area or skill will frequently attribute their strong motivation as a reason for achieving their learning goal.

There is also strong evidence of the inverse of the relationship between motivation and education, that low motivation to learn predicts low learning gains. Research suggests that negative or low motivation to learn is a reliable indicator of reduced confidence, expectation, and persistence to learn (Eccles, Midgley, & Adler, 1984). Seemingly related, the commonly observed lack of interest from students as they progress in grade levels correlates with a consistent decrease in motivation in school from third grade through high school (Cordova & Lepper, 1996). The same phenomenon of low motivation to learn predicting lower learning gains is also observed in adult learners (Baldwin, Magjuka, & Loher, 1991).

Why Use Digital Badges to Motivate Learning?

In our introduction to this chapter, we drew on a Frequent Flyer program's badges as a typical example of how a badge could motivate. But a closer parallel to how badges could motivate individuals to learn is the modern video-game system. For example, both Microsoft's Xbox and Sony's PlayStation game consoles have online networks where players can earn badges (named Achievements and Trophies, respectively) (e.g., Jakobsson, 2011). These badges are displayed in each player's online profile within the system. Players can review all of their earned badges when viewing their profile and can also review the badges earned by fellow players using the same console. The intended effect of these badge systems is to motivate additional game play both within a game and in the larger game ecosystem. Players might go back to a game, even after completing or "beating" the game, in order to earn additional badges that they can then add to their profile. The attraction to a single console system can remain high once a critical number of badges has been amassed; players likely feel that the archive of their earned badges is personally valuable because it represents their accomplishments and makes them visible to their game-playing peers.

Digital badge systems designed for education can possibly offer the same motivational effects by providing learners a badge to represent their completed learning objective. The badge can then be displayed in a variety of online profiles, both within the learning platform and outside of it. Learners could be encouraged to revisit a learning opportunity, even after completing the initial educational objective, in order to earn additional badges that represent additional learning. Learners could also see how their earned badges reside within a greater collection of digital badges around a specific learning goal, similar to the way they can see which badges are available to a certain genre of game. Badges can be displayed so that other learners or consumers of credentials (e.g., employers, teachers) could recognize a learner's earned badges. Learners could select new learning objectives based on the badges earned by their peers.

Models of Motivation to Learn for Badge Systems

Yet despite the prevalence and success of badge systems in commercial settings, it is not a given that these types of systems would apply just as successfully to educational settings. Motivation to learn is different than motivation to play a game or select an airline. For example, a classic taxonomy of motivation is the binary distinction of intrinsic and extrinsic (Sansone & Harackiewicz, 2000). Specifically, intrinsic motivation is defined as motivation that originates from within an individual, while extrinsic motivation originates from outside an individual. Learning motivation is often described as either extrinsic or intrinsic in origin. Applied to learning, intrinsic motivation is characterized by self-desire to learn or an internalized learning goal, while extrinsic motivation is characterized by an influence to learn from external sources (Deci & Ryan, 1985).

The distinction between intrinsic and extrinsic motivation to learn has proven useful in explaining some learning outcomes. For example, imagine students engaged in learning a foreign language. They might have a desire to learn a second language because they have a passion for the culture associated with the language, an example of intrinsic motivation to learn. Or students might be trying to learn a second language because it is a requirement of their school and they simply want to meet the requirement in order to graduate, an example of extrinsic motivation to learn. Research has revealed that intrinsic motivation to learn leads to larger learning gains than extrinsic motivations (Lepper, Corpus, & Iyengar, 2005). Consequently, it is more valuable to support and increase intrinsic motivation to learn rather than provide extrinsic motivators. This is a particularly important finding given that intrinsic motivation could be supplanted by an extrinsic motivator (Deci, Koestner, & Ryan, 2001).

Yet when applied to certain educational scenarios, the intrinsic/extrinsic model is less than optimal in explaining motivation. For example, let us say we have two students in a classroom. Student A, a competitive person, wants to learn more than student B, despite the fact that student A's assessments are determined independent of their relative performance to student B. We could make the argument that student A has an intrinsic motivation to learn since there is no direct external pressure on them to learn more than student B. However, it is also possible that student A would not be motivated to learn without student B. If student B transfers out of the class, student A will have no perceived competition and might not be interested in learning in order to master the content. Student A was motivated entirely by the goal of learning more than student B. This suggests that student B is an extrinsic motivator for student A. Applied to badges, the intrinsic/extrinsic model of motivation does not fully explain what motivates students to earn a badge. Applied to the same scenario, student A might be motivated to earn more badges than student B, which could mean that student A is intrinsically motivated to earn more badges based on an extrinsic factor (i.e., student B).

Thankfully, there are a number of learning motivation theories that can inform possible interactions between badges and learners' motivation. Achievement goal theory (Maehr & Zusho, 2009; Pintrich, 2000) suggests that motivation to earn badges can be described on two interacting scales of learning goals: approach to avoidance and mastery to performance. A motivation to learn based on a mastery goal is associated with the learner's interest. A performance goal is based on a desire to learn in comparison with how much other people are learning. Approach goals suggest that there is a motivation to achieve a learning goal, while avoidance goals represent a desire to not fail at the learning objective. Applied as a 2 × 2 matrix (Cury, Elliot, Fonseca, & Moller, 2006) (see Figure 6.1), learners could have a performance approach goal orientation and be motivated to earn more badges than their peers, or have a performance avoidance goal orientation and want to earn enough badges to be similar to their peers. Learners could have a mastery approach goal orientation where they earn badges that represent what they want to learn, or a mastery avoidance orientation where they are concerned with keeping the badges that represent their learning.

	Mastery	Performance
Approach	Goal is to earn badges that represent learning	Goal is to earn more badges than peers
Avoidance	Goal is to keep earned badges	Goal is to earn a number of badges similar to peers

FIGURE 6.1 Example of the 2 × 2 matrix of achievement goal theory applied to earning badges.

Another model of motivation that could explain how badges can motivate learners is expectancy-value theory (Wigfield & Eccles, 2000). Prior research indicates that an expectation for success when learning something, combined with the value placed on that learning, can predict how much people will learn. For example, if students expect that they can learn how to build a website and that building a website is important to them, then there is a good chance that they will be able to learn how to build a website. While this could seem rather obvious, it is important to recognize that the predictive ability of expectancy-value theory functions differently than other predictors of learning, such as a student's socio-economic status or gender (Fan, 2011). When applied to badges, expectancy-value theory suggests that earning a badge could motivate learners if the badge increases the expectation for learning the targeted material and if earning the badge increases how much they value the learning. For example, learners could receive a badge for finishing an online tutorial for JavaScript. They would then have an increased expectation that they could learn how to build a website because they have already mastered JavaScript, as indicated by the badge. In addition, the value of learning to build a website could also have increased since they are getting increased recognition of their learning in the form of a badge.

Many skeptics of digital badges are concerned with the potential for replacing learners' intrinsic motivation to learn with a badge. The worry is twofold: that once badges are no longer available for learning, learners will no longer be motivated to learn; and that learners who initially care about learning might become only concerned with earning badges. Cognitive evaluation theory, a subset of self-determination theory (Deci, Cascio & Krusell, 1975; Ryan, Mims, & Koestner, 1983), explains that the negative impact of external motivators occurs if learners perceive the motivator as extrinsic from their actions. Applied to badges, there is a viable concern that badges could negatively impact learners' motivation if the badge is seen as disconnected from the learning. However, if learners are able to connect their badges to their learning, then badges could support their motivation to learn by reinforcing their intrinsic motivation. The badge would act as an external motivator but not as an extrinsic one.

Badges and Motivation Research Findings

Although research on digital badges is sparse in comparison to other educational technologies, there are some studies that directly address how motivation theories can illuminate the design and implementation of badge systems. Abramovich, Schunn, and Higashi (2013) created badges for a computer-based intelligent tutoring system designed to teach algebra in the context of robotics. Badges were awarded for two basic types of use: basic participation with the tutor and for mastering algebra skills. For example, users could earn a badge for both the time spent with the tutor (i.e., participation) and for mastering proportionality (i.e., an algebraic skill). Using both achievement goal theory and expectancy-value theory, they found that different types of badges had different effects on learners depending on their prior knowledge and motivational goals. As they earned more participatory badges, students who had less prior ability in algebra grew more concerned with the number of badges they earned. In other words, the students with less prior knowledge had increasing performance avoidance goal orientation, a weak motivational goal for learning, with each participation badge. Higher performing students had higher levels of expectations of success as they earned more skill badges. The students with more knowledge had a higher expectancy of learning algebra with each skill badge awarded by the tutor. In summary, the authors found that badges can impact learner motivation but that the type of badge and the prior knowledge of learners predicted different types of changes to learner motivation.

A study by Wardrip, Abramovich, Bathgate, and Kim (in press) utilized expectancy-value theory and found that badges can facilitate interest-based learning by enabling students to engage in self-directed learning processes. Over the course of two years, the researchers investigated a badge system designed to allow middle-school students to pursue a variety of twenty-first-century skills. Students and teachers were interviewed on their use and perception of badges, with the investigators using different theories of motivation as a tool to uncover what the badge impacts were on student motivation to learn. One of the key findings from their study was that if badges are designed to allow learners to choose learning pathways, then it can be reasonably assumed they have chosen badges that they are motivated to complete. Thus the badge becomes an indicator of the motivational learning goals of the learner. For example, students chose badges that represented learning goals that they valued (e.g., learning how to collaborate with their peers) and skills that they believed they could learn (e.g., information literacy). Teachers could then determine what motivated their students to learn by looking at which badges students were selecting.

In regards to the potential that badges could be an extrinsic motivator and reduce motivation to learn, Filsecker and Hickey (2014) compared the use of badges in an educational computer game to the same game without badges. They found no difference in motivation levels between players of the version of the game with badges and players of the game without badges. While this study does not address the impact of badges in non-gaming settings, it does suggest that badges are not always extrinsic motivators and that providing badges does not necessitate a change in a learner's motivation when they have a strong initial motivation to learn.

Directions for Future Design and Research

Research on digital badges is far too limited to draw any definitive conclusions on the effect that badges can have on motivation to learn. Because there are only a few articles that use established motivational theories, it is premature to conclude that one theory of motivation is better than others for explaining how digital badges can motivate learners. Because different types of badges can have different motivational impacts on different learners, we suggest that designs for badge systems and research should use a variety of different theoretical lenses. This approach would increase the likelihood that we can measure the impact of different types of badges, and ultimately create a badge taxonomy. Badge designers could use such a taxonomy to build badges that target their desired motivational impacts (Hickey et al., 2014).

Our research on badges suggests that the motivational impact of badges is likely connected to learners' identity. However, we have yet to understand just how a badge design can leverage that connection. One area that we believe has promise is in building badges that utilize the cultural identity of learners, allowing learners to situate the learning goal associated with the badge within their culture. The advantage of this connection would be both in building on identity that is already firmly established and strengthening positive associations between learning and the students' identity. For example, we imagine digital badges awarded to students for learning how to collaborate not only within their academic communities but also within other communities that are part of their cultural identities.

We also believe that badges could be an interesting point of leverage for student engagement in schools since they may provide actionable information for teachers to guide instruction. In this chapter, we have discussed the ways that badges can support student motivation to learn, but supporting student engagement is also a practice of highly effective teachers (e.g., Alderman, 2013). Preliminary evidence suggests that, rather than supplanting teachers' role in motivating learning, badge systems can reveal what motivates individual students and enable teachers to utilize more effective strategies by leveraging that discovered motivation. Furthermore, because digital badges can be awarded for learning that is outside of traditional assessment, badges can also demonstrate students' interests in ways that are not traditionally evident to teachers. For example, a teacher might observe that a particular student earned a badge for public speaking skills. The teacher could then encourage that student to use public speaking skills in class, acknowledging student learning outside the classroom and building on what the student has already mastered.

Ultimately, we believe that badges can have a powerful, positive role in motivating students. We hope that this chapter helps badge creators and researchers understand that there are a variety of mechanisms that influence student motivation, which lead to a variety of ways in which badges may be motivating for students. If we can better understand the extent to which badges relate to students' identity development or achievement orientation, then we might provide guidance for designing badges that connect to and leverage those mechanisms for students' motivations. Consequently, we hope others join us in building and investigating digital badges that increase motivation to learn.

References

Abramovich, S., Schunn, C., & Higashi, R. M. (2013). Are badges useful in education?: It depends upon the type of badge and expertise of learner. *Educational Technology Research and Development, 61*(2), 217–232. doi:10.1007/s11423-013-9289-2.

Alderman, M. K. (2013). *Motivation for achievement: Possibilities for teaching and learning* (3rd ed.). New York, NY: Routledge.

Baldwin, T. T., Magjuka, R. J., & Loher, B. T. (1991). The perils of participation: Effects of choice of training on trainee motivation and learning. *Personnel Psychology, 44*(1), 51–65. doi:10.1111/j.1744-6570.1991.tb00690.x.

Broussard, S. C., & Garrison, M. E. B. (2004). The relationship between classroom motivation and academic achievement in elementary school-aged children. *Family and Consumer Sciences Research Journal, 33*(2), 106–120. doi: 10.1177/1077727X04269573.

Clark, R., Howard, K., & Early, S. (2006). Motivational challenges experienced in highly complex learning environments. In J. Elen, R. Clark & J. Lowyck (Eds.), *Handling complexity in learning environments: Theory and research* (pp. 27–42). Oxford, UK: Elsevier.

Cordova, D., & Lepper, M. (1996). Intrinsic motivation and the process of learning: Beneficial effects of contextualization, personalization, and choice. *Journal of Educational Psychology, 88*(4), 715–730.

Cury, F., Elliot, A., Fonseca, D. D., & Moller, A. C. (2006). The social-cognitive model of achievement motivation and the 2 × 2 achievement goal framework. *Journal of Personality and Social Psychology, 90*(4), 666–679.

Deci, E. L., Cascio, W. F., & Krusell, J. (1975). Cognitive evaluation theory and some comments on the Calder and Staw critique. *Journal of Personality and Social Psychology, 31*(1), 81–85.

Deci, E. L., Koestner, R., & Ryan, R. M. (2001). Extrinsic rewards and intrinsic motivation in education: Reconsidered once again. *Review of Educational Research, 71*(1), 1–27.

Deci, E. L., & Ryan, R. M. (1985). *Intrinsic motivation and self-determination in human behavior.* New York, NY: Plenum.

Dörnyei, Z., & Ushioda, E. (2013). *Teaching and researching motivation* (2nd ed.). New York, NY: Routledge.

Eccles, J. S., Midgley, C., & Adler, T. (1984). Grade-related changes in the school environment: Effects on achievement motivation. *Advances in Motivation and Achievement, 3,* 283–331.

Elliott, A. J., & Dweck, C. S. (2005). *Handbook of competence and motivation.* New York, NY: Guilford Press.

Fan, W. (2011). Social influences, school motivation and gender differences: An application of the expectancy-value theory. *Educational Psychology, 31*(2), 157–175. doi:10.1080/0 1443410.2010.536525.

Filsecker, M., & Hickey, D. T. (2014). A multilevel analysis of the effects of external rewards on elementary students' motivation, engagement and learning in an educational game. *Computers & Education, 75,* 136–148. doi:10.1016/j.compedu.2014.02.008.

Gibson, D., Ostashewski, N., Flintoff, K., Grant, S., & Knight, E. (2013). Digital badges in education. *Education and Information Technologies, 20*(2), 1–8.

Gottfried, A. E. (1990). Academic intrinsic motivation in young elementary school children. *Journal of Educational Psychology, 82*(3), 525–538.

Hickey, D., Itow, R., Schenke, K., Tran, C., Otto, N., & Chow, C. (2014). *Badges Design Principles Documentation Project Interim Report.* Indiana University. Retrieved from http://iudpd.indiana.edu/JanuaryReport.

Jakobsson, M. (2011). The achievement machine: Understanding Xbox 360 achievements in gaming practices. *Game Studies, 11*(1), 1–22.

Lepper, M., Corpus, J., & Iyengar, S. S. (2005). Intrinsic and extrinsic motivational orientations in the classroom: Age differences and academic correlates. *Journal of Educational Psychology, 97*(2), 184–196.

Maehr, M. L., & Zusho, A. (2009). Achievement goal theory: The past, present, and future. In K. R. Wentzel & A. Wigfield (Eds.), *Handbook of motivation at school* (pp. 77–104). New York, NY: Routledge.

Pintrich, P. R. (2000). An achievement goal theory perspective on issues in motivation terminology, theory, and research. *Contemporary Educational Psychology, 25*(1), 92–104.

Ryan, R., Mims, V., & Koestner, R. (1983). Relation of reward contingency and interpersonal context to intrinsic motivation: A review and test using cognitive evaluation theory. *Journal of Personality and Social Psychology, 45*(4), 736–750.

Sansone, C., & Harackiewicz, J. M. (Eds.). (2000). *Intrinsic and extrinsic motivation: The search for optimal motivation and performance.* San Diego, CA: Academic Press.

Wardrip, P. S., Abramovich, S., Bathgate, M. & Kim, Y. J. (in press). A school-based badging system and interest-based learning: An exploratory case study. *International Journal of Learning and Media.*

Wigfield, A., & Eccles, J. S. (2000). Expectancy–value theory of achievement motivation. *Contemporary Educational Psychology, 25*(1), 68–81. doi:10.1006/ceps.1999.1015.

7

WHAT VIDEO GAMES CAN TEACH US ABOUT BADGES AND PATHWAYS

Lucas Blair

In many ways, games and educational systems aim to accomplish the same things. Both are designed to move participants through an experience by equipping them with knowledge and skills. Both games and educational systems rely on goal setting, feedback loops, difficulty that scales along with participant experience, and incentivizing continued participation. Because of the similarities between the design and intent of games and educational systems, it shouldn't be a surprise that in many cases, they reach the same conclusions about the best way to accomplish that intent. Video games have a big head start on the digital badge community utilizing badges and pathways. The gaming community just uses different terminology for them. In video games, badges are called achievements and pathways are called skill trees.

There are thousands of games that have used these mechanics when accounting for all platforms. The story of each one of those little experiments is filled with successes, failures, innovations, and evolutions. Not only have game developers had a head start, but they are building systems for audiences on a massive scale that is bigger than anything that has been made for digital badges. Ignoring this kind of information is folly, but so far we have stuck primarily to academic explorations of the psychology behind digital badges and limited our case studies to the systems our community has made in the past few years. We are reinventing the wheel when another industry is already making supercars.

This chapter is organized by achievement and skill tree design techniques with game examples that illustrate them. Because the vast number of games that contain achievements and skill trees, as well as the limited amount of documentation on their designs, the majority of the examples in the chapter are taken from the author's experience as a player and designer. This chapter is not meant to discuss every aspect of achievement systems and skill trees in games. Nor is it a complete picture of everything that is going on in all games. The examples in this chapter are meant to be a collection of exemplars that represent patterns in the game industry, good and bad design decisions, interesting techniques, and the impact they have on players. Digital badge systems can be made better by understanding what video games have done with similar mechanics, and the lessons learned should be applied to systems being built today. This is especially true if badge earners are "gamers," a demographic that according to the ESA (Entertainment Software Association) is 59 percent of Americans. They will be used to the mechanics but may be underwhelmed by systems that do not utilize what they are accustomed to seeing in games.

Before we dig in, a few definitions and a little history are in order. Every example of achievements in this chapter will come from entertainment games after 2005. That year is when Microsoft coined the term "achievement" and began using achievements in the Xbox 360 Gamerscore system. Many other systems and game services followed suit within a few years, including PlayStation trophies, PC game cloud platforms like Steam, as well as social and mobile games. Skill trees, the gaming analogue of badge pathways, are older than achievements. For example, the strategy game *Sid Meier's Civilization* featured a technology tree, the precursor to the skill tree, in 1991. Soon they were adopted by other genres like role-playing games (RPG). Skill trees in games are not a collection or ordering of achievements as we think of badges relating to pathways. Instead, skill trees are a mechanism designed to allow players to unlock skills and enhancements in games at a controlled rate as they progress through game content. Skill trees can be compared to badge pathways because they represent all possibilities to players in a game. This is the same way that a badge pathway represents what badges earners can achieve within a system as well as the order in which they should be earned. Skill trees also act as a goal setting and planning mechanism.

Achievements

The differences between digital badges and achievements are mostly semantic. Each exists as an additional layer on top of some core experience they are meant to enhance. They represent a goal before they are earned and an artifact of the accomplishment afterwards. Also, they are both data rich and can provide important insights into earner behavior.

Achievements, just like badges, are awarded after certain performance criteria have been met, or when one or more tasks are completed. Most games strike a reasonable balance between achievements awarded for performance and achievements awarded for completing something. Many games, especially those that have a clearly defined start and end, also use achievements to mark milestones and show a player's progress to their peers. For example, an achievement for defeating a boss in a game is something that every player who beats that game will complete. Players cannot skip boss fights, so the achievements earned for them really only serve as proof of progression. The educational equivalent to these types of badges would be for completing a grade or graduating. More performance-based achievements may also exist for the same boss fight; for example, killing a boss and not losing health or using a difficult strategy can earn a player an achievement. These achievements are more difficult and the expectation is that players will return to the same fight over and over again in order to earn the achievement, even though they have already progressed past that point in the game. This is beneficial to players because they can set additional goals for themselves after the core experience is completed. From the developer's perspective, these require much less work to implement than creating new content. In education, badges that accomplish the same thing could be added at the end of a unit or semester to keep advanced students engaged. Players can also earn achievements through exploration of game environments or by collecting objects. These achievements are designed to increase playtime and encourage players to deviate from the main goals of the game. There are also achievements that are meant to challenge players by requiring performances that are above and beyond what an average player is capable of or at least interested in completing. These achievements can require flawless performances or rely heavily on luck, what players call RNG (random number generator). An example of this is the achievement "A Monument To All Your Sins" in the game *Halo: Reach*, which required the player to complete every campaign mission in the game on legendary difficulty without any outside help. Other achievements are difficult only because they require a lot of time to earn or "grind out." These achievements usually have less to do with skill than a player's willingness to do tasks over and over again. This can be seen in reputation quests in Massively Multiplayer Online (MMO) games or in the achievement "Seriously ..." in the game *Gears of War*. The "Seriously ..." achievement required players to kill 10,000 opponents in ranked multiplayer matches, a feat reported to take hundreds of hours of gameplay to complete. In education, badges that follow a similar design to these extreme achievements should be used sparingly. When used in games, they are typically only earned by a very small percentage of the player base and do not improve performance in enough players to be useful.

Once the spectrum of achievement difficulty within a system is defined, the next logical question is how many increments should be along that experience. The number of achievements in games is often related to the amount of content. For example, according to WoWHead.com, a popular *World of Warcraft* (WoW) information database, there are 3,113 character and 322 guild achievements in the game. WoW can contain this many achievements because the amount of content available to players is enormous. When deciding on the best number of digital badges, the lesson taken from games should be to have enough badges to give earners enough choices so they can differentiate themselves but not so many that they are overwhelmed. Another consideration is the range of player ability, what is acceptable as "passing," and what is expected to be the upper limit of performance. Strategies from games, like using meta and incremental achievements that increase the time spent on achievements, are a technique that some digital badges are already utilizing. Incremental badges are badges that have the same general requirements but increase the level of difficulty in set amounts. This limits the number of unique badges that have to be developed and also scales well with player ability. Meta badges are badges that are awarded for earning full sets of other badges. These are designed to encourage players to obtain all badges and are also a good technique to group badges that are related. In education when badges are chunked into meta-badges, the groups can often be tied to related learning objectives.

No matter how many achievements are in a system, almost all of them are awarded in recognition for something done well or completed successfully. However, some achievements are earned for doing something negative—for example, a player failing a certain number of times. Sometimes these achievements are perceived by the players as the developer playfully poking fun at them. Other times they can be an added annoyance to an already frustrating situation for the player. This is something that would be generally frowned upon in the digital badge world as well, especially in the realm of education.

However, another type of negative achievement that occurs in games may be an important exception to this general rule. Some games are punishingly difficult by design. Players are expected to perform flawlessly with very little margin of error and play levels over and over again because they fail so often. These types of games including *Super Meat Boy, The Binding of Isaac: Rebirth, Dark Souls*, and games from the "Roguelike" genre, let players know it is ok to fail. In these cases, the framing and context in which the achievements are awarded are very important. For example, *The Binding of Isaac: Rebirth* has an achievement called "The Scissors" for dying 100 times. This is an interesting methodology for getting players in a mindset that failure is a celebrated part of the game and everyone dies. Another interesting example, from the game *Dark Souls II*, is the achievement awarded the first time a player dies, called "This Is Dark Souls." This achievement sets the stage for a game in which players die hundreds of times to achieve victory. How different would a digital badge system for education be if it let earners know that they will fail continuously and that it is okay? These games teach us that badges in education for failure should be badges of honor and could be used to encourage risk-taking and unique strategies if they are framed properly.

The social aspect of achievements is a major contributing factor to their popularity in games. Achievements can be shared in many ways in video games. Immediate sharing of an earned achievement takes place in some games when the requirements are met and the achievement is officially received. These notifications are broadcasted to anyone in the immediate area. In some cases, like MMOs, they are also announced to the player's teammates or "guild." A more permanent sharing occurs when a player's earned achievements become part of their permanent profile and in many cases are available for other players to see. This acts as a record of the player's experiences. The collection becomes an additional identity for the player, especially when achievements are shared across characters or across games. This ties the accomplishments to the player and not the game character. The earned achievements are also an indicator of play style and past performance. This creates interesting scenarios where players exclude other players in co-op games because of their lack of certain achievements. "Link your achievement" is a common phrase in *World of Warcraft* seen by players before starting a PuG or "Pick up group" that comprises random players. The players use achievements as proof of capability. They want to be reassured that an inexperienced player is not going to be the weak link in their group. Players strive for efficiency, and having to teach someone how to do something is an inefficiency that many players will not tolerate. In some cases, this behavior creates a Catch-22 that prevents new players from gaining experience. This is a serious problem and has been present in *World of Warcraft* since the introduction of achievements; it is an important lesson for anyone implementing digital badges into group settings. The achievements players have are part of their identity, but so are the achievements players do not have. This issue has been lamented by players in other platforms as well. In an educational setting where students tend to form cliques and exclude others, it is important to consider the possibility of a badge system making those situations worse. Another interesting phenomenon occurs when another layer of value is placed on achievements like the Gamerscore on Xbox 360. This system assigns a numeric value to achievements and the total value of a player's achievements is called that player's Gamerscore. This system is one more step removed from the original game content. Because of this, some players strive to maximize their Gamerscore by finding the easiest achievements possible across all games. The lesson for educators is to remember that students, just like players, will always find the path of least resistance in a system in order to accomplish a goal. Earners become focused on the "score" and lose sight of the experience the designer intended them to have.

Earning achievements in games is not limited to individuals. Even beyond a group of players working in a team to earn individual achievements, as described above, is another level of achievement where players work to earn badges for an organization of which they are a part. "Guild" and "clan" are terms used to describe a formalized collection of players who work together in a game. Some games have created achievement systems at this level of player organization within the game. In MMOs, like *World of Warcraft, WildStar, and EverQuest II*, guilds earn achievements through the efforts of their members. The actual achievement does not stay in the individual player profiles but instead is attached to the guild itself. The player's association with the achievement is secondhand via their member-ship in the guild. Players can benefit from guild-level perks that are unlocked by the success of their guild. The idea of guild-level accomplishments could be incorporated into a classroom to encourage cooperation among peers. In this sce-nario, students would work together to accomplish some large goal that would be too large for any single student to achieve. For example earning an average grade above a certain threshold or completing large-scale projects as a class.

Skill Trees

Skill trees, as defined previously, are a collection of items that give players additional abilities and/or passive bonuses that can be unlocked while playing a game. The number of obtainable skills is typically greater than the number of skill points the player has to allocate. This creates several important effects on players. First, it forces the players to decide on a play style or an approach by deciding what skills they obtain and the order in which they attain them. It also gives the players a sense of ownership over the character they are playing because of their involvement in its customization. Finally, because the skill tree is a map of possibilities for the player, it creates a goal-setting environment where players decide on a "build" or an approach for which skills to obtain long before they have played enough to unlock them. This goal-setting behavior is an incentive for the player to return. Several important design factors in skill trees can change the effect they have on players.

The arrangement of a skill tree, hierarchically and visually, is deliberate and is much more than just an aesthetic design. How a skill tree is organized imparts information to the players before they begin to explore the game's contents. The shape can imply how many alternatives there are or imply where a player should start and expect to end. It may show players they can be good or evil, stealthy or brazen, a character that works well in teams, or one more suited for solo play. Skill trees come in many shapes and sizes, varying greatly across genres. The turn-based strategy game *Sid Meier's Civilization* used skill trees, or "technology trees," to visually show the progression of technology a civilization would experience as it becomes more advanced over time. These game timelines last from the Stone Age to the modern age and beyond. The game lets the players decide which technologies to invest in and then develop strategies based on the technologies they chose. For example, if a player's civilization was close to the sea, the player would invest in shipbuilding technology as opposed to a landlocked player who would not benefit from that technology. The tech trees in *Sid Meier's Civilization* were tied only to the specific match in which the player was involved. At the end of the game, the tech tree resets and the player begins with a new tree during the next game. The lesson for badge creators is to not just focus on designing at the badge level but also at the system level where collections of badges become pathways. The system view and the information it conveys is often the first thing an earner will encounter. That structure should help earners make decisions and understand what they are about to participate in.

Skill trees became even more potent when they were attached to characters. This attachment, unlike the more ephemeral strategy game tech trees, gave the skill tree a permanence that through the game character became attached to the player. It gave players a sense of ownership and a sense of identity. RPGs like *Diablo 2*, which was published in 2000, used simple three-column skill trees for each character type in the game. Each column contained 10 skills or passive enhancements and was labeled to identify the focus of that particular column. This style is still seen today in games like *Borderlands 2*. Since *Diablo 2*'s release, a multitude of RPGs have incorporated more complex skill trees with many organization types. Games like *Final Fantasy X* and *Path of Exile* use nonlinear, almost organic shapes that resemble mind maps. Their structures use the size and color of different nodes to denote relationships and hierarchy. Another RPG, *The Elder Scrolls V: Skyrim*, uses constellations as its skill trees with each skill being represented by a star and different constellations representing different aspects of gameplay. Other genres, like action games, have included simple linear skill trees that offer the players limited choices, but still allow players to augment certain skills or identify a playstyle they prefer. This can be seen in the 2013 release of *Tomb Raider*. Another unique example of linear skill trees in modern games can be seen in *Darkest Dungeon*, a rogue-like dungeon exploration game, in which players use linear skill trees to upgrade the buildings in a small town. Buildings with more upgrades provide the player's team of adventurers more effective treatment and items. When creating badge pathways it is important for designers to remember the sense of ownership earners will have over their decisions and how that will become a reflection of who they are within that context.

The size and pacing of skill trees are another important aspect of their design. If players move through skill trees too quickly they may be overwhelmed by the amount of new skills or the tasks they have to do to complete them. If they progress too slowly they may not feel their efforts are being rewarded. The frequency with which players unlock items is typically faster when they start an experience and slower the further they progress in a game. One of the justifications for this design is that players who are well into a skill tree are already committed to the experience and are likely willing to wait longer between achieving goals. Leveling systems in games are usually structured in a similar way. Skill trees are also paced so that the skills available to players are typically more powerful as they progress through the tree. This is done to ensure the game difficulty is balanced with player abilities. Another benefit of this design decision is that players desire more powerful skills. Placing those skills deeper into a skill tree requires the players to spend more time in the game. These design strategies are very similar to those used by instructional designers when designing a piece of curriculum. When creating badge pathways, consider the rate at which badges will be earned and increase badge difficulty along the pathway in alignment with player ability.

Some games group skills together based on player experience. An example of this can be seen in the game *Dying Light*, which contains clear labels for novice, adept, and expert level skills within the tree. The number of nodes in a skill tree is another important consideration. Some games have small focused skill trees with a limited amount of variability. An example of this is *Tomb Raider*, which has 24 skills spread across three categories. This game also allows individual skills within a tree to be leveled up more than once, a technique that many games use to get more out of shorter skill trees. This unlocks more powerful versions of the same skill. Players also have the option of using a single point to unlock a node in the skill tree and then moving on to more desirable skills further along. At the opposite end of the spectrum is a game like *Path of Exile*, which has 1,325 skills that players can spend only 120 points obtaining. One reason for the difference between these two examples is that they are from different genres. *Tomb Raider* is an action-adventure first person shooter. Players are not expected to spend hours analyzing an optimized build. The skill trees are meant to add a little boost to the players' chosen playstyle and give them a few customization options, whereas *Path of Exile* is an RPG, a genre known for having more complex skill trees and a player-base that is expected to invest a good deal of time customizing their characters. Another consideration is how many times designers expect players to go through the experience also called "replay value" or "replayability." A game like *Tomb Raider* will be played through only once by many players. So a solid initial experience is critical to the success of the game. Alternatively, in RPGs like *Path of Exile*, players are expected to make and remake multiple characters in an effort to find better strategies or experience the game in a new way. In some RPGs it is actually possible to have a build that will prevent players from completing the game, because the skills they have chosen make their character ineffective. The educational equivalent of this would be taking the wrong classes or learning the wrong skills for a desired career. This is why players spend a great deal of time planning, in and out of the game. Players accomplish this by using "skill calculators," a skill tree simulator outside of the game, to experiment with different builds.

The player behavior described above, sometimes called "min-maxing," or finding the optimal strategy or build, is worth further examination. This behavior challenges designers to build systems that do not have a single best technique, but instead offer players the opportunity to try multiple builds or strategies and still be competitive. The digital badging equivalent of "min-maxing" behavior may be finding the badge pathways that take the least amount of time or effort for the same rewards as other pathways. Alternatively, earners may find that one particular path has a better experience or is more rewarding in some way. If the majority of a population of badge earners is only experiencing a small segment of the available content, it could be problematic. Game players and badge earners often find the path of least resistance if given enough time. Also, the Internet allows them to share those strategies. Games solve this problem by constantly adjusting the skills available in trees based on community feedback, play testing, and data collection.

Conclusions

The statement that "thousands of games" use achievements and skill trees at the beginning of this chapter was not meant to be intimidating. It was meant to be exciting. This chapter is a glimpse into the realm of achievements and skill trees in games. There are many other design techniques that the badge community can adopt and case studies that should be examined. Use the examples in this chapter as a starting point to find those best practices and exemplars. Then, do what game designers do: Take the best ideas, make them your own, and improve upon them.

Games Referenced

MicroProse (1991). *Sid Meier's Civilization*, Publi. MicroProse.

Bungie (2010). *Halo: Reach*, Publi. Microsoft Game Studios.

Epic Games, People Can Fly, Black Tusk Studios (2013). *Gears of War*, Publi. Microsoft Studios.

Team Meat (2010). *Super Meat Boy*, Publi. Microsoft Game Studios.

Edmund McMillen (2014). *The Binding of Isaac: Rebirth*, Publi. Nicalis, Inc.

From Software (2011). *Dark Souls*, Publi. Namco Bandai Games.

From Software (2014). *Dark Souls II*, Publi. Namco Bandai Games.

Blizzard Entertainment (2004). *World of Warcraft*, Publi. Blizzard Entertainment.

Carbine Studios (2014). *WildStar*, Publi. NCSOFT.

Daybreak Game Company (2004). *EverQuest II*, Publi. Daybreak Game Company.

Gearbox Software (2012). *Borderlands 2*, Publi. 2K Games.

Blizzard North (2000). *Diablo II*, Publi. Blizzard Entertainment.

Square (2001). *Final Fantasy X*, Publi. Square EA.

Grinding Gear Games (2013). *Path of Exile*, Publi. Grinding Gear Games.

Bethesda Game Studios (2011). *The Elder Scrolls V: Skyrim*, Publi. Bethesda Game Studios.

Crystal Dynamics (2013). *Tomb Raider*, Publi. Square Enix.

Red Hook Studios (2015). *Darkest Dungeon*, Publi. Red Hook Studios.

References

Achievements (n.d.). Retrieved June 28, 2015 from www.wowhead.com/achievements.

Essential Facts About the Computer and Video Game Industry (2014). Retrieved June 28, 2015 from www.theesa.com/wp-content/uploads/2014/10/ESA_EF_2014.pdf.

8

INSTRUCTIONAL DESIGN CONSIDERATIONS FOR DIGITAL BADGES

Chris Gamrat, Brett Bixler, and Victoria Raish

This chapter outlines design recommendations for badges and groupings of badges. These recommendations are based on the authors' collaborations with multiple colleges and departments across Penn State University, involvement with various badging initiatives of the Mozilla Foundation and the Badge Alliance, and collaborative efforts with NASA Education since 2012.

This chapter follows a badge creation and implementation process that the authors have experienced and observed. This enables a designer to view the scope of badge design from a single badge to an entire group of related badges or "badge family." Digital badges are frequently not offered as isolated credentials but rather are made available by badge issuers as a suite reflecting entire learning experiences. It is recommended that designers think not only of the individual badge that they are developing but also how it might relate to a future offering within a badge family.

Organizational Goals and Purposes

When developing badges, it is useful to consider the overall goals of the issuing organization. Either an individual or a group designing and offering the badges should evaluate the purpose of the badges. Organizational strategy offers an opportunity for badge issuers to examine how they define a learning experience through a badge's design. After considering the goals of the badge issuer, there are many decisions for the design of each badge. Badges have great flexibility in how they can be designed; each badge requires considerations on the overall description, type of content, expiration, tasks, assessment, and relations both within and across badge families.

Digital badges have the capacity to explain a learning experience to others outside of the social context in which the badge was earned. As metadata stored in each badge is viewable by educators, learners, evaluators, and employers, it is important to clearly explain this experience in a way that will clarify the experience to those who might not be familiar with the subject matter. Inclusion of solid instructional objectives in the badge criteria is critical; doing so ensures the criteria outlines what tasks are involved or are required to earn a particular badge. Since each aspect of the badge's design will impact how others perceive the value of the badge, a designer should consider the following sections as a guide to designing badges.

Needs Assessment

A Learning Hierarchy Analysis (also known as a Prerequisite Skills Analysis) may be used in the needs assessment phase (Jonassen, Tessmer, & Hannum, 1999) to determine potential badges that support instructional goals and objectives of a particular scope. In this analysis, one starts with the most complex/highest level of learning and breaks it down into the prerequisite skills needed to accomplish it, as illustrated in Figure 8.1.

Tasks considered "previously mastered" fall below the dotted line. These tasks are not assessed in this instructional set. If a robust badging program has existed for some time, it may be possible to ask that potential badge earners for the current instructional set furnish previously earned badges as evidence of prerequisite mastery. Further elaboration on relationships between tasks, badges, and pathways appear later in the chapter.

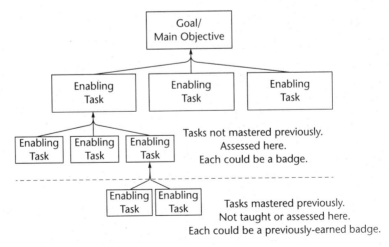

FIGURE 8.1 A Learning Hierarchy Analysis.

Badges and Existing versus New Content

Grant (2013) details several different types of badge systems, including the layered (the badge system is added on top of existing content) versus the integrated (the badge system and learning content are created together) approach. Similarly, new badges themselves may be added onto existing instructional content or created simultaneously with the content.

Badges with Existing Content

For existing instructional sets, the badge designer may have to deconstruct the entire curriculum and rebuild it from the ground up. Doing so ensures the badges are truly integrated and not just grafted onto the instruction. The badge designer may be able to use the addition of badges, if possible, as a great opportunity to redefine and improve the instructional set via the deconstruction—badge(s) addition—rebuilding process. However, the time and resources needed to deconstruct an existing instructional set are often not available.

Badges with New Content

Badges exist as a tool to capture formal and informal learning experiences. For example, the Penn State University Libraries have created an entire set of information literacy digital badges. Previously, information literacy instruction was often one-shot and not systemic (Raish & Rimland, 2016) and did not offer learners a way to capture their experiences. While there are other information literacy efforts delivering instruction online or using podcasts (Berk, Olsen, Atkinson, & Comerford, 2007), this example demonstrates that the design of instruction concurrent with building embedded assessments and visual representations of the skill earned was not possible until digital badges.

The design recommendations for creating new digital badges concurrently with new instructional content depend on the context and content of that particular setting. However, there are three broad-based considerations. First, it is important to create design uniformity within the badge family. Adding uniformity can help those both new and accustomed to badges to approach the badges as either an earner of the badge or as someone evaluating it according to a standard. The second recommendation is to consider how the alignment of learning objectives, tasks, required evidence, and assessments demonstrates that the badge activities reflect accepted norms of the learning context. Finally, consider user-design as a framework for creating a badge family. User-design involves bringing users into the design process and is recommended to ensure that the digital badges represent the needs and interests of potential stakeholders (Carr-Chellman, Cuyar, & Breman, 1998). While it is recognized that user-design efforts may fail, the results are often tremendous when it is successfully implemented (Hobbs & Klare, 2010).

Synchronous versus Asynchronous

Badges can be designed to have synchronous or asynchronous activities, or both. Even in individual badges, learners can be expected to cooperate with others to complete the badges. Choosing synchronous or asynchronous activities impacts the structure of that step of the badge; the communication method chosen will change the goals when designing that badge. For example, if a team project badge requires synchronous communication, then at least one step of the badge should address how they communicated synchronously. This badge step evidence could be an audio transcript, chat log, or a reflective response from each member. If the team project badge had asynchronous communication, the evidence could be forum posts, an email record, or changes to a Google Drive document. The design objectives of the digital badges should drive the decision between synchronous and asynchronous communication.

Expiration Dates for Badges

A badge designer may need to set an expiration date for a badge. For example, if the badge indicates a certification that must be renewed annually, the badge should be valid only for one year. If the badge system in use does not provide a method for automated badge expiration, one method to employ is a date/year in the badge title, such as "2014 Certification for X." Badge designers can also include more descriptive text in the badge description field, such as "This badge is valid until January 1, 2020." When the badge earner obtains re-certification, a new badge is issued.

Tasks per Badge

Badges need to be appropriately designed so that the activities are challenging to students without being cumbersome. This is difficult as the learners are going to be at different levels in their development. A badge designer must decide the number of tasks assigned per badge. From experience creating information literacy and teacher professional development digital badges, the authors recommend between four and six tasks per badge. Finally, designers may want to consider that assigning fewer than four tasks either signifies that each task is too complicated or that a certain activity is not worthy of a badge and deserves a smaller-scale recognition symbol such as a stamp (Gamrat, Zimmerman, Dudek, & Peck, 2014). More research is needed to determine overall recommended parameters for badge tasks.

Badge Assessment

Badges can be issued through either unrestricted or restricted award models. In an unrestricted model, a badge may be available to any individual who is interested in working on it. For example, badges might be offered to learners who work through an open education resource or a training module. These are easiest done when assessment of learner evidence is either automated or has a large capacity. Restricted award badges, on the other hand, might only be available for those specifically registered for a learning experience (e.g., camps, courses, and conferences). In each of these situations, badges can also be awarded through assessed and non-assessed mechanisms.

Badges may be awarded based on assessment and evaluation of presented evidence, or for some non-assessed criteria, such as attendance at a seminar. While assessed badges will most likely be more valued in academia, non-assessed badges have their place. As Carla Casilli (2014) writes, "All badges have some value." The trick is in properly presenting non-assessed badges in a way that illustrates their value.

Badge designers may want to visually indicate via badge image design the difference between assessed and non-assessed badges. Non-assessed badges require no assessment but act more as a form of recognition for participation. For badges like this, there may be benefit to a visual representation of the kind of activities completed. Additionally, designers may want to cluster non-assessed badges together into a meta-badge (explained in detail below). For example, if someone attends a dozen presentations on radio spectroscopy and earns an attendance badge for each, while there is no evidence of capability, there is a definite indication of interest in the subject.

Assessing badge evidence from a learner should follow accepted assessment processes for other, non-badged assessments. In particular, the learning objective, the tasks done to create evidence, and the assessment should all align with each other. Rubrics are an excellent, non-subjective way to define the criteria for awarding of the badge.

Badge Evaluation

Feedback is an important part of a learning experience (Hattie & Timperley, 2007). Badge designers will find it useful to consider both evaluation types and assessments workflows. A badge could be evaluated by a peer, single evaluator, multiple evaluators, automated evaluation, or a combination of these. Peer evaluations reduce the workload on faculty, staff, or instructors while at the same time improving the evaluation skills of students in a well-designed environment (Cho & Schunn, 2007). Limitations of peer evaluations revolve around the lack of experience in reviewing work and providing inadequate feedback (Cho & Schunn, 2007). Peer review can be useful both for lower-stakes badges and when it is desired to develop the skill of constructive criticism through a badge.

A single-evaluator model and multiple-evaluator model are similar. A single evaluator would receive all of the badge attempts for a particular badge and is responsible for giving feedback and approval. In a multiple-evaluator system, this responsibility is shared. It is critical in a multiple-evaluator system to have clear rubrics so that the evaluators are using the same standard and reasoning when providing feedback to the learner. A rubric would provide a better level of inter-rater reliability (Jonsson & Svingby, 2007) for badges with multiple evaluators.

It is important to balance each of these approaches to evaluation of badges so that the learner receives prompt and proper feedback without overburdening the badge issuers. A badge with automated approval will be viewed differently than a badge with a peer evaluator, which will be viewed differently than a badge with a professional evaluator. A careful design including all of these evaluation systems can allow for personalized feedback and adequate scaling of the badge.

Assessment Attempts

There are different foci for digital badges created by different communities. There are circumstances when it makes sense to limit the number of attempts a learner is permitted to make to earn a badge. This designed exclusivity may make the badge more valuable as fewer of these badges are earned, but it simultaneously reduces learner inclusiveness. Choosing to make a badge exclusive increases the pressure on learners and their opportunity for failure. The most important consideration in limiting one's attempts to earn a badge is how critically the badge designer values limited attempts versus unlimited attempts for that particular badge. Badges that can be earned through multiple attempts imply a lower-stakes environment for learners. Multiple attempts to earn could also be considered formative activities, whereas limiting the number of attempts to earn could be considered summative. For example, the same course could be led by two instructors; one that may allow multiple attempts with constructive feedback and the other instructor limits assessment to a single attempt.

A badge designer should also plan for a learner who submits evidence that does not meet the required criteria. Provided that the badge designer wants to give earners another attempt at earning the badge, detailed and personalized feedback and/or remediation can be provided as guidance for a second submission. The badge system in use might not inherently support this, so it may be necessary to develop additional communication structures surrounding the badge processes. Badge designers may be able to build in suggested remediation processes and references into the badge's descriptive fields or a supplemental web page.

Badge Structure

A competency-based design offers a simple binary choice for the evaluator of a badge. The learner either did or did not meet the criteria for the badge. When designing competency-based badges, the issuer should determine the level of performance required to reach "mastery" of the topic. This would involve developing a rubric with detailed performance criteria that would be used by both the badge designer and the evaluator of the learners' submissions. While there is value in issuing badges in this way, a badge issuer may also want to achieve other goals including offering distinction for learners and providing minimal performance levels.

Badge design can afford either competency-based evaluation (e.g., a driver's license) or levels of credentials that go beyond a basic level of performance (e.g., commercial driver's license). Depending upon the implementation of badges in a given context, these considerations can afford additional granularity and flexibility can be designed into the badge implementation with the designed badges. Stratification and hierarchy are two approaches that support a suite of badges around related topics.

Stratified

Stratified badge design offers an approach similar to that of traditional grading. A badge family could be designed with tiered credentials that are awarded for attaining different levels of work quality or performance. This offers a way to recognize effort that might not meet all of the highest-level criteria by capturing a learner's effort and involvement. Another example would be a gold/silver/bronze tier approach. Similar to grades, this demonstrates a level of mastery of the work and offers a means of recognition without perfection. Furthermore, as in the example of Gamrat et al. (2014) concerning teacher professional development, the badge design offered only two levels of stratification: badges and stamps, which involve more and less work, respectively. In this case, badge earners were able to decide the level to pursue.

Hierarchical

Hierarchical badges can be used to create a progressive series of learning challenges or to reflect skills that build on each other. Hierarchical design offers learners the ability to see both how the badges and content are related and the specific learning progression that the badge issuers are supporting. The transparency of a badge's description and evaluation criteria also supports the learners' ability to understand a badge hierarchy approach and determine what level would be appropriate for them. For example, a hierarchy might look like "Spanish 1, Spanish 2, and Spanish 3." Each badge would explain what is covered and build upon the previous one with greater depth and complexity. Learners would then know both where they fit within the hierarchy and what they might expect to be able to do in the future.

Meta-Badges and Pathways

A badge designer can require a variety of tasks in order for a badge earner to receive a badge. One or more badges might be required to earn another badge, which can be referred to as a meta-badge (Badges/FAQs, n.d.). A meta-badge consists of either another badge plus additional criteria/evidence, or two or more other badges as part of the criteria for earning the badge as shown in Figure 8.2. This structure affords the ability to create nested badges. Meta-badges support the summarization of effort by incorporating badges earned along the way. Rather than a learner displaying numerous earned badges, meta-badges can be offered as either culminating or capstone efforts that incorporate and represent previous work.

Learners can build digital badge pathways that can support a personal learning trajectory. Across badge families, it is useful for learners to see how badges they are earning connect to other badges. Recommended learning pathways would require collaboration between various badge stakeholders. Badge designers may also want to consider whether one badge can serve more than one role and whether learners can personalize their learning pathway and use badges from different badge families.

Figure 8.3 shows the relationship of badges in a single badge family and pathways for information literacy created by the Penn State University Libraries. This approach utilizes four meta-badges to provide a path to summarize parts of the overall experience. This offers a mechanism to show a learner other things they can do and learn after completing the first badge, the relationship between the activities, and how these can be summarized when they reach certain levels of completion.

Scalability of Badges for Program-Wide Considerations

Badge designers should incorporate the organizational goals that have already been identified for scope and growth of the badge family. The badge family design offers clarity and consistency as learners engage in the learning experiences.

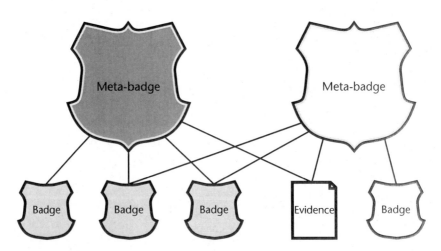

FIGURE 8.2 Possible relationships of badges to meta-badges.

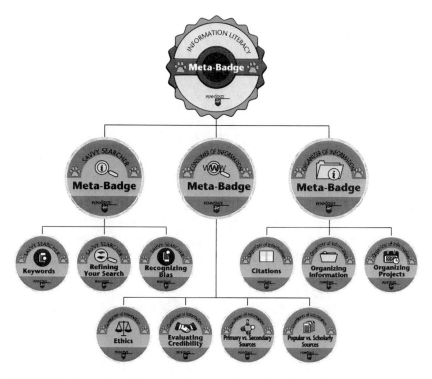

FIGURE 8.3   Penn State University libraries information literacy badges.

Badge designers can design ways in which a badge family can be developed over time, offering a way to grow from a family of 5 or 10 badges to 100+ badges if desired. The design of badge families does, however, raise concerns and considerations of scalability, including how many badges are created and how many evaluations are being requested.

Each badge that is created will require an evaluation as described above. Part of this decision will depend on the nature of the content and desired assessments. For example, when a department decides that creative writing papers have to be evaluated in a certain way to help the learners develop their skills, this could potentially impact the number of courses offered and each course's enrollment. Similarly, badge evaluations would need to have an organizational consideration with regard to the scale at which badge issuers can support an increase in offering either badges or reviews.

Conclusion

There may be those who question the value and worth of learning technologies and, in particular, digital badges (Resnick, 2012). However, as was illustrated throughout this chapter, the pedagogy and learning theories behind the design of the badges are more important than the technology itself. According to Rogers (2003), people need to see the relative advantage of an innovation to supplant a previously adopted innovation. Therefore, to increase the odds of adoption of digital badges and the likelihood that the badges can scale, it is important to have sound design processes to ensure a quality product. Future empirical studies will help to inform the research base on effective design of digital badges. The philosophy behind the design needs to be made as explicit as possible to strengthen the value of digital badges.

Badge design is a multifaceted process and badges can be designed to meet many goals. It is the design behind the use of the technology that directly affects the experience for learners. While traditional instructional design processes aid in digital badge creation, there are some unique considerations for the instructional design that surrounds the creation of digital badges. A quality design has to take into account several factors. Digital badge design must be considered within the existing learning context and organizational framework, and must adhere to guidelines that ensure they stand on their own and within a badge family. To summarize, designing for digital badges is a complex process and this chapter is intended to serve as but one resource to create quality badges.

References

Badges/FAQs (n.d.). Retrieved from https://wiki.mozilla.org/Badges/FAQs.

Berk, J., Olsen, S., Atkinson, J., & Comerford, J. (2007). Innovation in a podshell: Bringing information literacy into the world of podcasting. *The Electronic Library*, *25*(4), 409–419. doi: 10.1108/02640470710779826.

Carr-Chellman, A., Cuyar, C., & Breman, J. (1998). User-design: A case application in health care training. *Educational Technology Research and Development*, *46*(4), 97–114. doi: 10.1007/BF02299677.

Casilli, C. (2014, February 26). The myth of the lightweight badge. Retrieved from https://carlacasilli.wordpress.com/2014/02/26/the-myth-of-the-lightweight-badge/.

Cho, K., & Schunn, C. D. (2007). Scaffolded writing and rewriting in the discipline: A web-based reciprocal peer review system. *Computers & Education*, *48*(3), 409–426.

Gamrat, C., Zimmerman, H. T., Dudek, J., & Peck, K. (2014). Personalized workplace learning: An exploratory study on digital badging within a teacher professional development program. *British Journal of Educational Technology*, *45*, 1136–1148. doi: 10.1111/bjet.12200.

Grant, C. (2013, October 23). 5 buckets for badge system design: "You are here." Retrieved from www.hastac.org/blogs/slgrant/2013/10/23/5-badge-system-design-classes-you-are-here.

Hattie, J., & Timperley, H. (2007). The power of feedback. *Review of Educational Research*, *77*(1), 81–112.

Hobbs, K., & Klare, D. (2010). User driven design: Using ethnographic techniques to plan student study space. *Technical Services Quarterly*, *27*(4), 347–363. doi: http://dx.doi.org/10.1080/07317131003766009.

Jonassen, D. H., Tessmer, M., & Hannum, W. H. (1999). *Task analysis methods for instructional design*. Mahwah, NJ: Lawrence Erlbaum Associates, Inc.

Jonsson, A., & Svingby, G. (2007). The use of scoring rubrics: Reliability, validity and educational consequences. *Educational Research Review, 2*, 130–144.

Raish, V., & Rimland, E. (2016). Employer perceptions of critical information literacy skills and digital badges. *College & Research Libraries, 77*(1), 87–113. doi: 10.5860/crl.77.1.87.

Resnick, M. (2012, February 27). Still a Badge Skeptic. Retrieved April 27, 2015, from www.hastac.org/blogs/mres/2012/02/27/still-badge-skeptic.

Rogers, E. M. (2003). *Diffusion of innovation*. New York, NY: Free Press.

9

BADGING AS MICRO-CREDENTIALING IN FORMAL EDUCATION AND INFORMAL EDUCATION

Kyle Peck, Kyle Bowen, Emily Rimland, and Jamie Oberdick

Open badges have transformative potential in both formal and informal education. Traditional grading, reporting, and certification systems were created in a paper and pencil world, and the "micro-credentialing" potential of badges represents a disruptive technology that will increase the transparency and quality of educational products and services, while transforming communication about what has been learned. Because of their ability to convey more and better information than traditional types of educational records, open badges offer new opportunities to formal and informal educators, as well as to employers who might use them to understand the capabilities of potential employees. It has been predicted that badges will "reinvent the report card" and "transform the transcript" (Peck, 2013), and will "disrupt the diploma" (Hoffman, 2013).

While badges were designed to document what has been learned, grades are designed primarily to sort people (like eggs or meat). Grades institutionalize and perpetuate the idea of "failure" in learning, rather than progress to completion, and they often have more to do with compliance with rules and deadlines than with mastery. Grades summarize performance across multiple modules and types of content, masking whether a person has mastered individual concepts or skills.

Despite their limitations, for virtually every student, the acquisition of grades becomes a key and central part of their formal educational experience. Earning course grades is a symbolic achievement that represents the whole of a student's performance in a specific class. Course grades are married with "credits" that are used to quantify the amount, or literal number of hours, of class activities. As students move from course to course, their grades and credits are collected and reported on an official academic transcript. The student transcript is an important, official, and private document. It is the only document that students can use to show proof of the classes taken, grades achieved, and credits earned. Over time,

FIGURE 9.1   Comparing the college transcript to a retail store receipt.

the transcript has become the primary means of exchanging academic credentials between institutions.

When reflecting on the design and use of transcripts, it is interesting to see that, as shown in Figure 9.1, they are nearly indistinguishable from retail store receipts. Both attempt to detail and summarize a list of items as a means of providing "proof" of successful purchase. Like a receipt, each unit item is abbreviated and represented by a catalog number. This information connects the course to scheduling within the institution, but has limited meaning to anyone outside the institution reviewing the transcript.

In addition to the course numbers, transcripts and receipts both provide an abbreviated description of the purchased item. This description has just enough information to differentiate items on the list, but lacks the fidelity to even simply explain what may be included. In the case of course titles, there is no standard or formula for crafting them, which makes many indecipherable. Although some course titles attempt to add numbers to help show a sequence in learning (e.g., "Life Drawing 1" and "Life Drawing 2"), they typically do not explain whether this is a progression, extension, or replication of learning outcomes.

The fundamental challenge with academic transcripts is that they don't provide information about what a student learned, but rather an accounting of time spent. With a growth in student learning opportunities that exist across and outside of courses, the notion of credit transcripts may no longer be appropriate.

Badges represent an evolution in this concept that not only creates greater clarity around student learning, but can be a component part of the learning design process, becoming a source of motivation for students.

Another big difference between badges and report cards or degrees is the "granularity" or "chunk size" of what is being reported. Badges employ a grain size that effectively communicates that a valued unit of learning, representing knowledge, skills or attributes, has been demonstrated. Each badge describes something discreet that its earner knew and/or demonstrated the ability to do, while courses and diplomas combine many topics and are often confounded by other factors like attendance or class participation. As Hoffman (2013) put it, "So a diploma is essentially a communications device that signals a person's readiness for certain jobs. But unfortunately it's a dumb, static communication device with roots in the twelfth century. That needs to change" (paragraphs 15–17). While some fear that people will earn too many badges, and that there are so many trivial badges, reviewers will be inundated by the sheer number of badges, it should be remembered that applicants need not display all of their badges, just the most relevant. And the value of a badge can be instantly determined by clicking the badge to review the criteria for earning the badge, the caliber of the badge issuer, and any endorsements that might have been provided by employers, professional associations, or other groups. Additionally, there is speculation that the near future will bring automated systems that will be able to scan badge metadata and contribute to the initial screening process.

Badging in Formal Education

Interest in digital badges as a replacement for degrees or diplomas has, of course, started to capture the attention of formal education institutions. They would be remiss to overlook them, as new types of educational tools could serve to disrupt the longstanding framework of formal education (O'Shaughnessy, 2011). Interestingly, the U.S. government was among the early promoters of open badges, and even Arne Duncan (2011), U.S. Secretary of Education, referred to digital badges as being "transformative" to education, stressing that, "As we upgrade the crumbling infrastructure of our schools, we must also invest in the innovative learning technologies that can transform teaching and learning" (paragraph 9).

The term "transformative" is apropos because badges promote the idea that learning is much larger than what happens inside school walls, giving credence to organizations other than formal education providers (Duncan, 2011). Badges are also potentially transformative because they could replace the dismal "grades" issued by formal education providers, which often combine mastery of the knowledge and skills to be learned with compliance factors such as attendance and class participation, which diminishes the grade's ability to communicate mastery (Peck, 2013). In addition, badging can usher in the increasingly popular concept of competency-based education, including the ability to take and retake exams or to submit other evidence of mastery repeatedly, until the criteria are met. No longer must learning take the traditional assessment routine of standardized tests, since badges can become a form of embedded assessment, can place an emphasis on mastery of skills (much like the Common Core Standards), and can allow students to advance in a non-linear fashion (Farber, 2013).

Badging in Parallel with Degrees?

With new ways to learn and assess outside brick and mortar institutions, students and employers alike need and want recognition for learning, including much of the lifelong learning that often goes unrecognized in today's formal education systems. Badges can complement traditional degrees, which have been around for centuries and are not likely to go away soon. Graduates who enhance their formal degrees and certifications with badges could gain an edge by identifying specific skills employers may be looking for and by virtue of the ability of badges to include evidence or artifacts for review (Knight, 2013). Formal learning institutions already have power and authority over learning and degrees, but badges can provide additional opportunities and flexibility to graduates, benefiting both formal education institutions and their graduates.

Advantages of Badges in Formal Education

Aside from all the buzz that's being generated about badges, there are other clear advantages. Digital badges provide a level of *transparency* rarely seen in formal education. Badge earners can choose to include the *evidence* or artifacts used to earn the badge. Badges provide an unprecedented level of *granularity* for skills as well, allowing badge earners to hone in on the exact skills they want to showcase. Badges encourage various types of *higher-quality assessment,* above and beyond the hackneyed quiz format, allowing badge earners to develop other skills, such as writing, with the submitted evidence being verified by an authority. Badges also fold in well with new *competency-based* approaches to education that are gaining popularity (Kamenetz, 2015). As Bowen and Thomas (2014) put it, "Instead of saying, 'Time's up, you got a C!' We'd be able to say, 'Time's not up. Right now you're at a C level. What do you need to do to get to an A level?'" (para. 8). With badges, graduates and alumni walk away with *expanded portfolios of verified skills*, which they can confidently present to an employer.

Obstacles to Badging in Formal Education

There are, of course, obstacles to badges in education too, and they have their detractors. As with any new innovation, there is hard work to be done "up front," and there are investments to be made. Due to their novelty, there is quite a bit of initial input needed to create badges, including the development of learning outcomes, exercises, and assessments; assessing learning outcomes well; and developing the *technology infrastructure* needed to issue open badges and archive and retrieve the badge criteria and evidence. Teachers and higher education faculty are stretched thin as it is and therefore have *little time or incentive* to develop badges. Some worry that the high *transparency may help competitors*, creating fear that they may be giving away trade secrets by using badges. Although competencies are gaining popularity, there are still real questions of *how to define badges for more abstract areas* such as poetry. Finally, some educators fear that innovations like badges may mean *giving up their long-respected and desired role* of "sage on the stage."

In order to overcome these obstacles, there are a few considerations to undertake that could benefit formal education in the long run. If educators choose to ignore this type of disruption, it could mean ultimately missing the boat on the next wave of formal education trends. Institutions would do well to consider their areas of specialization and apply badges to those areas in order to create highly desirable and unique badges that will be prized and valued by students. Faculty, who worry about being displaced by badges, should be open to the idea of reframing their roles and recognizing the opportunity to develop higher-order skills themselves or retool their curricula.

How Badges Can Contribute in Formal Education

Based on his experience with digital badging first at Purdue University and now at Penn State University, Kyle Bowen has developed the model shown as Figure 9.2 illustrating some of the ways badging can be use in higher education, including curricular, co-curricular, cross-curricular, and open-curricular categories.

Other important roles digital badges can play are providing a *common currency* across institutions for students who want to transfer credits and avoid taking redundant courses, and serving as complementary credentials for learners who may already have or may not need degrees (Bowen & Thomas, 2014, p. 23).

The Case against Badging in Formal Education

Not everyone agrees that digital and open badges should be embraced in formal education. There seem to be three primary objections associated with the use of badges in education, in addition to the sheer amount of work that would need to be done to implement digital badges: (1) badges can be misused as extrinsic motivation to entice learners to engage; (2) the grain size associated with badges results in a granular approach in which the parts don't add up to the whole; and (3) there will be so many badges that they will lose their meaning.

In a post called "Still a Badge Skeptic," Mitchel Resnick (2012) objected to the fact that "in many cases, educators are proposing badge systems in order to motivate students" (para. 3). Resnick says he understands why they do it—"because

BADGES & MICROCREDENTIALS
In Higher Education

Student Badges and Microcredentials	
Embedded in *credit-bearing* learning	**Embedded in *non-credit* learning**
Curricular Recognize learning outcomes within courses.	**Co-curricular** Recognize learning or scholarship that occurs outside traditional courses.
Issued by faculty, programs, colleges, or university. *Examples:* Learning outcomes or competencies E-portfolio development Supports prior learning assessment Internship programs	Issued by student organizations, centers, research projects, or scholarship programs. *Examples:* Engaged scholarship Liberal Arts Citizens Student research Student organizations or events
Cross-curricular Recognize learning outcomes across courses or credentials. Issued by faculty, programs, colleges, or university.	**Open-curricular** Recognize learning outcomes in openly available structured courses. Issued by faculty, programs, colleges, centers, departments, research projects, or university.
Possible examples: General Education Outcomes Engaged scholarship opportunities	*Possible examples:* MOOCs Short courses Certificate programs Community engagement programs
Faculty/Staff Badges and Microcredentials	
Professional development Recognize learning as part of faculty/staff professional development.	***Certifications*** Recognize learning that may be required for faculty/staff member's role or position.
Possible examples: Training Organizational improvement opportunities Service recognition	*Possible examples:* Regulatory requirements Annual or renewable training

FIGURE 9.2   Categories of badge use in higher education.

students get excited and engaged by badges" (para. 3). He wonders how long that interest will last, and whether the extrinsic motivation they provide will "crowd out other sources of motivation, undermining opportunities for learners to develop sustained engagement with the underlying ideas and activities" (para. 6). This case is also well made by a children's book, *Franklin Wants a Badge*, which preceded the advent of digital badges, but has been posted as a VoiceThread conversation for digital badging enthusiasts and critics by Joseph and Halavais

(2012). The bottom line, as Resnick (2012) puts it, "Simply engaging students is not enough. They need to be engaged for the right reasons" (para. 4). Kohn (2014) expressed similar concerns and wondered about who really benefits from the use of digital badges, noting that the suppliers of the badges often have profit motives, and questioned whether these benefits are justified.

Open Badging in Informal Education

Informal education is "casual and continuous learning from life experiences outside organized formal or nonformal education" (ERIC, 2015). Government agencies around the world are attending to informal education, because, as Friedman (2002) reported in an address to the National Academy of Engineering, "over 70% of Americans are not in school," and "92% of any individual's lifetime is spent engaged in pursuits other than formal, curriculum-guided education" (para. 2).

The use of digital badges for learning began outside the formal education domain, instigated by a white paper titled "An Open Badge System Framework: A foundational piece on assessment and badges *for open, informal, and social learning environments*" written by Peer 2 Peer University and the Mozilla Foundation (2011). Although formal institutions have been rather slow to adopt digital badges, informal educational organizations around the world are embracing them.

For example, Cities of Learning (2014) describes its badging project that engages learners ages four to twenty-four in Chicago, Columbus, Dallas, Los Angeles, Pittsburgh, and Washington, DC, as "a new effort to network citywide resources to keep youth engaged in educational and career opportunities when school lets out" (Open Badges Blog, 2014, paragraph 5). Local partners in each city fund the project, and national support has been provided by the John D. and Catherine T. MacArthur Foundation, the Digital Youth Network, and the Badge Alliance (Open Badges Blog, 2014). The project offers "free or low-cost opportunities for youth to learn online or participate in programming at parks, libraries, museums, and other institutions" (paragraph 7), engaging learners in activities as diverse as fashion design, robotics, computer programming, and workplace internships, offering open badges for successful completion.

Another great example of digital badging in informal education is the Smithsonian Institution's "Quests" (Smithsonian Institute, 2013). The primary goal of this project "is to inspire youth to explore their own interests through a series of online activities and related incentive badges" (para. 4), and the secondary goal is "to enhance students' cognitive capabilities by incorporating knowledge and skill-building into the quests" (para. 5). Online conferences are incorporated into quests, the quests are interdisciplinary, and they are designed to offer students the opportunity to choose to pursue quests they care about most. The project also offers badges to educators and encourages educators to use quests either as part of a formal standards-aligned school curriculum or as a student-driven after-school activity.

Digital badging in informal educational contexts is happening around the world, and a list of badging projects in both formal and informal education can be found on a Mozilla Foundation hosted webpage titled "Who's currently issuing Open Badges?" (Mozilla, 2015b).

Badging in Workforce Preparation

While digital badges are beginning to make an impact in education, they are also starting to gain traction in the workplace. In particular, 2014 was a year of global growth for work-related badges. Mozilla's Open Badges project (Mozilla, 2015a) has sparked badging projects and initiatives in the United Kingdom, France, Finland, Serbia, Spain, Germany, Australia, and New Zealand. The Cities of Learning program, which teaches young people workforce skills, has grown from one summer program in 2013 to six in 2014 (Forester, 2014). "The Badge Alliance" was created to promote the use of open badges, and has gathered a set of existing workforce use cases to both document the value of badges and encourage the spread of their use (Derryberry, Presant, & Garon, 2014–15).

One workforce use case noted by Enkerli (2015) involves the Canadian government. Canada has a project known as Blueprint 2020, aimed at creating effective public service via a skilled public sector workforce. As of January 2015, they were piloting open badges for employees at Natural Resources Canada. They would convert their existing awards system that features paper certificates into digital badges via the digital badging management platform, the Open Badge Factory. There are plans to expand this form of badging to other federal departments.

So, what is attracting employers and human resources types to digital badging? A big reason is that digital badges are being viewed as a potential solution to one of the more significant issues facing employers today: "the skills gap." The skills gap refers to employers having difficulty finding employees who are qualified for the job openings, in both the technical and soft skills arenas. Jennifer McNelly, president of trade group The Manufacturing Institute, has noted that a survey done by the employee search firm Manpower found that 82 percent of manufacturers have reported issues finding skilled workers (WIECHE Cooperative for Educational Technologies, 2014).

McNelly said her organization is helping the manufacturing industry bridge this gap using digital badges as a form of certification, not only teaching new skills but also enabling individuals to transfer previously learned skills to the manufacturing world. For example, to make it easier for veterans to translate skills they learned in the military to the working world, the Manufacturing Institute offers the Military Manufacturing Badge. As of early 2014, nearly 4,000 transitioning veterans have earned this badge.

While there are badges for "hard skill" job requirements such as software coding and manufacturing welding, there are also badges for so-called "soft skills," sometimes referred to as "attributes" or "twenty-first-century skills." For example, the Missouri Customer Service Partnership, which includes state government agencies, customer-centric businesses, community colleges, and nonprofit organizations, is proposing the use of digital badges as part of a learning experience for youth new to the workplace. They offer 12 badges. The badge modules include communication, attitude, networking, teamwork, critical thinking, and social media (Forlaw, 2014). Professors at Penn State University are also developing badge sets that include systems thinking, global awareness, and empathy.

Another aspect of digital badges that is appealing to employers is a future where they make hiring choices based on more—and more accurate—information than what they currently can access. While some employers may balk at the idea of more information, because they have so many résumés and cover letters to sort through, there are plenty of benefits to the added information from badges. Instead of relying on the sparse information of college transcripts and perhaps inaccurate information from references, a set of digital badges could give an employer a clear idea of what skills an employee brings to the table, and how she or he gained those skills. There have been conversations among badging pioneers about a time when the evidence in badges becomes (with the badge holder's permission, of course) available in digital form to search engines, so that much of the sorting that human resource professionals now do manually will be done by computers, allowing them to turn over the initial screenings to data systems, freeing more time to go deeper into the differences that might separate top candidates. A great example of this is Carnegie Mellon University's "Cortex Principles of Advanced Programming, Level 2" badge. This badge provides information including when it was issued, the name, title, and affiliations of the teacher who verified the badge, the score on the student's final exam, and even a link to exam questions (Carey, 2012).

Although machine-based interpretation of badges is not part of the current implementation of badges, and although there might be issues with early attempts to allow computers to sort candidates, it seems inevitable that as badging matures, and as geographically distributed workforces become more common, machine-based interpretation of badges will make important contributions to the hiring process, and will boost the desirability of open badges (Alcorn, 2014).

So, what roles should employers have in developing badges? One role is identifying new subjects for certification. This could include badges that meet local employment needs, such as conversational Spanish in areas with significant Hispanic populations. Human resource professionals can provide input in both badge model discussions and creation of a taxonomy of badges. Human resource professionals will need to become more educated about badges and how they work, so they can become better prepared to weigh provided input on the skills they want to see certified by badges.

A new addition to the badging standard that may also improve the value of badges in employment decisions is the concept of *endorsements*. The Badge Alliance has an Endorsement Working Group that is developing a plan to allow endorsement of open badges and make endorsements more structured and practical. This will allow third-party organizations to support and promote relevant badges that they find most valuable to them, through endorsements that become part of the meta-data that is revealed when a viewer clicks an open badge. When this endorsement level is available and in widespread use, employers and professional associations (among others) will be able to tell people viewing badges that they have reviewed the criteria for the badge and the assessment processes and that they respect the badge as a valid form of certification. For example, if the Association for Educational Communications and Technology (AECT) was to endorse a set of badges awarded to instructional designers by universities, employers might be more likely to hire the designers prepared by those universities because they would know that they had skills that were identified as important by AECT and that AECT has confidence in the process used to develop and assess those skills.

Conclusion

As a new tool to document learning, digital badges are extremely versatile, providing more and better information, instantly available in digital form. The transparency they offer about *what is to be learned* benefits the learner (and the educator) and the information on *what has been learned* benefits both learners and potential employers. Digital badges offer the potential to make learning more personal, relevant, and learner centered, and to escort education to a performance-based system, transforming learning in schools, museums, after-school programs, clubs, and the workplace. Like any tool, digital and open badges can be used well or badly, but thoughtful use promises dividends for learners, educators, and employers alike.

References

Alcorn, S. (2014). Associations, the new lifelong learning hubs. *Associations Now.* Retrieved from http://associationsnow.com/2014/08/associations-the-new-lifelong-learning-hubs/.

Bowen, K., & Thomas, A. (2014). Badges: A common currency for learning. *Change: The Magazine of Higher Learning. 46*(1), 21–25. doi: 10.1080/00091383.2014.867206. Retrieved from http://dx.doi.org/10.1080/00091383.2014.867206.

Carey, K. (2012). Show me your badge. *The New York Times.* Retrieved from www.nytimes.com/2012/11/04/education/edlife/show-me-your-badge.html?pagewanted=all&_r=0.

Cities of Learning (2014). Cities of learning. Retrieved from www.citiesoflearning.org.

Derryberry, A., Presant, D., & Garon, G. (June 2014–February 2015). Workforce examples of badge use [Ongoing etherpad listing]. Retrieved from http://etherpad.badgealliance.org/workforce-badges-in-use.

Duncan, A. (2011). Digital badges for learning [Speech transcript]. *U.S. Department of Education.* Retrieved from www.ed.gov/news/speeches/digital-badges-learning.

Enkerli, A. (2015). Lab session summary: Implementing badges. Retrieved from www.vteducation.org/en/articles/digital-badges/lab-session-summary-implementing-badges.

ERIC (2015). Informal education. Retrieved from http://eric.ed.gov/?ti=Informal+ Education.

Farber, M. (2013). Badges and the common core. *Edutopia*. Retrieved from www.edutopia. org/blog/badges-and-the-common-core-matthew-farber.

Forester, J. (2014). The Badge Alliance at Mozfest [Blog post]. *Open Badges Blog*. Retrieved from http://openbadges.tumblr.com/post/104171168834/the-badge-alliance-at-mozfest.

Forlaw, B. (2014). Badges for job retention, continuous learning [Briefing for Badge Alliance Workforce Group]. Retrieved from www.slideshare.net/BlairForlaw/ badge-alliance-briefing-092314.

Friedman, A. (2002). Technology Literacy: What Informal Education Has to Offer. Speech to the National Symposium on Technological Literacy, January 17, 2002. Retrieved from www.nae.edu/Projects/24574/Symposium/AlanFriedmanRemarks.aspx.

Hoffman, R. (2013). Disrupting the diploma. *LinkedIn Pulse*. Retrieved from www. linkedin.com/pulse/20130916065028-1213-disrupting-the-diploma.

Joseph, B., & Halavais, A. (2012). Franklin wants a badge: A crowdsourced critique of badge anxiety [VoiceThread post]. Retrieved from https://voicethread.com/new/ share/3103017/.

Kamenetz, A. (2015). Competency-based degree programs on the rise. *nprEd*. Retrieved from www.npr.org/blogs/ed/2015/01/26/379387136/competency-based-degree-programs-on-the-rise.

Knight, E. (2013). Open badges transform the higher education and labor markets. *EvoLLLution*. Retrieved from www.evolllution.com/distance_online_learning/ open-badges-transform-higher-education-labor-markets/.

Kohn, A. (2014). Alfie Kohn on open badges [Video keynote address to the 2014 ePIC Conference]. Retrieved from www.youtube.com/watch?v=p_98XcxJqkw.

Mozilla (2015a). Badges wiki. Retrieved from https://wiki.mozilla.org/Badges.

Mozilla (2015b). Who's currently issuing Open badges? Retrieved from http:// openbadges.org/participating-issuers.

Open Badges Blog (2014). 6 big U.S. cities launch year-round citywide learning initiatives offering digital badges for youth [Blog post]. Retrieved from http://openbadges. tumblr.com/page/15.

O'Shaughnessy, L. (2011). Forget the college degree: Earn digital badges instead. Retrieved from www.cbsnews.com/news/forget-the-college-degree-earn-digital-badges-instead/.

Peck, K. L. (2013). Reinventing the report card. *AdvancED Source, Fall 2013*, p. 5. Retrieved from www.advanc-ed.org/source/reinventing-report-card.

Peer 2 Peer University & Mozilla Foundation (2011). An open badge system framework: A foundational piece on assessment and badges for open, informal, and social learning environments. *Digital Media and Learning Research Hub*. Retrieved from http:// dmlcentral.net/resources/4440.

Resnick, M. (2012). Still a badge skeptic [Blog post]. Humanities, Arts, Science, and Technology Alliance and Collaboratory (HASTAC) Blog. Retrieved from www.hastac .org/blogs/mres/2012/02/27/still-badge-skeptic.

Smithsonian Institution (2013). Smithsonian quests: Digital badging for the classroom and beyond. Retrieved from http://smithsonianquests.org/about/.

WIECHE Cooperative for Educational Technologies (2014). The manufacturing approach to digital badges [Youtube video featuring Jennifer McNeilly of The Manufacturing Institute]. Retrieved from www.youtube.com/watch?v=VEgwJwrK3qQ.

10

DIGITAL BADGES, LEARNING AT SCALE, AND BIG DATA

Barton K. Pursel, Chris Stubbs, Gi Woong Choi, and Phil Tietjen

Higher education in the United States is arguably unsustainable in the predominant model. Students physically attending a university for a four-year degree as the norm may someday become the exception. As tuition continues to rise, along with student debt, the average family income remains relatively flat. Interesting models are emerging, such as the Western Governor's University (www.wgu .edu/) that offers a competency-based approach to degrees. We also see an increase in adult learners taking degree or certificate programs completely online that are designed to fit into the busy lives of working adults. Projects like Stanford 2025 (Stanford University, n. d.) go so far as predicting when our current system will collapse, and then present possible futures. While badges do play a role in some of these examples, we see other trends in higher education that will undoubtedly somehow integrate or influence badges. In this chapter, we examine current trends, such as learning at scale and big data, and how they might intersect with badges to create unique opportunities for learners. Before moving into possible future states, we first examine how badges are currently influencing specific areas of education.

The Impact of Badges on Current Academic Practices

Since the dawn of the modern university, higher education has viewed itself as both "facilitator" and "assessor" of learning. But in response to rising tuition costs and an increasing number of students finding learning opportunities outside the traditional classroom, a new university experience is emerging. In this new paradigm, learning is left to the discretion of students to accomplish on their own. The role of the university, meanwhile, is more heavily focused on assessment and credentialing rather than teaching, allowing for a flexible and efficient, often less expensive, college experience. We see this trend playing out both in emergent higher education paradigms like Western Governors University (WGU) and in traditional settings, like the Flex Option (Board of Regents—University of Wisconsin System, 2015) at the University of Wisconsin (UW). As WGU describes it, their emphasis is on "showing what you know," rather than spending a great deal of time teaching specific content. In some ways, WGU has offered an opportunity similar to that offered to high school students by the AP examination structure, giving credit for performance.

These emerging models represent a substantial commitment to Prior Learning Assessment (PLA). While most universities have some process or procedure for PLA, it is rarely designed as an essential part of the student experience. Facilitating the process at scale involves careful mapping of the specific competencies that compose university classes to clear deliverables and methods of assessment. Put another way, it involves breaking the degree down into more discreet pieces. By doing so, universities open the door to a new category of students, for whom the barriers to traditional education were too high, by providing much shorter paths to a degree.

Once students, educators, or administrators are willing to cross into a university experience more heavily reliant on prior or "external" learning, it allows them to reexamine some of the traditional assumptions regarding higher education, such as the 15-week semester or the three-credit course. Imagine an oversimplified example of an introductory English course, 15 weeks long, broken down into five, three-week modules, consisting of grammar, composition, editing, supporting evidence, and audience connection. Prior to taking the course, Jane, a student, spent her summer working in the marketing department of a local business, where she was responsible for developing materials for public outreach. Jane's experiences are not sufficient to allow her to completely test out of the English course, but she already knows a great deal about audience connection through her summer work experience. There is little more she can gain from three weeks of content on audience connection. The traditional academic system does a poor job of accounting for situations like Jane's. But if courses were broken down into discrete competencies, it might allow Jane to more efficiently use those three weeks. Perhaps Jane could substitute a more advanced audience connection learning experience from a different "course" during that time period, or maybe shift more time to other courses or competencies. A more modular education will have many implications for students (both current and future), and support a culture of lifelong learning, something that educators agree is important.

The academic transcript and the diploma are traditionally the formal deliverables of the educational experience. And while they do convey valuable information, they only provide a surface-level glimpse of student knowledge. A grade in a course indicates only an overall score, but nothing about what specific areas of that course the student either struggled with or mastered. Nor does a transcript typically contain any information regarding non-academic experiences, such as co-curricular activities.

At schools like Northern Arizona University (NAU), we see a different benefit of breaking the curriculum down into more discrete pieces: transparency. NAU offers students a "Competency Report". This report details specific areas of student achievement in a far more thorough manner than a transcript, giving a detailed picture of what a student has learned and the degree of mastery. We also see this concept illustrated at The Pennsylvania State University, where the College of Liberal Arts' "Liberal Arts Citizen" initiative (Penn State, 2014) was created to capture student experiences in four co-curricular areas not measured by typical academic credentials: global perspective, engagement, initiative, and leadership.

These open, badge-like initiatives also blend well with the concept of e-portfolios. While universities often provide support for e-portfolio creation, little is done at scale to help support the generation of rich, meaningful content that fully encapsulates the totality of the college experience. Yes, you might have a platform to share your experiences, but what exactly should you say? Where should you begin? Badges can act as a starting point from which to share your experiences. If a badge is the proof, the e-portfolio can be the context that connects the dots between validated experiences. A university commitment to badges creates a foundation from which all students can easily develop a rich, evidence-based portfolio, supporting content creation in the same way that we support technology.

Digital badges represent a substantial shift in the way we view education. By breaking content and assessment into smaller pieces than the traditional course, badges make it easier and more transparent for learners to understand the expectations being placed upon them and increase the likelihood that they can apply existing experiences toward their post-secondary education. Not only can this reduce the time and cost associated with earning a degree, but it also introduces the possibility of a far more modular academia, less rooted in the three-credit course and the semester model, and instead tied to measuring knowledge. But the impact of badges on learning is certainly not limited to the traditional academic experience. In the next section, we'll examine ways in which badges might play a role in contexts that involve learning at a large scale.

Badges and Learning at Scale

The Massive Open Online Course (MOOC), at the time of this writing, is the dominant form of learning at a large scale. While MOOCs are still finding their place in higher education, they will soon start to mingle with badges in several interesting ways. Most MOOC providers issue students a certificate or statement of accomplishment upon the completion of a MOOC, though currently the percentage of students who earn this credential is relatively low, usually 6 to 10 percent

(Jordan, 2014). This statistic is very misleading; of the thousands (or tens of thousands) of students who enroll in a MOOC, many enter the course without necessarily intending to complete the course in its entirety. Students have different reasons for enrolling in a MOOC, such as to socialize with other students, to satisfy their curiosity about the content, or to learn a subset of the overall course content (Zutshi, O'Hare, & Rodafinos, 2013). This latter example is where badges will play a critical role in illustrating the knowledge and skills a learner mastered as part of a MOOC. As an example, consider a MOOC on English. Going back to our earlier example, the course might have five major sections: grammar, composition, editing, supporting evidence, and audience connection. As a student enrolling in this course, I already know a great deal about grammar, composition, and editing, so I only care about the content areas around supporting evidence and audience connection. If these modules are well designed and include a way I can demonstrate my competencies in these areas (perhaps through writing samples), I should be able to illustrate, through badges, that I have mastered supporting evidence and audience connection. Researchers from Google (Wilkowski, Deutsch, & Russell, 2014) suggest a similar design approach for MOOCs, where a MOOC is a learning experience that comprises a set of learning activities students can pick and choose from, creating a more meaningful, personalized learning experience. Successfully completing each activity can easily translate to a badge, and these badges then might be instantly published to LinkedIn, something that Coursera is already allowing LinkedIn users to do with statements of accomplishment earned in Coursera MOOCs.

One large obstacle to leveraging badges in a MOOC environment lies in the accurate assessment of knowledge on a massive scale. Currently, MOOCs often rely on simplistic evaluation methods, such as multiple choice quizzes and tests, or they rely on peer assessment, where students review one another's work. Quizzes and tests don't always work for measuring high-level knowledge, while novices grading novices in a peer assessment model is not always a valid way to assess mastery of high-level knowledge. Two potential methods to increase peer assessment validity in MOOCs, thereby strengthening the confidence we have in badges earned in MOOCs, are the credibility index in peer assessment and a human-computing approach (Pantic, Pentland, Nijholt, & Huang, 2007).

The credibility index approach (Xiong, Goins, Suen, Pun, & Zang, 2014) is a way to strengthen current peer assessment efforts, providing each student a credibility score as he/she moves through the course and assesses other students. If student A has scored 100 percent on the first three quizzes, and his/her assessment of a known-quantity assignment (a training assignment, assessed by a student then compared to the instructor's assessment of the same assignment) matches the assessment of the instructor, his/her assessment scores should carry more weight compared to student B, who scored a 70 on the first three quizzes, and has a two-point difference from the instructor when grading the known-quantity assignment. In theory, this type of peer assessment approach will provide a higher likelihood that an assignment was accurately assessed by a number of peers.

The field of human computing is starting to augment peer review systems in MOOCs through some of the work of Scott Klemmer (2014). Klemmer describes a peer review system that can machine grade student-submitted essays and assign both a score and confidence interval to that score, and then recommend a specific number of peers to also review the essays. The machine can even go so far as to recommend specific areas of an essay to focus on for the human graders. While this system theoretically increases the accuracy of the assessments, a challenge here is that the machine grading system often requires a great deal of student submissions that are already graded by an expert, to act as a comparison set of work for new submissions. So over time, a system like this will become more accurate, though getting a system like this started is a challenge.

In order for badges earned through MOOCs to be taken seriously by potential employers and university admissions offices, a scalable method of assessment, that is valid and reliable, must be present. The above examples represent two possible methods involving peer assessment and human computing, though other researchers are also exploring new ways to assess at scale that are not human resource-intensive.

Another area digital badges will start to impact is open educational resources (OERs). While there is no agreed-upon definition of the term, an OER has been generally described in terms of its chief governing characteristics: digital materials that are freely accessible and that can be re-used, revised, and remixed (McKerlich, Ives, & McGreal, 2013). Open textbooks, such as those offered by MIT's Open Courseware (Massachusetts Institute of Technology, 2015) and OpenStax College (Rice University, 2015), represent two common examples. But OERs can also include resources such as course curricula, modules, multimedia, blogs, and interactive simulations. In the future, perhaps existing OERs will provide the necessary content for learners to master in order to earn badges. For well-defined content areas, linking a badge to various open content on the web should be straightforward, and allow learners to access, for free, accurate content to help them master specific skills and competencies.

As badges begin to proliferate in various areas of education, and as adoption rises, the systems that host these badges will undoubtedly contain massive amounts of data that will provide various members of the badge ecosystem a great deal of insights. We explore this intersection of badges and big data in the following section.

Badges and Big Data

Imagine in the future that a few different badge platforms see large adoption, with hundreds of thousands, to possibly millions, of users. These platforms might be closely linked to companies with various web initiatives, like a new platform within the Google suite of apps or an expanded version of Mozilla's Backpack (Mozilla, n. d.). Or, these badge platforms might be new startups, akin to how

MOOCs emerged through companies like Coursera, EdX, and Udacity. A badge platform will be a repository of big data related to badge earners and creators. The platform will capture the metadata for everything related to digital badges, as well as how users navigate through the platform, browsing and earning badges. Hence, it is important to design effective strategies to manage and utilize these data. Fields such as learning analytics provide a starting point for exploring these data.

According to Siemens et al. (2011), learning analytics refers to "the measurement, collection, analysis and reporting of data about learners and their contexts, for purposes of understanding and optimizing learning and the environments in which it occurs" (p. 4). When interpreting this definition with regard to badges, it would mean measuring, collecting, analyzing, and reporting the metadata created by badge earners to advance their learning and learning environments to maximize learning outcomes.

Digital badges provide metadata that is traceable by the owners of the badge platform. These metadata are often included as part of a badge, when an earner publishes a badge to something like an e-portfolio. Metadata can also be analyzed to recommend a learning trajectory appropriate for each individual badge earner based on comparing specific user data to similar users, much like the way Amazon compares a user's purchase history to similar users in order to make recommendations.

The analytics will also be dynamic; they will change over time. For example, as specific skills become highly sought-after in the workforce, certain badges will begin to rise in popularity. Making these trends "discoverable" through analytics allows the platforms to constantly monitor, and recommend, badges that are relevant to a learner and also important to industry. A platform might begin to recommend a collection of badges based on data from previous badge earners. These badges might be intentionally related to a single collection (for instance, all the badges on a specific topic are created by the same source), or the platforms analytics engine might identify collections over time as users cluster around subsets of badges.

The data under the badge platforms, particularly the largest platforms, will also create opportunities for adaptive learning. Adaptive learning might use aspects of the data to create a personalized learning guideline for each individual, presenting the most efficient path to each learner's goals. The key to adaptive learning lies in how much data it will require to make suggestions. For instance, let's say an earner repeatedly fails to master a badge focusing on regression, a method of data analysis. The earner is working on a collection of badges that culminate in knowledge about inferential statistics, but is now stuck. The platform contains some level of historical data, and can identify other badge earners who appeared to have similar problems on the regression badge. Those historical earners often changed their badge trajectory, and moved into a different series of badges focusing on Microsoft Excel and various aspects of descriptive statistics. Through adaptive learning, the badge then recommends this alternative pathway to the learner struggling to master regression. A badge platform can theoretically provide the first level of learner support, attempting to adapt to learners' needs and provide new paths to completion.

The rich metadata under a widely used badge platform will also provide potential employers with a large amount of data to help identify and recruit talented employees. In the same way some MOOC providers help match successful MOOC students with companies, a large badge platform has the necessary data to match badge earners to employers seeking specific skills. A company might either contract with the badge platform to identify and connect learners with company recruiters, or perhaps a company might outright purchase a dataset from the badge platform owners in order to mine the data for potential employees. Coursera and Udacity offered such a service, providing data to companies about high-performing MOOC students.

In addition to providing companies a bridge to potential employees based on badge profiles, badge platforms can also utilize user data to make inferences about trends in the marketplace. For example, the badge platform owners might examine user data and discover that badges associated with 3D Art and Animation had a 50 percent increase in activity over a six-month period, while badges associated with programming in C+ saw a 75 percent decrease. This helps the platform owner continually monitor trends, and ensure badges that cover important and relevant concepts and content areas are continually available. The data might also uncover interesting badge pathways or trajectories, illustrating unique combinations of skillsets sought after by learners. For example, data might illustrate a linkage between learners who earn badges related to data science, geography, and cyber security. After discovering a large number of learners moving through these badges, the platform owner may raise the visibility of these badges, and attempt to connect people earning these badges to employers in the emerging field of geographic information systems (GIS). By identifying these emerging demands from learners, the platform owners can then populate the platform with new badges, directly addressing the trending content areas.

A challenge of an environment like this for employers is the confidence level they have with specific badges. In some instances, the data might suggest certain badges are very popular in a field or among users, but that specific badge may be poorly designed, and does not require the earner to reach a specific depth of knowledge to earn the badge. This also raises the question of who will be creating badges that reside in dominant platforms? Perhaps employers will create many of the badges, in an effort to strategically align recruiting efforts with specific knowledge that is a requirement of working at a company. Perhaps universities will begin creating badges, much like they create MOOCs now, which represent much more granular skills and competencies. Perhaps it will be a mix, where companies will collaborate with universities or platform owners, in order to create specified badges. Another question is: Who will be the assessors of badges in the dominant badge platforms? Also, who will create the content necessary to support the criteria earners need to demonstrate when earning a badge? Perhaps the badge platform will not host or reference any content, and other organizations will arise that provide the content, and align content from things like MOOCs or OERs to specific badges.

Conclusion

Many questions still exist about how badges, learning at scale, and big data will impact education. Still, clear connections can be drawn that provide hints at how these emerging trends will start to intertwine in the future, to make a positive impact on the accessibility and affordability of education. This chapter predominantly focused on higher education, because we currently see many different initiatives in higher education on a global scale that deal with badges, MOOCs, and big data. That's not to say the innovations are limited only to this space; badges are starting to play a role in both K–12 as well as professional development, and perhaps these areas will catalyze innovation around badges and other trends in education. Regardless of where we see these trends materialize, we firmly believe that badges, along with learning at scale and big data, will play a critical role in reforming a wide variety of current education models around the world.

References

Board of Regents—University of Wisconsin System (2015). UW flexible option: Competency-based degrees, competency-based education & learning. Retrieved May 12, 2015 from http://flex.wisconsin.edu/.

Jordan, K. (2014). Initial trends in enrollment and completion of massive open online courses. *The International Review of Research in Open and Distance Learning, 15*(1). Retrieved from www.irrodl.org/index.php/irrodl/article/view/1651.

Klemmer, S. (2014, March). Design at large. Keynote presented at the 4th International Conference on Learning Analytics and Knowledge, Indianapolis, IN.

Massachusetts Insitute of Technology (2015). MIT OpenCourseWare: Free online course materials. Retrieved May 12, 2015 from http://ocw.mit.edu/index.htm.

McKerlich, R., Ives, C., & McGreal, R. (2013). Measuring use and creation of open educational resources in higher education. *International Review of Research in Open and Distance Learning, 14*(4), 90–103.

Mozilla (n. d.). Mozilla Backpack. Retrieved May 12, 2015 from http://backpack.openbadges.org/backpack/login.

Pantic, M., Pentland, A., Nijholt, A., & Huang, T. (2007). Human computing and machine understanding of human behavior: A survey. In T. Huang, A. Nijholt, M. Pantic, & A. Pentland (Eds.), *Artifical intelligence for human computing* (Vol. 4451, pp. 47–71). Springer Berlin Heidelberg. Retrieved from http://dx.doi.org/10.1007/978-3-540-72348-6_3.

Penn State (2014). Be a liberal arts citizen. Retrieved May 12, 2015 from http://citizens.la.psu.edu/.

Rice University (2015). OpenStax College. Retrieved May 12, 2015 from http://openstaxcollege.org/.

Siemens, G., Gašević, D., Haythornthwaite, C., Dawson, S., Buckingham Shum, S., Ferguson, R., … Baker, R. S. (2011). Open learning analytics: An integrated and modularized platform: SOLAR. Retrieved from http://solaresearch.org/OpenLearning Analytics.pdf.

Stanford University (n. d.). Stanford 2025. Retrieved May 12, 2015 from www. stanford2025.com/.

Wilkowski, J., Deutsch, A., & Russell, D. (2014). Student skill and goal achievement in the mapping with Google MOOC. In M. Sahami, A. Fox, M. Hearst, & M. Chi (Eds.), *Proceedings of the First ACM conference on Learning at Scale Conference*, March 4–5, Atlanta, GA (pp. 3–9). New York, NY: ACM.

Xiong, Y., Goins, D., Suen, H. K., Pun, W. H., & Zang, X. (2014, April). *A proposed credibility index (CI) in peer assessment.* Paper presented at the annual meeting of the National Council on Measurement in Education, Philadelphia, PA.

Zutshi, S., O'Hare, S., & Rodafinos, A. (2013). Experiences in MOOCs: The perspective of students. *American Journal of Distance Education, 27*(4), 218–227.

11

IN THE EYE OF THE BEHOLDER

Value of Digital Badges

Zane L. Berge and Lin Y. Muilenburg

> Higher education is entering a new era, one in which some industry and nonacademic certifications are more valuable than degrees, transcripts are becoming credentials in their own right, and colleges are using badges to offer assurances to employers about students' abilities in ways that a degree no longer seems to do. (Blumenstyk, 2015, B4)

The contemporary workplace is characterized by rapid change, requiring people in the workforce to learn throughout their lives. Even for career pathways that begin with earning a degree, that situation no longer exists where education and training end. The need for lifelong learning has been a catalyst in the development of a large number of learning pathways to achieve professional and life goals, and there are more ways to achieve competency than only through earning a college degree (Bull, 2015). As the options for self-directed learning and competency development proliferate across multiple education providers, tracking that learning in a meaningful, easily accessible way has been problematic. Digital badges are one way to track learning and document evidence of mastering the skills and knowledge acquired along the way (Opperman, 2015).

Badges are symbols that indicate skills, accomplishments, characteristics, or interests and have long been used for these purposes. Most people are familiar with badges in the context of scouting for boys and girls. Merit badges have indicated an individual scout's demonstrated learning and performance in particular areas, in accordance with public, clearly articulated criteria and standards. More recently, *digital badges* have been used in education and training as online records to track the recipients' achievement and the issuers' standards to obtain the badge. The "core components of a badge include the information needed to determine its validity, authenticity, source, and value" (Finkelstein, Knight, &

Manning, 2013, p. 2). Digital badges used to document learning are versatile and make comprehensive digital information quickly accessible to earners and users of the badge system. Digital badges offer badge earners a finer granularity in representing their knowledge and achievements than do traditional diplomas and certificates. Learners have a more complete way to document achievements to those consumers who want to know about their skill set, such as potential employers or educators making decisions about admission to an academic program.

Throughout the pages of this book, you can read about the benefits offered by badging systems to badge earners, issuers, and consumers. Some of the advantages of badge systems include their use to develop individual pathways to learning, competency-based learning, and micro-credentialing, and the fact that the technology is available for anyone to use. You can also read about various barriers to implementing badge systems. Several of these obstacles exist because badging systems are new and all new systems are beset with obstacles that are worked out as the system matures. Other impediments involve stakeholders' resistance to change and how earners, issuers, and consumers perceive the value of the badging system. The focus of this chapter is on how badges and badging systems are *valued* by various stakeholders.

Value Defined

Money can be thought of as having a standard value. At any given time, all persons who have a legal U.S. dollar bill all have the same standard buying power to purchase goods and services. People simply say the value of their $1 bill is a dollar and pretty much everyone knows what is meant.

Besides currency, very few items have a standard value. Most things have value relative to a particular person and context. Craig (2015) talks about how the business model for the music industry changed significantly a little over a decade ago, when the practice of unbundling albums became common. No longer did consumers have to buy songs they wanted and songs they didn't want on a CD; they could purchase only the songs they wanted as digital singles. Since that time, this unbundling has caused the overall revenue of song purchases to drop 50 percent. Craig points out that similar transformational changes are occurring in the television and software industries and continues with these comments regarding higher education:

> The college degree is higher education's version of the bundle. In the tuition price of a degree program, colleges and universities combine a vast array of products and services—some educational, some not. As Anant Agarwal, CEO of edX, asked in a 2013 *Huffington Post* article, "Universities are responsible for admissions, research, facilities management, housing, health care, credentialing, food service, athletic facilities, career guidance and placement, and much more. Which of these items should be at the

core of a university and add value to that experience?" It's a good question; although these items don't add time-to-credential, as the academic program bundle does, they add to the cost. At the end of the day, this has the same effect on return on investment. (Craig, 2015, para. 4)

What does "add value" refer to in the paragraph above? Certainly not to a standard value, such as that of a dollar, because even the same academic program has a different value to each individual degree earner. It is a relative or perceived value being referred to. Badges have value that is relative to their *purpose* and to the *perspective* of the stakeholder being served. The digital badge's benefit, worth, and importance—its perceived value—is different because the perceptions of each individual regarding that badge are different. Thus, the impact a badge has is relative to the value perceived by the individuals and organizations involved in that particular badging system.

Major Purposes of Badges

"Badges serve, in different ways, to recognize a learner's work and encourage learning. Both organizational and learner goals are key components of determining the 'recipe' for any badge system" (Finkelstein, Knight, & Manning, 2013, p. 2). Along with these goals, badges have components that describe what the earner must do to be awarded the badge, the date the badge was awarded, the date the badge expires, and an official way to verify the validity of the award. While documenting the badge recipient's learning is the primary goal of a digital badge system, three main purposes of the system are generally the foci: (1) to act as an incentive to learners to engage in positive learning behaviors; (2) to map progress in learning and foster discovery; and (3) to signal completion and learning of an achievement with a credential that holds value (Gibson, Ostashewski, Flintoff, Grant, & Knight, 2015).

Motivating Learners

Students often become engaged when completing badges and even show excitement too, depending on their interest, their self-directedness, how motivated they are regarding content, the mechanics of how the badge is to be earned, and probably a dozen other factors (Resnick, 2012). Researchers, educators, and instructional designers are exploring the ways in which these factors relate to learner motivation in order to determine effective ways to use digital badge systems for educational purposes.

Mapping Learning Progress

"Badges are tools that are right for capturing accomplishments in a lifelong portfolio that includes proof-of-work, data, multimedia evidence, and a scope and sequence of accomplishments" (Cook, 2014, Archiving, para. 1). It is a new level of detail offered by badges that can map a person's learning pathway across a lifetime of learning. The archiving of learners' pathways and learning over time can document a rich experience for potential employers and other viewers.

From the badge issuer's perspective, a lot of time and resources goes into making a system in which the pathway(s) is logical for the learner to travel. As with any program development effort, getting the sequencing and prerequisites right helps to ensure that the learner has the knowledge and skills necessary to move to the next level of complexity.

Credentialing

Digital badges are a form of micro-credential. By that, we mean they are smaller in scope than degrees or certificates, which are the credentials most often awarded through the traditional academic credentialing systems. Because badges are smaller in scope, they have the advantages of being more flexible and less expensive to implement than the traditional systems. Of course, as with most new systems, badge systems lack the regulatory and accreditation mechanisms, making it more difficult for consumers of badges to assign them a value (Hicken, 2014).

These different functions of digital badges, sometimes in various combinations, drive much of the perceived value attributed to badges by stakeholders to the badging system.

Perpectives of Different Badge Stakeholders

For the discussion here, the three main groups of stakeholders to a badging system are: (1) badge earners (learners); (2) badge issuers (providers of education/training); and (3) badge consumers (e.g., employers, admissions officers at educational institutions).

Earners

Earners spend time and resources in demonstrating achievement of standards representing something they value or hope will have future value to achieving their life goals. Earners are the persons who demonstrate knowledge or achievement of the badge(s), according to the standards prescribed by the issuer, in order to be awarded a particular digital badge or badges.

Issuers

These are the organizations that issue the badges to badge earners. With open badges, any organization can use non-proprietary technology to create, issue, and verify digital badges. This allows the user or anyone else to verify achievements through the issuing organizations. Earners can combine badges from multiple issuers to tell a more complete story of their achievements. Since an *open* system allows verifiable recognition for the achievements of the earner and the issuer, a badge can hold value across as many organizations as find it useful to do so.

Consumers

Consumers of badging systems are usually looking to these systems to help with their decision making. Potential employers or admissions officers at all levels of educational institutions are among the greatest proportion of such consumers. Many consumers are keenly aware that traditional credentials are inadequate for their decision-making purposes. For example, the relevance of an earner's credential may diminish as the time since the credential was awarded increases. Consumers with such concerns are sympathetic to alternative credentialing systems. However, it is not entirely clear that the information stored with the badge is what is needed for decision support. Even if it is the right information, at this point, it is often tedious and time-consuming for decision-makers to locate and evaluate badges.

Each of these major stakeholders have a different perspective on badges driven by their motives and perceived value of the badge(s).

Framework for Badge Exploration

One way to frame a review of a badging system is to keep in mind the various stakeholders' perspectives and the purpose(s) that are most salient to each of their viewpoints. Given the three purposes of badges (to motivate learning, to map learner progress, and to signal completion), each of these purposes can have value (advantages/benefits), each must be evaluated (appraised, assessed), and each must be shown to be valuable (respected).

A badge's value is determined by several things. One important component is the perspective of the stakeholder in the value attached to the badge's purpose as detailed in Table 11.1. Some perspectives are fairly straightforward. The increased motivation for learning affects the badge earner more than any other stakeholder. Of course, the badge issuer considers this aspect, too, when designing the badge system. When considering the micro-credentialing purpose of badges and badging systems, it is pretty easy to conclude that this is of critical importance to all stakeholders.

Some perspectives are not as easy to determine. For instance, when considering the value placed on individualized pathways by consumers, in most circumstances all that is really valued is the terminal badge at the highest level. For a graduate program admissions officer, this would be similar to looking at a candidate's transcripts and seeing an award for a Bachelor of Science degree in an appropriate

TABLE 11.1 Value priorities of badges from different perspectives

Badge stakeholder	Badge purpose		
	Increase motivation for learning	*Individualized learner pathways (map individual's progression)*	*Micro-credentialing*
Earners	Of critical importance	Of major importance	Of critical importance
Issuers	Of major importance	Of critical importance	Of critical importance
Consumers	Of lessor importance	Of lessor importance	Of critical importance

Legend:
- Of critical importance
- Of major importance
- Of lessor importance

subject area. But under some circumstances, when the consumer is very familiar with the program and the intermediate steps involved in earning the terminal badge, following the pathway taken by the candidate may be important, too.

The point here is *not* that the relative levels of importance shown in Table 11.1 are the same for all badges in all badging systems. A badge has a particular profile and that profile changes depending upon the particular stakeholder's role and the motives that the individual stakeholder has for the badge.

Implications for Practice

Consider the tremendous impact (i.e., an indication of value) of the traditional forms of recognition (e.g., certificates, diplomas) to the stakeholders involved. There is a great deal of inertia and investment to the earners, issuers, and consumers of the current system of reward. It should be no wonder why the adoption of any alternative will be difficult and relatively slow. Yet, in spite of being firmly established, the traditional forms of recognition do have shortcomings given the changing needs of learners, such as recognition of achievements across a life span, mobility of credential granting across disciplines and settings, new forms of achievement/assessment, and individualized pathways to learning. "The value of a badge system lies in its ability to assemble evidence of different granularity and from different sources—diverse ways to gather proof of competence at both the individual and institutional levels" (Finkelstein, Knight, & Manning, 2013, p. 5). Digital badges are uniquely positioned to meet the needs of stakeholders in a rapidly changing educational landscape.

When considering each of the chapters in this book, especially when determining how some of the case studies might be applied to different settings, the reader is urged to determine the perspectives that the chapter writers take. Keeping the writers' perspectives in mind will help to sort through the underlying values ascribed within each chapter.

References

Blumenstyk, G. (2015, September 18). Next: When a degree is just the beginning. *The Chronicle of Higher Education,* B4–B7.

Bull, B. (2015, September 14). Why colleges should support alternative credentials. *The Chronicle of Higher Education. Next: The Credential Craze.* Retrieved from http://chronicle.com/article/Why-Colleges-Should-Support/232965/.

Cook, T. F. (2014). A badge won't make me care. *Sprout Stories.* Retrieved from https://medium.com/the-saxifrage-school/a-badge-wont-make-me-care-4200203c77de.

Craig, R. (2015, August 14). The great unbundling of higher education. *HigherEdJobs.* Retrieved from www.higheredjobs.com/blog/postDisplay.cfm?post=716&utm_source=09_16_2015&utm_medium=email&utm_campaign=InsiderUpdate.

Finkelstein, J., Knight, E., & Manning, S. (2013, July 16). *The potential and value of using digital badges for adult learners: Draft for public comment.* American Institute for Research. Retrieved from http://lincs.ed.gov/publications/pdf/AIR_Digital_Badge_Report_508.pdf.

Gibson, D., Ostashewski, N., Flintoff, K., Grant, S., & Knight, E. (2015). Digital badges in education. *Education and Information Technologies, 20*(2), 403–410. DOI 10.1007/s10639-013-9291-7.

Hicken, A. (2014, December 12). Digital badges for educational achievement. *Web Courseworks* [Blog]. Retrieved from www.webcourseworks.com/digital-badges-educational-achievement/.

Opperman, A. (2015, May 7). Are digital badges a new measurement of mastery? *Association for Talent Development.* Retrieved from www.td.org/Publications/Blogs/Science-of-Learning-Blog/2015/05/Are-Digital-Badges-a-New-Measurement-of-Mastery.

Resnick, M. (2012). Still a badge skeptic [Blog post]. Humanities, Arts, Science, and Technology Alliance and Collaboratory (HASTAC) Blog. Retrieved from www.hastac.org/blogs/mres/2012/02/27/still-badge-skeptic.

Young, J. R. (2015, September 14). Next: The credentials craze. *The Chronicle of Higher Education.* Retrieved from http://chronicle.com/article/Credit-for-Watching-a-TED/232973/?cid=at&utm_source=at&utm_medium=en.

PART II
Cases

12

COLLEGE AND CAREER READY

TK-12 Badging for Student Motivation

April M. Moore and Leanne Edwards

Digital badges are significantly different from existing practices of recognizing educational achievement, as badges honor student learning that may be non-traditional, include smaller skills and competencies, and reward completion of pathways. In contrast, current models of student assessment and recognition include formal and standardized tests and course grades posted to student transcripts. By incorporating digital badges, the Corona-Norco Unified School District (CNUSD) has integrated some of the most powerful components of gamification of student learning, capitalizing on the practices of the video gaming industry by recognizing students frequently and for smaller steps towards the ultimate goal of the game (or in this case, the course, pathway, and educational journey). In addition, the social nature of digital badges using the Mozilla Open Badge Infrastructure (OBI) allows students over the age of 13 to share their accomplishments through social media, thus rewarding students through their peer networks and simultaneously motivating their peers to explore and achieve in a similar manner. Four years ago, CNUSD took steps to design and implement a digital badging platform, 21st Century Badge Pathways (Corona-Norco Unified School District, 2014), which has been in place for the past two years at CNUSD. There are now more than 26 active pathways and 162 active badges in the CNUSD system. Over the past two years, more than 413,000 badges have been earned by students in transitional kindergarten (TK) through twelfth grade (TK-12) at 49 school sites.

Our journey to implement digital badges began in 2011 when CNUSD was preparing to launch an ambitious college and career readiness initiative, Passport to Success (P2S) (Corona-Norco Unified School District, 2012). One of the 10 largest school districts in California and the largest in Riverside County,

CNUSD serves approximately 53,000 students in grades TK-12. With 49 schools and a large geographic region, administrators in the Educational Services division were seeking ways to motivate students and reward them along their journey to college and career readiness. The P2S initiative was initially designed as a physical passport on which students would earn 12 stamps as they achieved various milestones in their journey. However, with the advent of digital badges and Mozilla's OBI, a team was convened to design a badging platform that met the privacy needs of a public school district and integrated the gamification that digital badging offers.

Inspired by the Digital Media and Learning (DML) competition hosted by the MacArthur Foundation, HASTAC (Humanities, Arts, Science and Technology Alliance and Collaboratory) and the Mozilla Foundation, a collaborative Digital Badge Design Team from CNUSD met to discuss the design elements and draft an entry to the DML competition. This team included curriculum and instruction administrators, teachers on special assignment, and a variety of information technology (IT) administrators, including the database administrator, network engineer, and the director of technology.

The Digital Badge Design Team sought to design a program that would engage students in their educational journey to college and career readiness. The adults in our school district were highly motivated for students to become ready for college success and career advancement, but our students had varying levels of interest and engagement in the process, especially at the intermediate level (seventh and eighth grades). In reviewing research and best practices, we determined that a TK-12 focus on college and career readiness was critical and chose to use digital badging as the hook to engage students. Initial focus groups with intermediate students showed a high interest in video gaming and an interest in transferring gaming components such as badging into the school environment.

Once we felt this was a worthwhile endeavor for supporting student learning and motivation, we began outlining the core functionality desired in a TK-12 badging platform. The following technological priorities were identified: (1) keep student-level data on our school district servers; (2) push a minimum of information to a badging portal; and (3) clearly identify criteria for badges. This third priority would allow IT personnel to automate reports that issued badges on a large scale rather than manually issuing badges, something that would not be sustainable for our large district.

Once the Digital Badge Design Team had an outline of the basic structure of the badging system, we had one key philosophical question to answer: What is worthy of a badge? A series of focus group meetings involving a range of administrators and teachers from curriculum and instruction, assessment and accountability, and school sites resulted in a clear consensus: The students would earn badges for scoring proficient or advanced on assessments, showing growth on assessments, demonstrating academic behaviors, and performing community service.

To promote student motivation, badges would be issued in pathways. Thus, when a student earned one badge, the student would see further badges available in a similar area and the criteria necessary to earn them. It was further determined that we would launch our badges district-wide with 12 key college- and career-ready badges: three at the elementary level, three at the middle level, and six at the high school level (see Figure 12.1).

Analysis

As we looked to personalize learning and motivate students towards college and career readiness, we saw digital badges as a way to connect formal learning and district priorities to gamification and student interests. One target group we desired to motivate was intermediate students, particularly males. These students tended to play video games and understand the concept of digital badges and leveling up. With the launch of our college and career readiness initiative, recognizing students for achieving a variety of milestones along their educational journey in the form of digital badges was a natural fit.

To incorporate multiple gamification components, we planned to include points with each badge earned and a points store for each school where students could redeem their points for tangible rewards. After discussion with a Microsoft badging and gaming researcher at the DML conference, we understood better how to structure the points, using them to hook the learner early on rather than having later cumulative badges worth the most points.

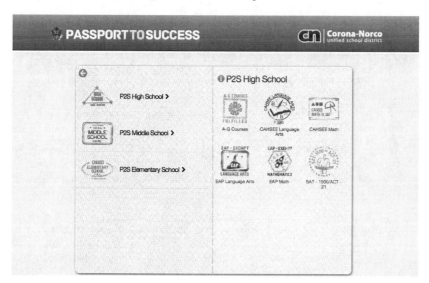

FIGURE 12.1 High school Passport to Success digital badge pathway (CNUSD, 2012).

Used with permission from Corona-Norco Unified School District.

Instructional Design Considerations and Processes

While CNUSD was not selected to advance to the next round of the DML competition, two representatives from the Digital Badge Design Team attended the conference in spring 2012. Through networking with other competition participants, we formed a partnership with software development company Forall Systems, Inc. and its CEO, Dr. Karen Jeffrey. We were further able to secure start-up funding from our district collaborative and thus began development on our digital badge platform: 21st Century Badge Pathways.

Technical Design Considerations

The initial Digital Badge Design Team expanded to include members of Forall Systems, Inc., and the design and mock-up process began. Key design consideration topics included Family Educational Rights and Privacy Act (FERPA) and student security, automation through the student information system (SIS), sustainability (pricing and technology), badging connectivity through Mozilla's OBI, and future enhancements through an open-source platform.

FERPA and student security. In order to protect our student information, we determined to keep all student data—including assessment, participation, and attendance data—within our SIS. Our database administrator would create reports (exported as .CSV files) that indicated when a badge was to be issued to a student. In addition, criteria for badges would be clear but generic. Thus, if a student earned the CAHSEE Language Arts badge, the criteria showed that the student must "Receive a score of 380 or higher on the English-language arts section of the California High School Exit Exam during the 10th grade year" (see Figure 12.2). However, the student's actual score on the exam would not be released.

To ensure student privacy, students log into their accounts using a secure username and password combination. A student may access all badging information within our platform, and if the student is 13 years of age or older, the student may publish the badge to their Mozilla Backpack for further sharing and showcasing.

Automation through SIS. Automation of badge issuance was another key requirement for the badge platform, and information technology administrators and Forall Systems, Inc. designed the issuing process such that periodic exports from our existing SIS would be uploaded into the badge platform via three simple .CSV files: (1) a list of schools and their codes; (2) student account data; and (3) badge issuance data (Tables 12.1–12.3).

Sustainability, badging connectivity, and future enhancements. The remaining technical design considerations were addressed through the open-source nature of our platform. We wanted to capitalize on the Mozilla OBI to promote badging connectivity and similarly determined to launch our platform as open source to ensure long-term sustainability of the program. We ultimately planned to host the platform on our own district server, but initially opted to have it hosted by our software developer during the design phase.

CAHSEE Language Arts

Description: The California High School Exit Examination (CAHSEE) is administered to 10th grade students and consists of a scale score range of 275-450. The Language Arts portion of CAHSEE consists of five strands of multiple-choice questions : Word Analysis; Reading Comprehension; Literary Response and Analysis; Writing Strategies; English Language Conventions. The assessment also includes an essay. Although 350 is considered a passing score, students should strive to attain a score of proficient or above (380-450) since the goal is to become 'college ready'.

English-Language Arts Study Guide
http://www.cde.ca.gov/ta/tg/hs/elaguide.asp

Criteria: Receive a score of 380 or higher on the English-language arts section of the California High School Exit Exam during the 10th grade year.

Done

FIGURE 12.2 Description and criteria for CAHSEE Language Arts Badge (CNUSD, 2012).
Used with permission from Corona-Norco Unified School District.

TABLE 12.1 Data table of school information (CNUSD, 2014)

School Code	School Name
310	John Adams Elementary

TABLE 12.2 Data table of student information (CNUSD, 2014)

School Code	Student ID	Grade	First Name	Last Name	Birthdate	Username	Password
310	1234567	2	Johnny	Appleseed	4/11/2007	Jappleseed	Apple1234

TABLE 12.3 Data table for badge issuance (CNUSD, 2014)

Badge Uniq	Student ID	Badge ID	Issue Date
10001	123456	CN0000	6/10/2013

By paying for the upfront development cost to our specifications, it was our intention to create a robust platform that met the unique needs of TK-12 education organizations in a cost-effective manner. In this way, we hoped to support future enhancements to the open-source platform in a collaborative model. As more TK-12 education organizations signed up to use the platform, 21st Century Badge Pathways, each could contribute content, technological enhancements, and other benefits to the entire user community.

Instructional Design Considerations

While the technical badge issuing and viewing platform was being developed, simultaneous conversations were taking place in the district's curriculum and instruction (C&I) department regarding badge design, criteria, and implementation process. In focus group conversations, the philosophical question quickly arose: What is worthy of a badge? Some administrators wanted to ensure that every student earned a badge and thus advocated for a low threshold for issuance. Each student would earn a badge for taking a particular standardized exam, but their level of achievement would be indicated with a different badge color. With the five performance bands of our statewide assessment model (Advanced, Proficient, Basic, Below Basic, Far Below Basic), they advocated that all students should earn a badge. However, when we recalibrated the purpose of the badging program, tied to our college and career readiness initiative, we came to the consensus that "Proficient" or "Advanced" scores should be our target. Since badging was designed as a student motivation component, cheapening the badge such that everyone earns a badge every time would defeat the purpose.

In addition to earning badges for proficient or advanced scores, we agreed that we wanted to reward students showing growth in achievement, such as moving from a score of "Below Basic" to "Basic" or being re-designated from an "English Learner" to fluent in the English language. Finally, there were other achievement categories that we desired to recognize—such as student leadership, community service, or extra-curricular activities—and to acknowledge these areas, we would work closely with individual schools to create and issue badges.

To further promote student motivation in earning badges, badges were to be issued in pathways. Thus, when a student earned one badge, it would trigger access to a larger pathway or a sequence of badges in that same area. The student would see more available badges and the criteria necessary to earn them.

Development

We launched the badging platform district-wide in spring 2013 with 12 key college- and career-ready badges: three at the elementary level, three at the middle level, and six at the high school level. To accompany the launch, we developed a series of marketing materials using the passport theme of P2S for use within the district: student pamphlets with log-on information, parent fliers with infographics on the types of badges available, and resources for teachers and site teams for developing badges. To assist with the launch of the open-source platform in July 2014, we also crafted generic marketing materials using the colorful 21st Century Badge Pathways look and feel. These editable documents are shared with other educational organizations as they consider adopting the 21st Century Badge Pathways and joining our user group.

Implementation

With the cutting-edge nature of digital badging, we found it imperative to execute implementation of our badging in a systematic and dynamic way. Without proper awareness, something so new could easily flounder. In order to ensure district-wide familiarity between all stakeholders, we followed a process that took place in several phases.

Presentation/Awareness

Our initial phase to activate implementation was a presentation/awareness phase. During this time, the P2S program was presented to CNUSD district and site-based administrators during monthly administrators' meetings. In addition to the specifics on how the program works and integrates with our SIS system, the principals were informed of the district-wide badging as well as the future capacity for school-site specific badging. The principals were responsible for then determining who their "digital badge site ambassador" would be. Some principals chose themselves, their assistant principals, student advisors, a lead teacher, or a secretary or clerk to become the ambassador for their site. Promotional printed materials (and digital files) were created and given to the principals in their meeting to be distributed to parents, students, and staff regarding the launch of the P2S program. In addition, a dynamic website was developed (http://p2s.cnusd.net/) and targeted to stakeholders to enhance the understanding and the impact digital badging can have on our community of learners.

Digital Badge Ambassador Community

Once digital badge site ambassadors were determined, additional meetings and presentations were held to clarify the program as well as the roles and responsibilities of each ambassador. Ensuring an understanding of the P2S program, the purpose of badging, and the marketing plan was the initial focus of our meetings. As the ambassadors became more familiar with the program, we expanded the focus to include developing future district- and site-level badges and implementing the points store.

To assist in P2S implementation and facilitation with digital badge site ambassadors, a lead ambassador was selected at each school level (elementary, intermediate, and high school). These lead ambassadors were given additional administrative privileges in the badging platform and leadership responsibilities in the implementation process. This structure further enhanced communication and cohesion. To promote online collaboration, we utilized the online project management tool, Basecamp, which housed critical forms, images, and badge proposals submitted by site ambassadors.

District Badges

The initial launch consisted of district-wide badges that were automated using our SIS. We chose to begin this endeavor to address our district's college and career readiness goals and ensure access to all students. District-level badges at the elementary level comprised those awarded by trimester for outstanding attendance, behavior, and work habits. At the intermediate level, students could earn badges for scoring proficient or advanced on the California Standards Test (CST) in seventh grade, scoring proficient or advanced on the College Board's ReadiStep exam in eighth grade, as well as completion of an individual learning plan. District-level badges were awarded to high school students for scoring 1500 or higher on the SAT or 21 or higher on the ACT, scoring exempt on the Early Assessment Program (EAP) hosted by the California State University in math or English/language arts, scoring proficient or advanced on the math or English/language arts portions of the California High School Exit Exam (CAHSEE), and successfully completing the A-G course sequence as outlined by the University of California. The district-level badges provided a solid foundation in terms of badge criteria, point values, and consistency for the next phase of our launch: site-level badges.

School-Site Badges

School-site badges allow each school site to highlight the courses available and the skills students are mastering that are unique to that school. To illustrate, one of our intermediate schools offers courses to seventh and eighth graders in Robotics, 3D Modeling, Video Production, Web Design, Adobe Photoshop, and Adobe Illustrator. These elective courses are not only unique to that school, but also are advanced, assisting students to learn college- and career-ready skills. Digital badging for completion of these courses is an example of what the district hopes to promote. As site ambassadors developed badges with their school teams, badges were submitted to their lead ambassadors for review regarding consistency of focus, appropriate point value, and opportunities to share badges between school sites.

While challenges to site-level badges were anticipated at the time of launch, the specific idiosyncrasies that have arisen could not have been foreseen. For instance, due to the design and the usage of our SIS to automate badges associated with specific course codes in the master schedule, we have found some inconsistencies between schools using the same course code to teach similar but not equivalent courses. This has resulted in a few instances of students being assigned badges for skills they did not learn or master. We have worked with our software development partner to further customize the issuance of badges and pathways to restrict badges to a specific school if needed.

School Points Store Launch

Our current phase in digital badging is the implementation of a points store available at each school. We chose to be strategic in the timing of the launch of each points store as they were designed to be site-specific. Sites were encouraged to work with community partners to procure and distribute items to be "purchased" by students. As sites have the capacity and readiness, the district team turns on their points store, allowing students at that site to redeem their points for the tangible rewards available to them. Site ambassadors or another administrator will manually input the actual, physical inventory available, and the badging platform monitors student points redemption.

Evaluation

In March 2014, a group of 112 eighth and ninth grade students were surveyed on their interest in the digital badges, and the initial research findings were shared with the international badging community in a follow-up report. The findings indicated that students in intermediate and high schools were very motivated to earn digital badges, with unique interests for female students desiring academic and subject-specific badges (Moore, Cuicchi, and Jeffrey, 2014). Specifically, 87 percent of students stated that they were "motivated" to "very motivated" to earn badges. At pre-test, only 4 percent of students knew they had earned any digital badges. However, after logging in to see the badges that had been automatically issued to them, on the post-test, 92 percent of students indicated that they had already earned badges. Eighty percent of students said that they were "likely" to "highly likely" to revisit the badging website again to learn more about the badges. Female students were most interested in academic, subject-specific, and STEM (Science, Technology, Engineering, and Math) badges. Male students were interested in all types of badges. In fact, six males said that they wanted to earn every badge available.

A subsequent survey of more than 300 seventh graders was conducted in October 2014 on the students' knowledge of and interest in digital badging (Edwards, 2015). Results of this survey are shown in Figure 12.3. As in the initial survey, 89 percent of respondents were "somewhat" to "very" motivated to earn badges, and motivation levels differed for males and females. Of the 183 male respondents, 77 percent indicated that they were "motivated" to "very motivated" to earn badges, with their overall motivation at 89 percent. While the 176 female respondents had similar overall motivation at 87 percent, the intensity of their motivation was lower. Females were nearly equal in their answers of "somewhat" motivated (25 percent) and "very motivated" (26 percent), with "motivated" accounting for 36 percent of our female respondents (Edwards, 2015).

In consideration for the types of badges students wished to earn, we surveyed students to ensure that we were badging for the skills, courses, and extracurricular activities that our students cared about. Although students wanted to be rewarded for their overall academics with Honor Roll badges, students frequently named their elective courses. In fact, of the 398 individual responses, only 14 students referred specifically to their core classes in Language Arts (12 responses) and Math (2 responses). This may indicate that students wished to be badged on what makes them unique (the skills they are learning in electives), not necessarily on what is common between them and their peers (core classes).

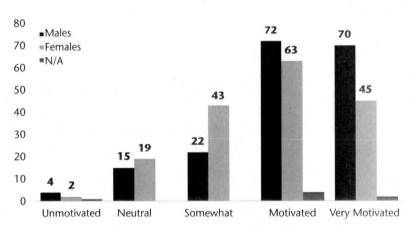

Motivation to Earn Badges By Gender

FIGURE 12.3   Motivation of seventh graders to earn badges (Edwards, 2015).

Conclusions

Digital badging has incredible potential in TK-12 education as a motivational factor for student learning and owning their educational journey. By working collaboratively and thoughtfully with a diverse team of stakeholders, CNUSD was able to have a successful launch of badging district-wide, with follow-up phases focusing on site-specific badges and tangible rewards earned by redeeming points.

By designating a core team of lead ambassadors, serving as digital badge champions and pilot leaders, the work continued moving forward. As students and community members became introduced to a functioning badging system, new life was infused in the project.

Seeing the data, some of the first quantifiable data available from TK-12 badging initiatives, has been reassuring to the core team. Digital badging is motivating to our students, including an intermediate-student population that is often difficult to motivate. As they indicate their interests and desires to earn badges, explore pathways of badges, and take ownership of their learning, we can indeed say that this has been a worthwhile journey. The destinations and possibilities on their journey, using their Passport to Success, are limitless!

References

Corona-Norco Unified School District (2012). *Passport to success.* Retrieved from www.cnusdp2s.com/browse/.

Corona-Norco Unified School District (2014). *21st Century badge pathways: 2014 Summer institute.* Retrieved from www.cnusd.k12.ca.us/Page/28894.

Edwards, L. (2015, March). *Pre and post survey of P2S: 7th grade students.* Presentation to Corona-Norco Unified School District Site Ambassadors in Eastvale, CA.

Moore, A., Cuicchi, L., & Jeffrey, K. (2014, April). *P2S pre and post survey data.* Presentation to Corona-Norco Unified School District Open Badges Research + Badge System Design Community in Norco, CA.

13

LEARNING WITH DIGITAL BADGES IN FORMAL, INFORMAL, AND CROWD-SOURCED SETTINGS

Christine Chow, James E. Willis, III, and Daniel Hickey

The Design Principles Documentation (DPD) project (Hickey, Otto, Itow, Schenke, Tran, & Chow, 2014) at Indiana University's Center for Research on Learning and Technology followed the badge development practices of 29 grantees in the 2012 Badges for Lifelong Learning competition, sponsored by the MacArthur Foundation's Digital Media and Learning (DML) initiative and the Gates Foundation (HASTAC, 2012). The DPD project documented the *intended* practices as outlined in their DML project proposals and then conducted structured interviews to document *enacted practices* that DML projects were able to establish with their badge systems. The DPD project paid particular attention to the contextual factors that allowed some intended practices to be enacted but not others. The data produced by studying practices of recognizing, assessing, and motivating learning in digital badges was then organized into more general design principles. The more contextual information from the DPD data makes these principles useful for others (Hickey et al., 2014; Archive for Badge System Analysis, 2014).

Analyzing the DPD project data has led to a number of preliminary conclusions about badge system design. When comparing the extent to which each of the 29 DML projects was able to create the learning ecosystem they had envisioned in their proposals, the projects that associated badges with informal and social learning were generally more successful, compared to the projects that awarded badges for more formal learning outcomes. Comparing the success of each project in relation to the amount of new programmatic and technological development directly impacts the infrastructure outcomes. The DPD data revealed that the projects that only had to layer badges into the existing learning content and learning technology were generally more successful than the projects that attempted to create content and technology along with the badges.

This case study examines three 2012 DML grantees. These projects were selected because they all focused on younger learners and they generated examples of the nuanced, but ultimately important, interactions between the intended badging practices and project contexts. Two awardees were the Milwaukee-based aquaponics program, AQUAPONS, and the Providence After School Alliance (PASA); both AQUAPONS and PASA aimed to associate their badges with formal school credit. The third project was the web-based MOUSE Wins! program for mentoring New York City high school students who were learning to help manage the digital networks in their schools. The MOUSE Wins! project was particularly noteworthy because it aimed to establish the value of their badges more informally and communally, as the information the badges contained circulated in the digital network associated with the project.

Isolating and comparing the data for three projects amongst the 29 available programs provides compelling findings in the area of building community into badge systems. The most salient findings deal with the *value* of badges, the *validation* of badges, and the *community* provided through badges. The data indicates that challenging practices often carry the most lasting and beneficial outcomes.

The evidence in this case study comes from several sources. Most of the evidence was gathered by the DPD project (Hickey et al., 2014; Archive for Badge System Analysis, 2014). This included detailed analyses of the project proposals (MOUSE Wins!, 2012; Providence After School Alliance, 2012a; Providence After School Alliance, 2012b; Sweet Water Foundation, 2012) and extended interviews conducted at three intervals: initial project start-up, midway, and at the end of funding. Most of this evidence is captured in detailed case studies for each project that can be viewed at the DPD website (Archive for Badge System Analysis, 2014). Other evidence was obtained from the answers each project provided to a set of standardized questions as final reports at the HASTAC website (HASTAC, 2015).

Aquapons and Digital Badges in Formal Learning Environments

The Sweet Water Foundation proposed the AQUAPONS project to promote education on aquaponics and sustainable agriculture. They developed a program for high school teachers to implement with their students, connecting informal after-school science learning to formal education. The project aimed to offer hands-on project-based learning experiences to promote learning in the subjects of science, technology, engineering, and math that students were expected to master in the science classrooms of Milwaukee's urban secondary schools (Sweet Water Foundation, 2012).

AQUAPONS translated its existing aquaponics curriculum to the badge system, incorporating specific tasks at the aquaponics facility. In the design, AQUAPONS mapped badges to their own set of standards with the goal of aligning to the Common Core State Standards. They narrowed down their badges to four categories: *Plants, Fish, Water,* and *Design & Build* (see Figure 13.1). Additionally, the badge system designed a multi-tiered badge structure, with learners progressing through four increasingly more challenging levels: Advanced Beginner, Competent Performer, Proficient Performer, and Expert. Learners earned three types of ascending badges from Skill Badges that represent distinct skills to Content Badges that sum up all of the skills achieved in a content area, and finally, AQUAPONS badges for achieving all of the content badges at a specific level (Otto, 2014), as shown in Figure 13.2.

The design of the badge system was created by using the principles associated with constructivist learning, conventional apprenticeship learning, the Dreyfus Model of Skill Acquisition (Dreyfus & Dreyfus, 1980), and Bloom's Taxonomy (Bloom, 1956).

In December 2012, the Sweet Water Foundation enlisted a programming team who adapted the curriculum to the badge system. The team released the prototype in late spring 2013 and tested the system with students over the summer. The team constructed a public-facing website, *aquapons.info*, on the WordPress platform and used the Mozilla's Open Badge Infrastructure to issue badges (Otto, 2014).

AQUAPONS also brought together a team to train teachers and students to use the badge system (see Figure 13.3) to develop their knowledge about physical and biological interactions in an aquaponics system and manage its health and balance. From the project efforts, AQUAPONS reported intermittent use of the

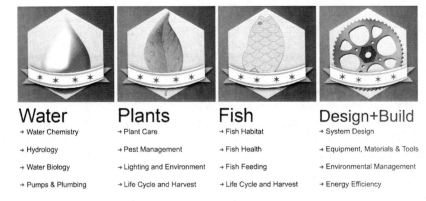

AQUAPONS
An explanation of the badge system

Badge Categories:

Within the aquaponics training system , four categories have been identified. These parts and their associated tasks give a full experience with aquaponics.

Water	Plants	Fish	Design+Build
→ Water Chemistry	→ Plant Care	→ Fish Habitat	→ System Design
→ Hydrology	→ Pest Management	→ Fish Health	→ Equipment, Materials & Tools
→ Water Biology	→ Lighting and Environment	→ Fish Feeding	→ Environmental Management
→ Pumps & Plumbing	→ Life Cycle and Harvest	→ Life Cycle and Harvest	→ Energy Efficiency

FIGURE 13.1 Badge categories of the AQUAPONS badge system.
Used with permission from Sweet Water Foundation.

AQUAPONS

An explanation of the badge system

Levels of competency: As a user progresses through the system, gaining skill and proficiency, the system gives them a reward that reinforces their success within the community.

Junior	Senior	Journeymon	Master
Act on the basis of context-independent elements and rules which they have learned to identify and interpret on the basis of their own experience from similar situations	Characterized by the involved choice of goals and plans as a basis for their actions; goals and plans are used to structure and store masses of both context-dependent and context-independent information/data	Identify problems, goals and plans intuitively from their own experientially based perspective. Intuitive choice is checked by analytical evaluation prior to action	Characterized by a flowing, effortless performance, unhindered by analytical deliberations; behavior is intuitive, holistic, and synchronic, understood in the way that a given situation releases a picture of problem, goal, plan, decision, and action in one instant and with no division into phases.

FIGURE 13.2 Levels of competency of the AQUAPONS badge system.
Used with permission from Sweet Water Foundation.

curriculum and badges. Tensions surfaced between the content and the badge system's target demographic because significant segments of students were in special education and reportedly needed more support for self-documentation and self-reflection than the program had anticipated. The Sweet Water Foundation wanted to support teachers and administration, so they sought to understand how to integrate the badge system in schools without changing their curricular programs. The AQUAPONS research indicates that teachers should implement the badge system with students with relevant prior experience and use only content that is inherently relevant to their course curriculum (Otto, 2014).

In 2014, the original AQUAPONs website and badging system ceased use as a learning and recognition platform. The website was transformed into a static content repository for teachers wishing to use the materials, and the program shifted its energy into providing informal summer-programming to young people as part of the *Cities of Learning* initiative, issuing badges instead through the platform established for that initiative (Sweet Water Foundation, 2015).

FIGURE 13.3 Users of the AQUAPONS badge system.
Used with permission from Sweet Water Foundation.

PASA and Digital Badges in Informal Settings

The Providence After School Alliance (PASA) network of after-school programs attempted to use badges to award formal credit for learning from an informal setting. PASA offered 10-week programs in which students completed interest-related projects and then earned badges for their accomplishments outside of school. The students chose subjects they wanted to learn, affording them flexibility to explore as opposed to following an established curriculum. In this sense, the badges acknowledged students for skills and abilities that might otherwise be overlooked (Chow, 2014b).

PASA collaborated with the Providence Public School District to align the after-school curriculum with school-based standards, enabling Providence schools to award youth formal credit for earning badges. PASA implemented their badge system through *The Hub*, an after-school system for high school students (Chow, 2014b). PASA described that "the Hub connects Providence youth to opportunities throughout the city, hosts new programs and builds policies and processes with PPSD [Providence Public School District] that provide course credit for ELO [expanded learning opportunities] that occur after school" (Providence After School Alliance, 2012a, para. 2). At the outset of the badge effort, PASA indicated the need for a uniform way to capture and assess students' expanded learning opportunities and experiences. PASA sought to document evidence of learning with digital badges, envisioning that badges would serve as guideposts for learners and create pathways that extend to college and lifelong learning (Chow, 2014b).

The project creators intended to design a tiered badge system, starting with Progress Badges for accumulating a certain number of points that eventually led to Recognition Badges as the culmination of an achievement. However, this plan proved too complex because of the learner analytics needed to document the various steps of students' learning pathways leading to badges. In response, the initiative streamlined their efforts to focus on the core experience and award an overall badge that represents the students' learning experiences (Chow, 2014b).

In the system's development phase, the team built the technical infrastructure of the badge effort and the capacity to push Open Badge Infrastructure-compliant badges out to the Mozilla Backpack. Badges are accessible on hubprov.com only after the learners have entered the eighth grade. Middle-school students were offered physical forms of badges and year-end parties to recognize their achievements. Building the infrastructure posed a set of barriers in securing district-wide access to technology, raising the concern that this limitation can exclude students from access to opportunities (Chow, 2014b). Alex Molina, PASA Deputy Director, explained:

> We work with schools that don't even have computers or laptops, or there's no wireless access, and young people go home where there's no access to technology either … the reality is that we're working in an urban environment, and [on] the idea of badges, a lot of urban centers or cities are not going to be ready five, ten years down the line." (Chow, 2014b, para. 67)

As part of the badge system, PASA utilized the Rhode Island Program Quality Assessment to measure program quality and maintain the standards and rigor of youth development programs through the use of a rubric. To gauge learning, youth presented their work to a panel of judges at the end of the six-week program. The judges then used rubrics to assess the projects and decide whether to award badges in recognition of the youths' achievements (Chow, 2014b). Besides this, the effort delineated that "[f]or daily management and participant tracking, attendance, and monitoring participation trends, PASA uses a web-based program management tool—YouthServices.net" (Providence After School Alliance, 2012a, para. 12). The program also relies on the Survey of Academics and Youth Outcomes (SAYO) from the National Institute on Out-of-School Time to ensure program quality (NIOST, 2015). The larger point here is that issuing badges for formal school credit *also* required formal systems for: (a) assessing student work; (b) verifying attendance; and (c) documenting program quality.

PASA's initial success at using badges to award formal credit for after-school learning was widely noted and landed the project on the front page of *Education Week* (Fleming, 2013). However, some of the after-school providers found the initial badge system cumbersome, and turnover of key staff made it hard for PASA to maintain that system while at the same time incorporating new content and criteria. Rather than backing off on the formality of the badges system (as many other DML projects did), PASA paused its badging program in 2014 while the development team systematically added new features needed to streamline assessment of student work and documentation of program quality (such as putting the SAYO survey online) (Durham, 2014).

MOUSE Wins! and Digital Badges in Crowd-Sourced Settings

Using crowd-sourced recognition, MOUSE Corps constructed a badge recognition system, MOUSE Wins!, which promoted the development of computational and workplace literacies for students. An after-school program, MOUSE aimed to nurture design and technological skills in high school students in New York City (Chow, 2014a). MOUSE programs tapped into students' interest in media and technology and then mobilized them "as teams of level-one help desk experts supporting technology and media in their schools by day and thriving as a community of peers whose combined skills and interests are shared and applied while 'geeking out' after school and online" (MOUSE Wins!, 2012, para. 1). The MOUSE Wins! badge system provided a place where a community can come together to share ideas and experiences (Chow, 2014a). Project administrators explained, "[l]earning in MOUSE programs starts during the school day and supports students in carrying over interests into out-of-school time" (MOUSE Wins!, 2012, para. 14). The learning experience was carried through the school day and beyond to the online community.

MOUSE recognized talent and expertise through crowd-sourced means. Specifically, the badge system designed Community Wins! (see Figure 13.4) to recognize youth for their community participation and accomplishments. The project implemented Peer2Peer Awards under the umbrella of Community Wins!, enabling peers to award micro-achievements, or Wins!, to one another within the categories of Creativity, Technical, Inspiration, and Motivation. MOUSE Wins! intended for this practice to reflect the peer recognition of team contributions in the workplace, demonstrating the importance of recognition by one's colleagues and senior professionals. With the capacity to issue Wins!, peers can attest to one another's skills and abilities and encourage each other in the learning process. In this respect, MOUSE Wins! offered a crowd-sourced setting where youth in the community play a role in the credentialing process (Chow, 2014a). MOUSE Senior Program Manager Meredith Summs explained students' progress from "users of technology to specialists in applied technologies and ultimately to makers and creators" (Chow, 2014a, para. 12). This practice promoted greater engagement between learners and builds reputation and trust amongst peers.

In technical development, the project created features for its website, like Wins!Tracker, to document the badges earned, and Kissmetrics, to monitor user analytics on the mousesquad.org website. The Wins!Tracker assessment tool was created for educators to monitor the performance of their students and to understand how to structure the learning environment. These features enabled MOUSE administrators to derive insight into the interests and behaviors of their participating youth (Chow, 2014a).

In Spring 2011, MOUSE partnered with Mozilla's Open Badge Infrastructure to link the profiles of youth to other social network sites and present badges publicly. MOUSE released the Wins!Tracker assessment tool in summer 2011, offering an aggregate view of student performance in a given group (Chow, 2014a). To build in feedback loops, the effort detailed that "[t]he interface allows check-ins on student progress during certification work (see Figure 13.5), 1:1 communication functionality to offer feedback, and an 'award' control that allows the facilitator to approve certification when complete" (Chow, 2014a, para. 35). MOUSE fostered a growing community of social and distributed learning.

MOUSE administrators confronted bandwidth limitations and infrastructure constraints in building an online portfolio system. Because the project used the open-source Drupal content-management framework, system design was limited by the Drupal modules used to create the system. Like many of the DML projects, MOUSE was thwarted in its efforts to include public links to learner work because that work resided behind a password-protected firewall. Additionally, questions remained regarding how to move data over to an upgraded badge

FIGURE 13.4 MOUSE Community Wins!
Used with permission from MOUSE Inc.

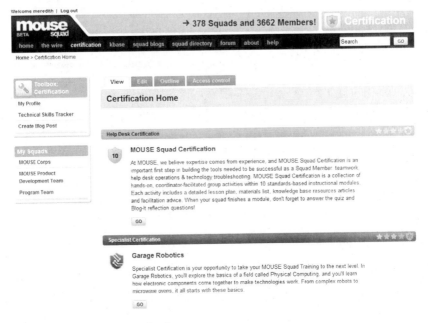

FIGURE 13.5 MOUSE certification.
Used with permission from MOUSE Inc.

system and what the implications would be for users and the badges they already earned. Nonetheless, as of early 2015, the MOUSE Wins! badge system remained an integral part of the larger MOUSE ecosystem, and was continuing to evolve with the larger programs (MOUSE Squad, 2015).

Findings across Three Projects

Studying the intended, enacted, and formalized practices across AQUAPONS, PASA, and MOUSE illustrates important findings from the larger study about how badges contribute to learning in formal, informal, and crowd-sourced ecosystems. These findings help bring out crucial sociological aspects of the open badges movement that seem easily overlooked. Olneck (2012, p. 1) pointed out that the movement "entails an exceptionally weak classification of knowledge," which means that it "proliferates and disperses authority of what learning to recognize" and "provides a means of translation and commensuration across multiple spheres."

The findings of the DPD project (Hickey et al., 2014), including the three projects detailed here, support Olneck's proposition that badges work best in informal spaces:

> Badge proponents claim that long-institutionalized ways of representing learning, e.g., grades, credit hours, diplomas, degrees, and certificates, carry

very little information, and fail to capture and recognize the full range of what people know and can do, much of which is acquired out of school and informally. (Olneck, 2012, p. 2)

Badges, he goes on to argue, achieve two goals: "capturing and communicating learning, knowledge, and know-how at a much more granular level than conventional credentials or marks of achievements, and for ensuring creditability based on direct evidence of accomplishment" (Olneck, 2012, p. 2).

With respect to Olneck's former goal, PASA aligned their curricula to standards so earners may achieve academic credit, which shows the skills and knowledge to be assessed (Chow, 2014b). AQUAPONS aimed to motivate students by ensuring that they had value to employers by publicizing portability of learners' acquired skills; further, they show students the possible career outcomes of their aquaponics experiences (Otto, 2014). To Olneck's latter goal of "ensuring credibility based on direct evidence of accomplishment," the validation of badges via experts helps to contribute further to the question of value. Expert recognition is important in community-driven ecosystems because it not only provides validation, but it also upholds standards. Community judges help validate the specific claims of evidence in earners' badges. For example, both PASA and MOUSE formalized systems by tying learning artifacts with expert recognition (Chow, 2014a; Chow, 2014b). Additionally, peer validation supports claims of learning. All three programs formalized assessment activities involving human experts, and PASA and MOUSE used a combination of human and computer experts (Chow, 2014a; Chow, 2014b). The results include bringing together the community of learners, peers, and experts to validate learning artifacts.

While a community of learners is certainly important for motivation, it is also appreciable to underline the tension with individual needs. A major finding is an express importance for learners to be able to take control of their own learning. Using badges to map learning trajectories allows learners to have a sense of control; visual demonstration of the pathways helps motivate learners. For example, AQUAPONS offered leveled badges to demonstrate proficiency, prestige of accomplishment, and commitment (Otto, 2014). Such leveling also promoted incremental scaffolding to providing learning structure. MOUSE built the capacity for earners to acquire Wins! by adding up to badges, which reflects how structured learning can help recognize skills and the growth of individual abilities (Chow, 2014a). Setting the goals of user-created badges and the display of goal trajectory are difficult to implement and, perhaps, best suited to specific types of programs. However, implementation of user-created badges helps motivate self-directed learning. PASA implemented this practice, which may increase earners' connection with the credential, possibly motivating further learning and participation (Chow, 2014b). The practice of displaying a goal trajectory has proven difficult for PASA, though, because connecting in-school and out-of-school data through recognition and progress badges is still underway.

The tension of community participation and individual needs is best conveyed in skills acquisition and potential for new activities. Complex learning environments can benefit from badges because incremental achievement can lead to reflection and skills acquisition. AQUAPONS formalized the recognition of diverse learning by requiring a set of skills from different areas to illustrate how different concepts functioned in balance with one another (Otto, 2014). Similarly, MOUSE formalized a system to recognize hard and soft skills in their Wins! program (Chow, 2014a). Providing incentives like new activities and internships is important but difficult to formalize in practice. New activities or internships may stem from badge learning, but providing a structure to replicate those incentives proves problematic. Likewise, recognizing educator learning is difficult because infrastructure concerns, prior planning, and value-adding can be taxing on a badge system. In both instances, AQUAPONS and PASA intended to enact these practices, but infrastructure limitations and concerns meant concentrating effort on other project goals (Otto, 2014; Chow, 2014b).

These nuanced interactions led to perhaps a key finding: Building community *into* the badges through reflection, assessment, and demonstration of learning is challenging but necessary. Building community is not limited to the badge system or its participants, but rather anyone who interacts with a badge. Community provides context for the earner, structure for the program, and robust evidence for those examining learning in the badge. It is difficult to build a system where participants can discover other learning activities and learners. This often requires technological development outside of the immediate badging ecosystem. As an example, the purpose of e-portfolios is to demonstrate skills; however, incorporating them into badge systems can be difficult. Building in the technical specifications for public-facing materials can quickly extend beyond the intended practices. AQUAPONS employed a portfolio system to capture learning artifacts, but a very limited publicly facing page means that often the learner and instructor only see the portfolio; AQUAPONS is exploring other social media sites to display achievement (Otto, 2014).

Building community also means incorporating peer assessment and self-reflection. Managing peer assessment can be challenging if conducted outside of the badge system (via email, for example). All three programs intended to incorporate peer assessment, with PASA's and MOUSE's system specifically designed for peers to recognize each other's learning, including feedback in PASA's system (Chow, 2014a; Chow, 2014b; Otto, 2014). Self-reflection is an important part of the learning process, but implementing it with badges can be difficult for organizations that serve populations with minimal access to technology. While AQUAPONS regarded self-reflection as critical to encouraging participant conversation amongst each other, PASA encountered difficulties with district-wide access to technology (Otto, 2014; Chow, 2014b). Though certainly a challenge, this latter point explicitly highlights the fact that engaging with the community, whether locally or digitally, has a dividend effect of promoting further learning through interaction. AQUAPONS provided activities that led to external possibilities like internships; MOUSE's practice of awarding Wins! promoted further interaction amongst participants (Otto, 2014; Chow, 2014a). The community of learners, then, benefits from greater interaction with peers, content experts, instructors, and those examining learning artifacts. This is accomplished through careful consideration of the individual and group needs as they are built into the badging infrastructure.

Conclusion

The badge development projects of AQUAPONS, PASA, and MOUSE illustrate how digital badges can help implement formal, informal, and crowd-sourced learning environments (Hickey et al., 2014). The organizations assessed the needs of their target audience in designing the badge system, taking into account a number of factors like learner characteristics, activities, constraints, and existing considerations of the program and curriculum. One of the major findings of the overall DPD research is that it is generally easier to layer badges into the existing content and technology than concurrently create both the badges and the content and technology (Archive for Badge System Analysis, 2014). Additionally, the DPD research shows that badges often work best in informal spaces (Hickey et al., 2014). As shown by AQUAPONS, PASA, and MOUSE Wins!, creating a community of support in badging environments nurtures learning and balances the needs of the group and the individual.

References

Archive for Badge System Analysis (2014). Design Principles Documentation Project. Retrieved from http://dpdproject.info/details/category/badge-system-analysis/.

Bloom, B. S. (1956). *Taxonomy of educational objectives. Vol. 1: Cognitive domain*. New York, NY: McKay.

Chow, C. (2014a). MOUSE Wins! In *Badge system analysis, design principles documentation project*. Retrieved from http://dpdproject.info/details/mouse-wins/.

Chow, C. (2014b). PASA pathways for lifelong learning. In *Badge system analysis, design principles documentation project*. Retrieved from http://dpdproject.info/details/pasa-pathways-for-lifelong-learning/.

Dreyfus, S. E., & Dreyfus, H. L. (1980). *A five-stage model of the mental activities involved in directed skill acquisition* (No. ORC-80-2). California University Berkeley Operations Research Center.

Durham, A. (2014). The new face of badges: PASA and Boston team up to re-envision digital badges. Retrieved from http://mypasa.org/2014/09/11/the-new-face-of-badges-pasa-and-boston-team-up-to-re-envision-digital-badges/.

Fleming, N. (2013, February 6). R. I. students gaining 'badges' and credits outside school. *Education Week*. Retrieved from www.edweek.org/ew/articles/2013/02/06/20credits.h32.html.

Hickey, D., Otto, N., Itow, R., Schenke, K., Tran, C., & Chow, C. (2014). Badges design principles documentation project interim report. Indiana University. Retrieved from http://dpdproject.info/files/2014/05/DPD-interim-report-v4-january.pdf.

Humanities, Arts, Science, and Technology Alliance and Collaboratory (HASTAC) (2012). *Digital Media and Learning Competition 4*. Retrieved from www.hastac.org/dml-competitions/2012.

Humanities, Arts, Science, and Technology Alliance Collaboratory (HASTAC) (2015). Retrieved from www.hastac.org/.

MOUSE Squad (2015, June 29). Summer microproject: The wheels of Spinvention [web log]. Retrieved from http://mousesquad.org/wire.

MOUSE Wins! (2012). MOUSE Wins! Badge-based achievement system for national youth technology leadership: DML stage 1 proposal. *Digital Media and Learning Competition*. Retrieved from http://dml4.dmlcompetition.net/dml4.dmlcompetition.net/Competition/4/badges-projects.php%3Fid=2701.html.

National Institute on Out-of-School Time (NOIST) (2015). The survey of academic and youth outcomes. Retrieved from www.niost.org/Training-Descriptions/survey-of-afterschool-youth-outcomes-for-staff-and-teachers-sayo-s-and-sayo-t.

Olneck, M. (2012). *Insurgent credentials: A challenge to established institutions of higher education*. Paper presented to "Education in a New Society: The Growing Interpenetration of Education in Modern Life" at Radcliffe Institute for Advanced Study, Harvard University, Cambridge, MA, April 26–27, 2012.

Otto, N. (2014). Sweet Water AQUAPONS. In *Badge system analysis, design principles documentation project*. Retrieved from http://dpdproject.info/details/sweet-water-aquapons/.

Providence After School Alliance (2012a). Pathways for lifelong learning: DML stage 1 proposal. *Digital Media and Learning Competition*. Retrieved from http://dml4.dml-competition.net/dml4.dmlcompetition.net/Competition/4/badges-projects.php%-3Fid=2773.html.

Providence After School Alliance (2012b). Pathways for lifelong learning: DML stage 2 proposal. *Digital Media and Learning Competition*. Retrieved from http://dml4.dml-competition.net/dml4.dmlcompetition.net/Competition/4/badges-projects.php%-3Fid=3227.html.

Sweet Water Foundation (2012). Sweet water AQUAPONS: DML stage 1 proposal. Retrieved from http://dml4.dmlcompetition.net/dml4.dmlcompetition.net/Competition/4/badges-projects.php%3Fid=2655.html.

Sweet Water Foundation (2015). Sweet water AQUAPONS. Retrieved from http://sweetwaterfoundation.com/aquapons/.

14

AFTERSCHOOL AND DIGITAL BADGES

Recognizing Learning Where It Happens

Sam Piha

If the growing afterschool movement is to prosper, these programs must be recognized as important places of learning. The use and awarding of digital badges to recognize the learning that takes place within these programs represents an excellent strategy to accomplish this.

When we use the term "afterschool," we are referring to those youth programs that take place after the school day and/or during the summer months and that can be based in a school or broader community. These programs are primarily informal learning settings. Key stakeholders include youth and their families, educators, community leaders, youth workers, youth and family advocates, funders, and policymakers.

A small number of afterschool systems and programs are using digital badges to acknowledge exemplar programs as well as the learning by their youth participants and adult staff. However, because the use of digital badges is fairly new, finding information on resources, best practices and technical assistance is difficult. To address this problem, Temescal Associates launched a *Center for Digital Badges* (Temescal Associates, 2015).

This chapter provides a description of the Center for Digital Badges (CDB) and case studies of two of our digital badge projects conducted in partnership with the California School-Age Consortium (CalSAC) and Central Valley Digital Badge (CVDB) Project.

The CDB and our partners believe that by using digital badges to acknowledge the learning of staff and youth participants, benefits will accrue in several areas:

- Because program leaders must think through and explicitly state what learning will go on in specific program activities or clubs that are being recognized by a digital badge, this specificity raises the bar for learning accountability.
- The awarding of digital badges defines the learning that goes on in programs for outsiders, which is vital if afterschool programs are to be recognized as important places of learning. These badges are important, visible evidence that afterschool programs take learning seriously.
- The adult program staff members often acquire important knowledge and skills through professional development and years of experience. Youth acquire valuable skills and knowledge through their participation in specific afterschool activities. Both deserve an artifact that documents their learning and—importantly—can be shared with peers, future employers, and those allowing admittance to higher education.

To increase our own understanding, we consulted with a number of groups that had more experience awarding digital badges. They included the Badge Alliance, the Mozilla Foundation, the Privacy Technical Assistance Center, Los Angeles Unified School District, Providence After School Alliance, and Norco-Corona Unified School District in California. We also initiated a number of digital badge pilot projects with various groups. They included the California School-Age Consortium, California Teaching Fellows Foundation at Fresno State University, Youth Institute at the YMCA of Greater Long Beach, Central Valley Afterschool Foundation, and the Fresno and Tulare County Offices of Education. These projects enabled us to explore the issues in presenting badges to exemplar programs, adult staff, and youth participants in afterschool programs. We selected digital badge partners using the following criteria:

- Shared understanding on the importance of digital badges for the afterschool movement;
- Capacity to develop clear learning goals, criteria, and evidence needed for each badge;
- Capacity to award and manage badges over time; and
- Willingness to work closely with CDB in the design of the badges and development of the larger badge project.

The CDB is designed to advocate for the use of digital badges and promote state and local policies and guidelines that are supportive of digital badges. The CDB is also working to promote the recognition by others that digital badges are valuable evidence of learning, and to serve as a clearinghouse on the most up-to-date information on best practices and where they are being applied.

Finally, the Center is dedicated to contributing to national and global discussions on digital badges and providing direct assistance to afterschool organizations and programs wishing to issue digital badges.

Case Study #1

Overview

The focus of this case study is our pilot project with the CalSAC in their creating a digital badge system. The CDB subcontracted with Public Profit, a local training and evaluation organization, to assist us in this effort.

CalSAC is dedicated to supporting and advancing the out-of-school time field by connecting professionals, enhancing competency, and building community. CalSAC provides training, leadership development and advocacy opportunities to staff serving children and youth. CalSAC was looking to award digital badges to recognize the training investment of their participants. According to CalSAC Executive Director, Ruth Obel-Jorgensen, "Developing the digital badge system also helped us think through how we communicate our projects to a larger audience" (R. Obel-Jorgensen, personal communication, February 2015).

CalSAC chose to issue badges to trainers first, with the eventual goal of issuing badges to all staff from afterschool organizations who participate in trainings. They have begun this by issuing badges to staff who completed a year-long leadership fellowship.

Design and Implementation

The CDB provided assistance to CalSAC in moving through the following steps:

Ask "why?" We assisted CalSAC by offering an orientation to staff and offering pre-readings to ensure that everyone had a common understanding of what digital badges are and the benefits that they provide to those who receive them. These information resources were gathered from the Mozilla Foundation, the Badge Alliance, and the Center for Digital Badges. Because implementing a digital badge system takes a significant amount of work, it is important that everyone knows and agrees on why a digital badge system would benefit the program. Are the badges intended to acknowledge learning, motivate recipients, or something else?

Determine learning goals, criteria, and evidence. We consulted with CalSAC's leaders on which activities warranted the awarding of a digital badge. It is vital that organization and program leaders think through the learning goals (knowledge and skills that will be acquired). "One of the important considerations in the design of the badge system was establishing criteria for the badges that were easy enough to achieve and that would not intimidate the participants, but challenging enough to carry weight" (R. Obel-Joregensen, personal communication, February 2015).

CDB consulted with CalSAC leaders on this process and provided planning tools to develop the needed criteria and evidence that was required for each badge. Planning tools can be found on the CDB website (Temescal Associates, 2015) and Open Badge Designer website (MyKnowledgeMap, 2015). To assist in this process, the CDB adapted planning tools based on our conversations with representatives from Mozilla.

CalSAC leaders decided to develop a multi-tiered digital badge system. It includes the recognition of staff serving as CalSAC trainers according to their length of service, level of activity, and leadership roles they have fulfilled. These roles include serving as a mentor, leading a "train the trainer" institute, and contributing to curriculum development. Figure 14.1 presents an example of badges that represent years or hours of service as a trainer.

A second tier recognizes trainees who have participated in long-term, more extensive projects. These projects go deeper to develop the capacity of the participants and the agencies for which they work. They are referred to as "capacity" badges. For instance, the capacity badge entitled *Leadership Development Institute* is awarded when a participant completes "a year-long cohort-based fellowship for emerging leaders of color focused on creating more responsive programs and policies for out-of-school time and early education programs" (California School-Age Consortium, 2015). A complete display of the badges awarded by CalSAC can be found on their website (California School-Age Consortium, 2015). For an example of capacity badges, see Figure 14.2.

FIGURE 14.1 CalSAC trainer badges recognizing years or hours of service.

FIGURE 14.2 CalSAC capacity badges.

Training participants can also receive a badge for building their competency to work with children and youth. This "competency" badge is awarded on completion of a certain number of hours in training sessions. For instance, the competency badge entitled *Working with Children and Youth* requires participating "in 8 or more hours of training in CalSAC's Working with Children and Youth series" (California School-Age Consortium, 2015). For an example of competency badges, see Figure 14.3.

Determine how badges will be managed and awarded. The management and awarding of digital badges requires some kind of application to track the badges, the required criteria, the means to award the badges, and the names of awardees. We researched several digital badge software applications focusing on short- and long-term cost, ease of use, and compliance with legal issues governing the sharing of data. We decided to use the ForAllRubrics application.

CDB staff assisted CalSAC in deciding how their digital badges would be managed and awarded, and who on their staff would be responsible for managing this digital badge system. The CDB raised funds to support CalSAC's work and trained their staff on how to use the badge management application (ForAllRubrics) to manage and issue badges. The CDB also conferred with CalSAC leaders to ensure that they were aware of federal and state legal issues regarding permission and confidentiality. The badge system hosting was a big part of CalSAC's consideration. They wanted a system that was easy to use by staff and their constituents.

Determine how badges will be created and by whom. Badges can be designed by the client using existing badge design applications such as the Open Badges Designer. CalSAC leaders decided to have the CDB custom design their badges. CalSAC viewed this option as a way to further align badging initiatives. It was important for CalSAC to maintain branding, as well as design elements that corresponded to the badge titles. This was guided by a badge design rubric that the CDB provided. See Figure 14.4 for the badge component map that we provided to CalSAC. The badges that were created by CDB were done using Adobe PhotoShop and Illustrator.

Deliver badges to recipients using Mozilla backpack. There are several entities that are awarding digital badges. The Mozilla Foundation created a "badge backpack" that enables badge earners to store and collect all of their badges regardless of where the badges came from. The CDB designed a digital tutorial on how

FIGURE 14.3 CalSAC competency badges.

BADGE BORDER   BADGE BODY TEXT

BADGE BODY   BADGE ICON

BANNER   BANNER TEXT

FIGURE 14.4 Badge component map developed by CDB.

to create a Mozilla "badge backpack" and retrieve their digital badge. This was then given to the CalSAC leaders to distribute to their badge recipients.

Once badge recipients have "pushed" their earned digital badges into their backpack, they can share their badges with others by using social media (Facebook, Twitter, etc.) or placing the link to their backpack on their résumés or applications for higher education. We instructed the CalSAC staff on how to assist their badge recipients in this process. We also developed a digital tutorial for them to use with their awardees.

The CDB used several technologies in our digital badge work, which is described above.

Evaluation

The pilot project with CalSAC did not include a formal evaluation. They gauged the success of their efforts by tracking the number of awardees who downloaded their badge and the degree to which they shared their badge with others. "There was an initial excitement about the idea and implementation of a digital badging system. However, there continues to be a lack of full understanding of the badge ecosystem" (R. Obel-Jorgensen, personal communication, February 2015).

Conclusions

The use of digital badges is new to the afterschool community. In order for a badging initiative to be successful, stakeholders must understand the value of digital badges and how they can be used. To accomplish this, these messages have to be heavily reinforced. "One of the challenges is communicating about badges and getting buy-in. We held a webinar, sent emails and created user guides. The process of accepting the badges and then sharing them remains a challenge for recipients" (R. Obel-Jorgensen, personal communication, February 2015). She added,

> We need to raise awareness of digital badges and make the case for their value. This also means ensuring that there is alignment and connection with other badge initiatives statewide and nationally. Finally, support with securing funding for ongoing development and management will also be important for programs to sustain their badging initiatives. (R. Obel-Jorgensen, personal communication, February 2015)

For program leaders planning to initiate a badging system, Obel-Jorgensen advised that the planning phase is really the most important, and that taking the time to get as many details on paper ahead of badge creation really helps move things along.

The CDB will endeavor to address these challenges through our continued development of materials and tools. We will also form a work group consisting of other organizations in California interested in working together to raise awareness of digital badges, align our collective work, and connect with other badge initiatives.

Case Study #2

Overview

This case study focuses on the use of digital badges to recognize high school afterschool programs that are exemplary in demonstrating the Learning in Afterschool & Summer (LIAS) learning principles (Learning in Afterschool & Summer, 2015). These principles promote the necessity for learning activities to be active, collaborative, and meaningful, to promote mastery, and to expand the horizons of the participants. This project was a partnership between the CDB, Fresno County and Tulare County Offices of Education, the Central Valley Afterschool Foundation, and the California Teaching Fellows Foundation. Each organization served as a member of a work group, which we labeled the Central Valley Digital Badge (CVDB) project. This group also included an advisor from the California Department of Education After School Division. In an interview with Lori Carr (2015) from the Fresno County Office of Education, she explained the objectives of this project.

> We entered into this project to recognize programs for exhibiting quality as defined by the LIAS learning principles. Our objectives include reinforcing the use of LIAS learning principles as a best practice, driving the field towards quality, recognizing quality programs and their staff, and perhaps most importantly, increase youth ownership and impact.

Design and Development

This project was unique in that it required not only the design of orientation trainings but also the means for gathering evidence to qualify a program as an exemplar in demonstrating the LIAS learning principles. This included the development of application forms, a scoring rubric for applications, a rubric to guide observations, and the preparation of observation teams to verify and score what they noted in their program observations. Observation teams were prepared through a one-day leadership and best practices training. We also made sure that youth were involved in the observation teams.

Afterschool programs were awarded digital badges for each of the learning principles they demonstrated based on the scoring of their applications and site observation. The digital badges used in this project were designed by Youtopia and issued by the LIAS project in partnership with the CVDB project. Because the LIAS project was already familiar with issuing digital badges, this project did not require additional training on the use of the digital badge software. See Figure 14.5 to view the CVDB badges.

Implementation

Programs interested in applying for recognition were required to participate in an orientation to digital badges and the specifics of the CVDB project. Applying programs were also asked to recommend youth who could join the observation teams that visited the applying sites. These observation team members participated in a one-day leadership and observation best practices retreat led by ARC. After further training by the Fresno County Office of Education, the observation teams conducted site visits to each of the applying programs.

The high school afterschool programs that earned digital badges also received a framed certificate, a letter of recognition from the California Department of Education After School Division, and press coverage. Their district superintendents and school principals also received notification of their awards.

The biggest challenge, according to Lori Carr, was scheduling workshops for staff and youth and then following up to make sure all applicants received training:

COLLABORATIVE   ACTIVE   EXPANDS HORIZONS   MEANINGFUL   SUPPORTS MASTERY

FIGURE 14.5 LIAS badges used by Central Valley Digital Badge (CVDB) project.

The biggest surprise was how much youth gained from the experience. Youth shared their enthusiasm for having a set of clear standards to evaluate programs. They left the training inspired and equipped to assess and impact programs in meaningful ways. (L. Carr, personal communication, February 2015)

Evaluation

The pilot project with CVDB did not include a formal evaluation. According to Carr, "Based on anecdotal evidence, the digital badge program assessments assisted program leaders and youth identify strengths and weaknesses in activity content and delivery" (L. Carr, personal communication, February 2015).

Superintendents and principals expressed their appreciation for this project recognizing program quality rather than just compliance:

> They were also grateful to have positive feedback to bring before their School Boards. Site Leads and staff were proud of the program and motivated to expand youth involvement. Youth observers were empowered to influence program design and proud to recognize program accomplishments. They now have higher expectations for program and a tool for measuring quality. The sites are more intentional in using the LIAS learning principles when building classes and designing lesson plans. (L. Carr, personal communication, February 2015)

Conclusions

This project was very successful in engaging a small number of high school afterschool programs. Ms. Carr's advice to people thinking about using digital badges to recognize exemplar programs is, "Don't wait. Recruit partners and set a window for planning and launching a digital badge system for programs and/or youth!" (L. Carr, personal communication, February 2015).

The CVDB Project is currently engaged in a second round of this recognition project. Our advisor from the California Department of Education suggested that in the next round, we need to determine the real costs of badging in afterschool programs so that we can best determine how it can be taken to scale. We are now seeking to measure the actual time and costs required to launch a digital badge project similar to the one described above.

Case Study Comparison

The CalSAC project recognized level of engagement, completion, and competency of trainers and trainees based on specific training and development programs. The CVDB project case study is different in that it recognizes exemplar programs that demonstrate the LIAS learning principles. As a result, the CVDB project required a unique set of tools and processes to verify which programs warranted an exemplar status and badge. Because neither project awarded badges to youth, they did not need to be concerned about federal or state legal issues.

Both projects acted as "pioneers" in the use of digital badges in afterschool settings. They will benefit by future efforts to raise awareness and the value of digital badges to outside institutions, and the increased use of digital badges by the afterschool community. Both projects relied on anecdotal evidence to gauge their success and neither conducted a formal evaluation process.

References

California School-Age Consortium (2015). Digital Badges. Retrieved from https://calsac .org/projects/digital_badges.

Learning in Afterschool & Summer (2015). Learning in Afterschool & Summer. Retrieved from http://learninginafterschool.org.

MyKnowledgeMap (2015). Open Badge Designer. Retrieved from www.openbadges.me.

Temescal Associates (2015). Center for Digital Badges. Retrieved from www .centerfordigitalbadges.com.

15

DESIGNING DIGITAL BADGES FOR AN INFORMAL STEM LEARNING ENVIRONMENT

Eve Klein and Katie Davis

This chapter outlines a case study at Pacific Science Center in Seattle, Washington. Using an approach inspired by participatory design (Carroll, Chin, Rosson, & Neal, 2000; Kensing & Blomberg, 1998), the design team constructed a digital badge system for an out-of-school science, technology, engineering, and math (STEM) education program that aims to support high school students' college and career readiness. The project included a series of focus groups and interviews with youth participants, program leaders, and the designers of the badge system. Participants shared their attitudes towards digital badges, and the youth participants were invited to offer feedback about two prototype iterations of the badge system.

Project Overview

Pacific Science Center (PSC) opened its doors during the 1962 World's Fair and was one of the first hands-on, exploration-based science centers in the country. The *Discovery Corps* (DC) youth development program began at PSC in 2005 to build confidence, life skills, and STEM knowledge and interest among its participants. The program recruits high school students in the Seattle area and trains them to staff public-facing positions in the Science Center's exhibit spaces. DC draws together students from a wide range of racial, ethnic, and socioeconomic backgrounds. During this project, there were 61 youth active in DC activities, who hail from 31 different schools (public and private) in the Seattle area. Of the active youth, 17 self-identified as Asian, 12 as Black/African American, 13 as Multiracial, 13 as White/Caucasian, 3 as Other, 2 as Hispanic/Latino, and 1 as Pacific Islander.

Many students learn about the program by word of mouth or from a school counselor or teacher; teens are invited to apply as rising freshmen and are encouraged to stay for the full four years of high school. The youth who join DC are not necessarily those who are already drawn to STEM fields. Instead, many DC members are drawn to the reputation of the program as being the source of a strong, close-knit supportive community, and to the value of being able to put PSC's name on a college application. Crucial to the diversity of the program, DC youth are paid after volunteering an initial 100 hours with the program. The program is carefully crafted around a career ladder and a range of benchmark accomplishments that serve as gateways to the next ladder rung; youth participants are given a clear set of tasks they must accomplish before they are able to move through the ranks. The program is led by two supervisors, both of whom were interviewed during the course of the project.

As the capstone project in their Informatics program at the University of Washington, three undergraduate students developed a small-scale digital badge system prototype to suit the needs of the DC program. The team was responsible for the conception and construction of the badge system outlined here.

The Need

Learning in informal environments is typically more flexible than formal learning structures and allows students to engage in interest-driven learning, often within a social community (Bevan, 2013; Ito et al., 2013). The value of informal learning experiences for an individual is increasingly recognized, but this shift presents several new challenges: finding a way to offer credit for participating in high-quality, robust informal learning experiences; a way to link more effectively the learning that is taking place in various settings, both formal and informal; and a way to enable learners to manage their own skills to create a narrative version of their qualifications and goals (Fullerton, Menking, Lee, & Davis, 2014; Ito et al., 2013). Digital badges have been proposed as an alternative to traditional transcripts and certificates because they are better able to represent "twenty-first century" skills, like communication and systems thinking, which are highly valued in the current economy (Gibson, Ostashewski, Flintoff, Grant, & Knight, 2013; Rehak & Hickey, 2013; Riconscente, Kamarainen, & Honey, 2013). These skills are often gained outside of the formal education system and are not effectively represented by traditional transcripts or résumés.

Other Benefits of Digital Badges

All of the youth interviewed during the course of this project acknowledged that the paper-and-pencil system currently employed by DC to track youth progress through the program is inadequate and susceptible to error. Currently, the two program supervisors are tasked with tracking the individual progress of more than 60 youth, which understandably results in delays in processing and sometimes lost or misplaced documentation of progress. The two supervisors we interviewed described the tedious and impractical analog methods of tracking and documentation. They also said that they sometimes feel they struggle to keep track of Corps members as closely as they would like, and are sometimes startled to discover that a particular member is either succeeding or struggling outside of the typical rates of progression. Students and supervisors agreed that the program would benefit from a digitized tracking system. We also hoped that a badge system might serve as a tool to help youth visualize and understand learning pathways, i.e., where they stand, what steps come next, and what they should expect to learn and do in the future.

Analysis

The analysis that informed the design and development of the badge system focused on whether and under what circumstances students would be inclined to use digital badges. During two focus group sessions, we asked questions that assessed students' prior knowledge of badge systems, word associations, attitude, and interest.

Question 1: Have you heard of digital badges? What have you heard?

When asked if they were familiar with the concept of digital badges (outside of the present project), both groups unequivocally said "no." The groups were then asked if they were familiar with the idea of "achievements" or "endorsements" and they began to offer examples. The most frequent responses were games or game platforms, including Flappy Bird, Farmville, Pokemon, and Steam. Students saw these badges as a way to "hook people in," and a source of "income for the game-makers." A student also mentioned Khan Academy, which she used to improve her math performance in school.

Question 2: What do you think of when you hear the word "badge"?

Both groups cited Boy and Girl Scout badges, then began to describe what a badge of any kind might signify or represent. Responses fell into a few categories:

- badges as an indication of mastery;
- badges as a *personal* matter of pride;
- badges as an indication of belonging or participation;
- badges for the purpose of ranking or comparing to others;
- badges as an indication of seniority or time invested; and
- badges for access, e.g., to "let you go through locked doors."

Both groups recognized that the DC program currently uses what is effectively an analog badge system. After volunteering for 100 hours or being certified to facilitate certain programs, youth participants earn a small metal pin, which they can affix to their employee lanyard.

Question 3: Imagine you could use a badge system for Discovery Corps—is that something you would be interested in?

The teens were shown several examples of badge systems including Quiz Up, LinkedIn endorsements, and Angry Birds, and were asked about their interest in this kind of achievement system. In the first group, the teens agreed that they would be interested if badge systems were widely used or were linked to the college Common Application. But, as one teen put it, "if it were just, 'Oh I have these badges on this one site,' and no one else uses it, it's not going to be as effective."

This feedback prompted us to construct a badge system that was, in essence, bi-modal. Portions of the DC badge system are intended to be a reflection of a teen's progress *within* the program, whereas other features are intended to translate smoothly *outside* of DC.

Design and Development

The Digital Badge System

The DC badge system consists of a custom website through which students can see their earned badges and track their progress. The undergraduate team took the lead on the design of the badges and built their visuals loosely around PSC branding. The badges themselves are both fun and professional-looking. In developing the badge system, the team aligned the technical infrastructure with Mozilla's Open Standards for digital badges. Upon logging into the system, users see a welcome page with a navigation pane and an image of the badges already earned (Figure 15.1). The home page also includes a few at-a-glance features: Place-holders for future badges and a progress bar are both intended to help youth quickly assess their progress and standings.

The skills and jobs associated with the DC career ladder served as the basis for developing the badge system prototype. To differentiate between badges earned at different levels of the career ladder, distinct shapes were assigned to each level. For instance, triangles were used for the initial Discovery Corps Assistant (DCA) level badges, while squares were used for the next level, Discovery Corps Interpreter (DCI). At each successive level, another side was added to the shape to signal a student's movement up the ladder. Circles, diamonds, or "badge" shapes were used for personal goals and skills so that they would be visually distinct from ladder badges. Specific metadata were enumerated for each badge, including the student's name, badge name, date of issue, issuer, and specific skills associated with the badge.

FIGURE 15.1   System dashboard (homepage).

The three primary types of badges are career, skill, and personal. Various career and skill badges can be earned at each level of the career ladder (see Figures 15.2 and 15.3). For instance, Ocean Acidification Discovery Cart is a career badge that DC youth can earn when they have reached the Discovery Corps Senior Interpreter (DCSI) level. Relevant skill badges associated with this career badge include content knowledge, public speaking, and long-term engagement. In addition, youth have the potential to advance within particular skills. For example, if they are particularly motivated to develop their public speaking skills, they can complete various jobs involving this skill and thereby advance from an apprentice through to a master skill badge in public speaking. A master badge in public speaking includes evidence of a student's full range of experiences and achievements in public speaking. In this way, the valuable but often undocumented skills that youth acquire through their participation in the DC program become visible within and outside of the PSC.

During our focus group conversations, many youth described specific personal accomplishments they had achieved through their participation in the DC program. Recognizing these personal achievements as important, identity-shaping experiences, we devised a third category of personal badges that youth can define and work towards on an individual basis. For example, one girl described her fear of handling cockroaches and how she was very proud of overcoming it. She would have the opportunity to create and work towards a personal badge involving overcoming this fear. Personal badges support youth's STEM-related identities by recognizing their individual accomplishments and giving them agency over their learning experiences.

One teen described a desire to see the progress of others so that he could learn what steps his peers were taking to move up the ladder, and many of the teens expressed interest in a profile page that could be seen by others inside or outside of DC (only one teen raised privacy concerns). In response, the designers built a more robust internal social network with primary focus on profile pages that

FIGURE 15.2 Career level badges.

FIGURE 15.3 Skill badges.

are visible to other DC members. Future iterations of the system might offer the option of enabling public access to this page and the ability to turn it on or off at the discretion of the individual user.

Implementation

While implementation was not a component of this project, we did ask program supervisors for their thoughts about the practicalities of adopting the system. They underscored that for badges to gain a foothold in DC, it must be clear that the system will ease, rather than increase, the strain on often limited resources at the Science Center. The two supervisors noted that they do not have the capacity to take on an *additional* system unless it is clearly an improved way of accomplishing the core duties of the work they already do. An additional—and significant— barrier to implementation is access to technology, which is currently limited for DC participants.

Evaluation

Because this case study focuses on the design of a badge system prototype (and not the implementation of a badge system), we focus here on the formative evaluations that guided the design process.

Usability Testing

Once the undergraduate designers had developed a rough model of the badge system, we conducted a series of usability tests with the youth individually, and later with the two DC supervisors. During usability testing, the youth were invited to tour the badge website on their own, and were then asked to share their thoughts about the system. Some feedback was incorporated into the design of the system itself, as described above. We additionally hoped to learn more about the value youth might ascribe to digital badges that recognize their skills and achievements in out-of-school learning activities. Several key themes emerged that gave us greater insight into how these badges might be perceived or used if adopted in the future.

DC Cultures and Values

Many youth focused on ways to further incorporate aspects of DC culture into the system. Most notably, many of the youth (four out of six) requested the addition of badges that acknowledge earned "kudos" (a way of complimenting or thanking coworkers) and badges for internships. After their first or second year in DC, youth are invited to apply for a range of summer internship positions with other departments at PSC or other institutions. Kudos and internships are both important in the DC culture, and this request suggested that the teens were eager to see the badge system align with the values of the DC community. If the badge system is adopted in the future, these two components are likely to be added.

Motivation

The two DC supervisors saw great benefit in building visible pathways for students who might otherwise not push themselves to pursue the next step in the career ladder. The supervisors suspect that if less-motivated youth not only see the next steps, but also see that their peers are progressing through these steps, they will be motivated to move up too, rather than be left behind.

Despite this potential, one student did express concern about the exact nature of the motivating power of badges:

> I think [badges] could also *not* be useful in the sense that … if you have tangible goals as far as medals or trophies or badges, then sometimes people go after an activity or a pursuit in order to get those tangible things and kind of lose vision of other things in the pursuit of getting like ten badges or twenty badges. And so instead of like going to the Science Center and experiencing it for what it is … you go in with the idea of like, 'Oh I want to get these skill sets. And if I don't, then I'm a failure' … you may lose some of the nuanced part of being part of the Science Center.

The student's concern is astute, and the question of intrinsic versus extrinsic motivation is the subject of ongoing education research (Hickey & McCaslin, 2001).

Establishing Badge Validity

Students recognized the value of third-party verification of skills, but all of them alluded to concerns about standardization and credibility at some point during the focus group conversations. When a badge is awarded, it is necessarily based on the judgment of an individual or a group of individuals. Students wondered how the rigor behind badges could be compared across institutions and how the credibility of the awarder could be established.

Beyond DC

A dichotomy emerged when teens were asked who they might engage through a badge system. All of the students converged on the idea that "[the system] has to be something that we can apply to a lot of things, not just Science Center."

Participants were particularly excited about any opportunity to link badges to the college application process or to college credit. But as previously described, the teens expressed a simultaneous desire to produce badges that are deeply specific to DC culture. They also expressed a resistance to using badges to bridge their personal and professional lives, discussed below. These sentiments are not mutually exclusive, but they do represent an extra layer of complexity for those looking to design badges that will be appealing to youth.

Social Media

The design team initially planned to build badges that could be exported to other social media sites, such as Instagram, Facebook, and Twitter. During the focus group conversations, the team learned quickly that the youth were not interested in mixing their work and social lives in this way, and so that feature was removed. With one exception, the teens expressed a resistance to linking any kind of professional badge system to their personal social media use. Several alluded to the idea of not wanting to "brag." The teens also said that constant, small-scale updates would likely be "annoying" to their friends.

Connecting Activities

When asked to consider when and where they chose to discuss their time in DC, the youth were clearly able to draw vivid lines in their minds—divisions between those with whom they might discuss their accomplishments and those who occupy a social role that is distinctly separate from DC. Students were all open to the idea of connecting to friends within their immediate DC circle, but were almost unanimously wary or opposed to the idea of sharing their DC accomplishments (badges) with non-DC friends. Opinions about sharing badges with their teachers and parents were split. There was unanimous support for sharing information with potential employers or colleges.

The supervisors explained that there may actually be value in the separation of the DC experience from other parts of teens' lives. Parents are invited to family events at the Science Center once or twice a year, but—as the program supervisors put it—"we build up the culture to be 'this is your thing. This is not your parents' thing.'" There may be a similar value to the distinct separation of DC and school. Some of the youth involved in DC are those who struggle with the structure and impersonal nature of the formal education system; keeping DC separate gives them an alternate opportunity to thrive. This opportunity to explore distinct "selves" is an important part of being a teenager and may impact efforts to connect learning experiences (Davis & Fullerton, in press). An ideal connected learning landscape would give youth the opportunity to draw connections between experiences while giving them the ability to control how and when they publically display different aspects of themselves. Though it may introduce design challenges to badge system developers, a bi-modal—but deeply integrated—system is most likely to be embraced by teens.

Conclusions

Through this project, we found that youth respond well to the ownership and personalization of education that badges may well afford. The DC members interviewed embraced the inward-facing component of the system; badges as a way to organize the internal bureaucratic workings of their program seemed like an obvious and needed next step. Given the daily operational challenges that the DC supervisors face, we were gratified to find that the system may well improve program organization and simultaneously help motivate program participants.

Despite this enthusiasm, participants still expressed skepticism when asked to imagine large-scale adoption of badges, perhaps because a larger network of badge systems is still too abstract to embrace fully. The DC youth and supervisors were all asked if they thought the broader network of badges will truly take hold, and each group responded that it depends on the commitment and involvement of a few high profile groups, including universities and the Common Application administrators. Until badges gain a critical mass of prominent users and supporters, it may be a challenge to encourage smaller groups with limited resources to develop and adopt badge systems voluntarily.

Our conversations with DC youth and program supervisors revealed a notable tension: On the one hand, the youth in the DC program wanted to tailor the badge system to reflect the values of the program, incorporating personal badges and kudos. At the same time, the youth also embraced the idea of badges with standard and verified value that could be recognized and accepted by external evaluators (e.g., college admissions officers or future employers). While these two facets may seem at odds, the lesson here may be that effective digital educational systems need to have a familiar, comfortable, and localized social community, but must also have components that are recognizable and usable by external stakeholders like college admissions officers and prospective employers. The interaction with DC youth and supervisors provided valuable insights into the design process, illustrating the importance of including the intended users in developing digital badge systems.

References

Bevan, B. (2013). *LOST opportunities: Learning in out-of-school time.* Dordrecht: Springer.

Carroll, J. M., Chin, G., Rosson, M. B., & Neale, D. C. (2000). The development of cooperation: Five years of participatory design in the virtual school. In *Proceedings on Designing Interactive Systems: Processes, Practices, Methods, and Techniques* (pp. 239–251). New York, NY: Association for Computing Machinery.

Davis, K., & Fullerton, S. (in press). Connected learning in and after school: Exploring technology's role in the diverse learning experiences of high school students. *The Information Society*.

Fullerton, S., Menking, A., Lee, C., & Davis, K. (2014). *Stakeholders' perceptions of the opportunities, challenges, and value of digital badges in education*. Paper presented at the annual meeting of the American Educational Research Association, Philadelphia, PA.

Gibson, D., Ostashewski, N., Flintoff, K., Grant, S., & Knight, E. (2013). Digital badges in education. *Education and Information Technologies*, pp. 1−8.

Hickey, D. T., & McCaslin, M. (2001). Comparative and sociocultural analyses of context and motivation. In S. S. Volet & S. Järvelä (Eds.), *Motivation in learning contexts: theoretical and methodological implications* (pp. 33−56). Amsterdam: Pergamon/Elsevier.

Ito, M., Gutiérrez, K., Livingstone, S., Penuel, B., Rhodes, J., Salen, K., ... Watkins, S. C. (2013). *Connected learning: An agenda for research and design*. Digital Media and Learning Research Hub. Retrieved from http://dmlhub.net/sites/default/files/ConnectedLearning_report.pdf.

Kensing, F., & Blomberg, J. (1998). Participatory design: issues and concerns. *Computer Supported Cooperative Work* 7(3): 167−185.

Rehak, A., & Hickey, D. T. (2013, May 20). Design principles for recognizing learning. *RE-MEDIATING ASSESSMENT*. Retrieved from http://remediatingassessment.blogspot.com/2013/05/digital-badge-design-principles-for.html.

Riconscente, M. M., Kamarainen, A., & Honey, M. (2013). *STEM Badges: Current terrain and the road ahead*. New York, NY: New York Hall of Science. Available at http://badgesnysci.files.wordpress.com/2013/08/nsf_stembadges_final_report.pdf.

16

MEASURING NURSING STUDENTS' MASTERY OF HEALTH CARE COMPETENCIES

Andrea Thomas, Jason Fish, Pamela M. Karagory, and Kristen Kirby

Case Overview

As an administrator who hired nurses in the health care industry, Pam Karagory often wished for better ways to assess new graduates' knowledge, skills, and attitudes, which weren't fully illustrated by their resumes or academic transcripts. In one instance, she remembers hiring a nurse who had graduated from a competitive private college with a 4.0 grade point average (GPA) and another who had graduated from a less-renowned public university with a 3.4 GPA. The nurse with the lower GPA exceeded Karagory's expectations in every way; the nurse with the perfect GPA, on the other hand, was terminated after only three months. Although a lot of time and money was invested into orienting someone who was brilliant, that didn't translate into a competent employee. Experiences like this make clear that, although important, transcripts don't always convey crucial competencies such as teamwork and critical thinking.

Curriculum Revision

In 2012, Karagory and Kristen Kirby, both clinical assistant professors in Purdue University's School of Nursing, completed a comprehensive revision to their curriculum so that it aligned better with the standards set by the Institute of Medicine and the American Association of Colleges of Nursing (AACN).

As part of the revision, the faculty decided to implement new and innovative processes and experiences at the sophomore level. The idea was to provide students the opportunity at a very early part of their educational trajectory to start making connections between what they were learning clinically and what was happening in the real world of health care. As health care organizations began to navigate a new health care reform program that included quality and safety metrics as part of patient satisfaction, there was mounting pressure on educators to ensure that their students developed critical skills. Additionally, it was more important than ever that students be well-prepared to become leaders in a rapidly changing field.

To that end, the faculty developed a framework that required students to go out into the community and conduct quality improvement projects. After connecting with local health care stakeholders, the students performed assessments, identified gaps in school and community health care systems, and created proposals for solutions. They also created PowerPoint presentations and shared their ideas with audiences comprising physicians, attorneys, and other community members. It was work that Karagory and Kirby had traditionally seen at the senior level, but their second-year students embraced the challenge and demonstrated excellence in competencies such as public speaking, leadership, writing, and critical thinking. In fact, several schools and health care facilities implemented the students' solutions. Although the faculty had high expectations for robust learning outcomes, they had not fully anticipated how rich and granular the students' learning experiences would be. It was clear that a single grade awarded for the project, or even a final grade at the end of the semester, presented a severely limited picture of their students' accomplishments.

That's when they started to discuss developing a mechanism to capture students' work and the learning that occurred throughout the semester. They also wanted to enable students to display their achievements for potential employers.

Purdue's Passport

Also in 2012, Information Technology at Purdue (ITaP), Purdue's central IT organization, began developing a technology intended to help students define their own learning paths and keep track of their progress. The idea was to build a system that would measure student success based on mastery of specific and pre-defined skills, as opposed to the traditional 4.0 grading scale, which represents largely how a student did compared with others in a class without much context to show what they actually learned (Thomas, 2012).

The tool, Passport, is a learning assessment platform and electronic portfolio (e-portfolio) system that uses digital badges to validate an individual's achievements and competencies. With the public Passport profile (Figure 16.1), learners can selectively showcase the badges they have earned and include biographical and contact information. They also can export badges to their open source Mozilla Backpack or post on Facebook and LinkedIn (C.V. Wright, personal communication, March 31, 2014).

While Passport was being piloted in several science and engineering courses at Purdue, Karagory and Kirby were still searching for a better mechanism to measure students' academic achievements. They were surprised and delighted to discover that a tool with the functionality they sought had already been

FIGURE 16.1 The public Passport profile allows learners to showcase the badges they've earned and include biographical and contact information. Individuals also can export badges to their open source Mozilla Backpack or post on Facebook and LinkedIn.
Used with permission from Purdue University. Created by Brianna Lencke.

custom-designed at their own institution. Shortly after their discovery, they reached out to representatives from ITaP, who began guiding the faculty through the process of implementing Passport into their curriculum.

Partnership

Karagory and Kirby decided to partner with ITaP on a suite of badges that would help nursing students detail their learning and accomplishments for potential employers (see Figure 16.2). With input from three high-performing undergraduates in Purdue's College of Health and Human Sciences, the team developed a set of mandatory and optional health care-related digital badges housed within ITaP's Passport application.

One of the first mandatory badges enabled students to demonstrate the ability to improve the safety and quality of patient care and lead health care teams effectively. Challenges in the badge are associated with real-world safety and quality improvement modules developed by the Institute for Healthcare Improvement (IHI) Open School (Thomas, 2014). One optional badge recognized the community safety and quality improvement projects that had been added to the sophomore curriculum during the program revision. Other optional badges recognized IHI certifications on patient safety, leadership, and family-centered care.

FIGURE 16.2   Purdue's Passport application displays a collection of mandatory and optional health care–related digital badges that may be earned by nursing students in the university's College of Health and Human Sciences.

Used with permission from Purdue University. Created by Brianna Lencke.

Analysis

Having student buy-in was a critical aspect of implementing the nursing badge program, which is why the instructors asked students Kelly Dyer, Megan Nowaczyk, and Elizabeth Oldenburg, pictured in Figure 16.3, to participate from the outset. These three individuals were selected to participate primarily because of their exceptional academic performance and their emergence as leaders among their cohorts. Additionally, these three had amassed a collective range of academic experiences—including research and extracurricular activities—that could be well represented by digital badges. Because most badges were optional, the faculty believed it would be crucial for students to understand the value that completing the badges would add to their educational experience and career prospects. They were hopeful that these students' early engagement would encourage them to serve as ambassadors during the later phases of implementation.

For Nowaczyk, a senior in the College of Health and Human Sciences, it wasn't a tough sell. She says her proudest academic moment occurred a week after her team presented its final project to a community school board, when she learned the school would implement her recommended health care solutions. Her badge contains evidence of the hard work she put forth on the project.

> Having more opportunities to show employers all the different skills we've acquired is a huge benefit. Badges are something new and innovative that not a lot of other universities are implementing, so anything that helps us stand out from the crowd will motivate my classmates and me in the future. (Nowaczyk as cited in Thomas, 2014, para. 13)

The nursing students and instructors hope to expand their set of badges and develop a framework within Purdue's School of Nursing that will allow more students to participate. Although students typically understand and appreciate the benefits that Passport offers to their learning and career goals, one of the biggest barriers to broad implementation relates to preconceived notions about the purpose of badges because the word has various associations.

For example, the idea of badges is embedded for some generations in terms of Girl Scouts, or the "everyone gets a trophy" mentality. But that is not the case with the system that has been implemented at Purdue. There were no intentions to give up or exchange students' competency as clinicians by including Passport into the curriculum. Instead, badges take education a step further by helping students demonstrate their excellence.

One potential barrier for adoption is that some faculty members may be reluctant to adopt new technologies due to the perceived time commitment required, which is why it's crucial for badge platforms to be intuitive and easy to use. Especially in higher education, where program silos exist, it's important for instructors to persevere when introducing cutting-edge technology and ideas.

FIGURE 16.3 Representatives from Purdue's School of Nursing (from left) Kelly Dyer (student), Pam Karagory (clinical assistant professor), Elizabeth Oldenburg (student), Kristen Kirby (clinical assistant professor), and Megan Nowaczyk (student) have implemented Passport badges to measure academic learning and achievement. Used with permission from Purdue University. Photograph by Kevin O'Shea.

Design

Passport is designed to illuminate students' learning connections in a digital portfolio. Each badge icon includes metadata such as who issued the badge, how it was earned, and when it was earned. Individuals can also attach deliverables including essays, certificates, presentations, and more to provide context that shows what they actually accomplished.

This is valuable because many health care organizations now hire nurses only if they've completed bachelor's programs like Purdue's. They also expect the graduates to have more than just the necessary clinical skills. At Purdue, badges are one way to show that graduates possess leadership skills and other desired qualities, while also setting them apart from graduates of other programs.

"I know that our Purdue nursing students are going to be the best hires, but an employer is not going to distinguish between an A from other schools and an A from Purdue" (Karagory as cited in Thomas, 2014, para. 8).

Moreover, the health care industry also now views what used to be considered soft skills—such as leadership, communication, and interpersonal and professional interactions—as essential for nurses to be successful. Badges can illuminate students' talent in areas such as innovation and research, as well as their commitment to safety and patient-centered care. Additionally, data that provide specific details about what the students did and the impact they had on the community will help employers visualize the ways in which prospective hires can identify tough problems and develop solutions.

Mandatory Badge

Karagory and Kirby, with the help of ITaP, designed their mandatory health care badge to align with IHI's Open School Certifications in Safety and Quality. To earn the badge, students log in to the IHI website and complete four modules associated with patient safety, teamwork and communication, the culture of safety, and fundamentals of improvement. They have 13 weeks during the semester to complete the modules and are required to upload their certificates to the Passport application. With this badge, students can show evidence that they've developed fundamental knowledge and skill competencies related to safety, systems thinking, quality improvement, and inter-professional communication.

Optional Badges

A primary benefit of Passport is that it enables students to go above and beyond the expectations laid out for them in course syllabi and earn recognition for their extra efforts.

One optional badge, for instance, requires students to design, implement, and evaluate a small test of change in their daily work routine using an experiential learning method (Plan-Do-Study-Act). This is specific to the Quality Improvement LEAN Healthcare A3, which is a problem-solving framework intended to identify issues from the perspective of a patient. To earn the badge, students must create a non-linear, continual process graphic representation that includes five sections: define, measure, analyze, improve, and control.

Another optional badge may be earned by students who write and submit a 250-word self-reflection on two of the following discussion points: the impact of health care errors on patients, families, and providers; mechanisms to encourage safe patient care transitions; examples of ways in which a culture of safety can help improve the care they provide; and constructive approaches towards responding to errors. This activity helps demonstrate students' written communication skills and their ability to compare life experiences with academic knowledge to infer differences and similarities, as well as acknowledge perspectives other than their own.

Students also had the opportunity to earn several other optional badges by completing IHI Open School certifications on patient safety, improvement capability, leadership, and more.

Development

Passport was created to be flexible so that it could accommodate faculty and students in ways that best fit their teaching and learning style. Passport badges are designed to integrate with Mozilla's Open Badge Infrastructure, which is what enables students to display their accomplishments on their Mozilla Backpack, Facebook, or LinkedIn. The team that developed Passport is constantly seeking feedback from users and making adjustments to meet evolving needs. ITaP's strategy with Passport, and with other tools in its suite of learning applications, is to create the minimum viable product to avoid wasting time and resources on an idea that may not work. In other words, ITaP created the first version Passport with just enough functionality to be usable in the classroom. After the tool was released, however, staff collected input from pilot participants that helped shape future iterations of the app. ITaP is now partnering with several Purdue faculty members on research studies to measure the impact that Passport has on student learning and motivation.

Implementation

Kevin O'Shea is an educational technologist who helps tailor ITaP's teaching and learning applications to faculty and student needs. When Karagory and Kirby first reached out to his team about Passport, O'Shea met with the faculty and their students to demonstrate the tool. Once the professors decided to adopt Passport, they worked with ITaP Web application programmer Casey Wright to design the badges they envisioned. At the beginning of each semester, O'Shea and Wright give students an overview of Passport and badges.

Successes and Challenges

Making one badge mandatory ensured that the entire sophomore nursing cohort would have at least some interaction with the tool. However, one positive surprise was the high number of students who expressed a desire to complete optional badges—even after the semester had ended. Many students who had heavy workloads were unable to balance the completion of optional badges with their course work. Instead, they requested that the instructors keep Passport open during the summer so they could earn the badges during their downtime. The instructors happily agreed.

About 50 percent of the sophomore nursing students went on to complete at least one of seven optional badges, and many completed more than one. Students' voluntary participation in completing the optional badges after the semester is over indicates that students see value in the ability to illustrate their learning. It also underscores the idea that learning can't be measured exclusively by papers, tests, and transcripts.

There are anecdotes of hiring managers literally flipping a coin between two prospective nurses who looked the same on paper. In today's environment, many health care organizations have taken the position that they'll hire only baccalaureate-prepared nurses. With that comes a responsibility for educators to up the ante beyond just the clinical competency to that bigger piece of helping students develop as leaders and agents of change. Documented learning experiences, like what Passport provides, can help tip the scale in favor of a nurse who otherwise shares the same GPA and degree credentials as other applicants.

Still, one pervasive challenge associated with Passport is helping employers understand the ways in which the tool can help them hire individuals who align with their organization's mission, vision, goal, and employment needs. Moving forward, it will be crucial to ensure that the criteria, evidence, and expectations associated with all of Purdue's badges continue to be rigorous. Because most of the health care industry has not yet seen these types of systems, it's going to take some time before hiring managers can fully appreciate the value of badges.

Evaluation

The first nursing cohort to use Passport included 93 students who completed the mandatory badge. The optional badges had varying completion rates; one optional badge was completed by two students, for example, while another was completed by 20. As of the spring semester of 2015, Karagory and Kirby had collected mostly anecdotal evidence about Passport's success in their nursing program. However, they are conducting data-driven research that explores students' perceptions of badges, motivation to complete them, and impressions on whether badges will enhance their employment opportunities. Part of the study will require students to complete surveys based on research by Abramovich, Higashi, Hunkele, Schunn, and Shoop (2011), as well as Keller's (2010) ARCS model, which includes four steps for supporting motivation in the learning process: attention, relevance, confidence, and satisfaction. In the meantime, students' voluntary completion of optional badges serves as an initial sign of their value. The goal is to expand the use of badges more broadly throughout Purdue's nursing program, which may produce additional opportunities to measure Passport's effectiveness.

Conclusions

A substantial component of Passport's success is that the badges are linked to outcomes that have direct value to students, which is why Karagory and Kirby encourage other instructors to focus on the benefits that badges offer to the learner when considering this type of curriculum change. Kirby also recommends that other individuals who wish to implement a similar badge infrastructure start slowly. For example, it's easier to begin with a single class or project and build out an entire curriculum over time. Karagory adds that educators who wish to pursue innovative teaching and learning strategies have to be courageous and committed to their goal. Adopters should be prepared to face criticism and resistance from skeptics about learner-centered education initiatives, especially when new technology is involved.

These types of initiatives demand that instructors empower students to be champions of their own learning. It's important to understand the inherent value in measuring learning however and wherever it occurs, and to avoid being held hostage by the old paradigm of measuring learning exclusively with tests and papers.

For the instructors at Purdue, the most difficult part of the project was finding the time to establish badges as a part of the nursing curriculum. Now that it's in place, however, both professors agree their endeavor was well worth the effort. Kirby points specifically to several projects her students completed in the community that help demonstrate the competencies they developed. One of her clinical groups, for example, created a peanut allergy policy for a local school corporation after finding out that the policy hadn't been updated since the 1970s. The new policy specified roles and expectations for teachers, cafeteria workers, bus drivers, and other ancillary staff and was implemented immediately after the students completed the project. In another case, students collaborated with the Indiana State Department of Health to develop a policy and organization to make free pregnancy tests available at a rural health department. By earning badges associated with these projects, the students have a visual representation of the work they completed, which they can share with future employers.

Graduates from Purdue's nursing program have frequently reported that the quality improvement work they completed as students had a profound impact on their post-college success in the health care industry. From now on, students will have a resource that tells a story about their achievements, gives them a leg up in interviews, and helps them stand out among their peers.

References

Abramovich, S., Higashi, R., Hunkele, T., Schunn, C., & Shoop, R. (2011). *An achievement system to increase achievement motivation.* Paper presented at the Games Learning Society 7.0, Madison, WI.

Keller, J. M. (2010). *Motivational design for learning and performance; the ARCS model approach.* New York, NY: Springer.

Thomas, A. L. (2012, April 23). Professor, ITaP seek faculty to collaborate on new learning technology. *ITaP Newsroom.* Retrieved January 20, 2015 from www.itap.purdue.edu/newsroom/news/professor_itap_seek.html.

Thomas, A. L. (2014, April 17). Nursing faculty and students implement Passport badges to measure learning, achievement. *ITaP Newsroom.* Retrieved January 15, 2015 from www.itap.purdue.edu/newsroom/news/140417_passport_nursing.html.

17

LIFELONG LEARNING STARTS AT SCHOOL

Competency-Based Badge Systems within the Transdisciplinary Experience at Purdue Polytechnic

Iryna Ashby, Marisa Exter, Sorin Adam Matei, and Jeffrey Evans

In addition to professional domain knowledge and skills, today's employers look for cross-disciplinary knowledge, holistic thinking, self-directed lifelong learning skills, creative and critical reasoning, multi-tasking, collaboration, and proactive use of technology that can help new graduates quickly adapt to the changing needs of the global market (Felder, 2006; Litzinger, Lattuca, Hadgraft, & Newstetter, 2011; Morell, 2010; National Academy of Engineering [NAE], 2004). To provide students with a flexible and adaptive skill-set, a new transdisciplinary experience (TDE) was created within the Purdue Polytechnic at Purdue University. This experience was the first step towards the recently approved Transdisciplinary Studies in Technology degree (Purdue Polytechnic, 2015). Designed by a multi-disciplinary faculty group with input from industrial partners, the TDE is the first competency-based program at Purdue and one of the few in the U.S. (Mili, 2014). In the Fall of 2014, the program welcomed its first cohort of 36 freshman students with diverse professional interests in technical and engineering fields, including mechanical engineering and technology, computer graphics technology, computer information technology, and aviation.

Design of a Competency-Based Program

The design of the transdisciplinary experience was aligned with six core values: viewing the student as a whole person with individual talents and strengths; diversity in thinking, knowing, and learning; openness, collaboration, and cooperation to embrace and share creative powers; access to education for students with diverse backgrounds and professional goals; student autonomy in exploring knowledge and skills; and risk taking (Purdue Polytechnic, 2015).

It was envisioned that students will go through four phases during their academic career: exploration of foundational competencies; knowledge formation and development of a personalized mission; deep immersion into one discipline; and ongoing refinement of skills reflected through advanced badges (Mili, 2014). *Learning experiences* were organized around topical themes rather than around specific learning objectives or competencies, and each learning experience allowed students to develop and provide evidence of mastering cross-cutting competencies such as "written communication" or "design thinking." Such overarching competencies allowed for a deeper holistic understanding of a problem and a creative multi-faceted approach to solutions (Purdue Polytechnic, 2014).

The proof of competency attainment differed from the established grading system, which focuses on extrinsic and sorting-based assessment, and penalizes students for not giving the "right" answer (Reigeluth, 2012). Fear of making a "punishable" and "irreversible" mistake can hinder risk taking and motivation, resulting in dependence on an instructor and diminished likelihood of digging deeper beyond the required scope. Finally, the lack of transparency and granularity of the traditional grading system makes it incapable of depicting a full picture of a learner's achievement and learning path (Pearson Learning Solutions, n.d.), which would allow graduates to be more competitive in the current job market. For example, even if a potential employer is generally familiar with the content for a given class listed on a transcript, an employer will have no way of telling what skills and knowledge were truly mastered and which were not understood or misunderstood by a student.

Each TDE competency was represented by a "badge" that operationalized and certified that competency. Using badges to credential granular skills and experiences (or microcredentials) allows students and mentors to focus on the creation of validated and trusted individualized granular learning paths for each student, which encourages mastery learning, recognition of embedded learning experiences, and identity curation through students' ability to "own" their learning experiences (Finkelstein, Knight, & Manning, 2013; Purdue University, 2012). Because the adoption of badge-based credentialing in the TDE allowed students to take responsibility for their own learning paths, it was expected to encourage self-directed learning—an important step in preparing students to be able to adapt to the rapidly changing needs of today's employment.

Design and Development of Learning Experiences

A multidisciplinary group of approximately 15 faculty were involved in the design of the overall program. Then, the development of individual learning experiences and corresponding competencies was tasked to smaller groups of instructors, who worked closely with the design team to ensure alignment with the overarching program goals and values. During the first semester, the focus of the TDE was on two major learning experiences:

- A *Seminar*, co-designed and co-taught by faculty from the Purdue Libraries, Purdue Polytechnic, and the College of Liberal Arts. The intent of the seminar was to guide learners through the discovery of self and the world through engagement in projects that stimulate creativity, empathy, critical thinking, information literacy and written, oral, visual and auditory skills.
- A *Design Studio*, co-taught by a faculty member from Purdue Polytechnic and a faculty member from the Theater program specializing in scenery technology and engineering. The *Design Studio* used a studio model, which included ongoing design review and critique by instructors and peers to support the development of design thinking and skills and domain-specific competencies.

In addition to the discovery learning and learning-by-doing pedagogies, students also had access to more structured foundational knowledge, e.g., speech preparation and delivery taught as part of the Seminar. These modules were available throughout the semester to help students gain a deeper understanding of core topics and provide a starting point for further exploration.

Competencies and Badge Development

Through an iterative process, core competencies were identified within both technical and liberal arts domains based on the University Foundational outcomes defined by the Purdue University Senate, as well as the Essential Learning Outcomes and Association for American Colleges & Universities (AAC&U) value rubrics (see Figure 17.1) (AAC&U, n.d.; Purdue Polytechnic, 2015). The competencies were further categorized in accordance with the Purdue classification of competencies: *developing* (foundational and general skills, e.g., skills gained earlier in the student career); *emerging*; and *proficient* (mastery of advanced skills in the professional domain) (Purdue Polytechnic, 2015). The developing competencies identified for inclusion in the first semester encompassed argumentation, visual communication, narrative building, speech organization, rhetorical persuasion, grammar and orthography basics, English composition, techniques for auditory messages, principles of engineering design, and domain-specific competencies for students pursuing a particular major. While some competencies were aligned with the outcomes of traditional classes in each domain, additional ones were added to provide a richer learning experience to support creative and critical thinking and problem solving.

The system selected for badge development and display of badge e-portfolios was Purdue's Passport. Named as a top innovation for 2013 by the Center for Digital Education (Purdue University, 2013), Passport serves as a learning management system that allows for creation of interactive course content, artifact

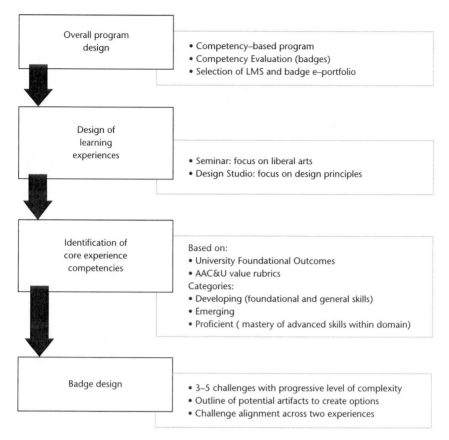

FIGURE 17.1 Design process outline.

evaluation, and feedback provision using a wide range of tools. Course instructors and students are provided with built-in support to navigate through the system, review and upload materials, complete tasks, and award and accept badges. Learners can design an individualized list of gained skills and competencies developed at school and in informal settings by making badges public through the Passport and sharing with their Mozilla Backpack or social networks, like LinkedIn and Facebook (Purdue University, 2014). It is envisioned that once badge portfolios are publicly available, employers can search, evaluate, and reach out to potential employees by performing nuanced searches.

Implementation

Working towards Badges

To help students ease into the new system during their first week of classes, the instructors created a *Gateway Badge*, which included challenges similar in structure and requirements to those used in the Design Studio and Seminar experiences. Unfortunately, the novelty of completing the *Gateway Badge* led students to over-complicate the task. To overcome this challenge in the future, more scaffolding prior to this activity is needed to make a transition toward the competency-based model easier for students. For example, we are planning on creating badge and challenge maps, outlining connections with higher-level goals, and providing recommendations on self-regulated learning.

The badge structure was similar across both the Seminar and Studio learning experiences. Each badge consisted of three to five challenges that progressed from simple tasks designed for novices to more complex activities to refine skills. Within each challenge, students had a range of options to make the activity more applicable to their individual needs and interests. For example, the first challenge of the *Developing Argumentation* badge (required for Seminar) was to engage in a formal training session in which students learned to identify and use valid versus invalid syllogism and arguments, diagram an argument to build a solid persuasive case, and use argumentation skills to construct a speech. They also had an opportunity to practice these skills by critiquing video clips containing persuasive messages and engaging in further discussions on the topic. The skills gained in the first step were then put into practice in subsequent challenges. Students were required to use a combination of strategies to make a valid, coherent, and convincing argument on a topic of their own choice. They then had to present their speech either in class or outside of class to a group of peers, and provide critiques on speeches made by their peers. Regardless of where the presentation took place, a video was recorded and submitted as an artifact within the badge. Some students found that having to present their work in class served as a good way to practice and obtain feedback from peers and faculty. Students also felt that badge requirements served as a natural soft deadline for their projects, which helped them better organize their learning.

To build on their activities across the two learning experiences, students could apply the skills they developed in one learning experience towards the other one. For example, if students worked on projects in the Design Studio to address the problem of food deserts, they could build their argumentative speech for the Seminar around that topic. Additionally, due to the inherent interconnectedness of some competencies, a number of projects and corresponding artifacts could be included as part of evidence to meet the requirements of several badges within the same learning experience (e.g., Seminar). As an example, a written project that exhibited elements of critical awareness could be used towards both the *Critical Thinking in Writing* and the *Developing Storytelling* badges. It should be noted, however, that the number of options available and the non-linear process served as sources of confusion and stress for some students. Faculty were requested to give multiple explanations, particularly in the beginning of the semester.

In addition to the required badges, students could elect to work on badges across disciplines outside of their immediate domain of interest to gain diverse competencies and skills. For example, mechanical engineering students could gain skills in graphic design or programming languages and receive recognition through badges. Likewise, if they wanted to develop additional skills not available within the current badge set, they could work with instructors on independent projects focused on specific skills and earn additional badges. While during the first semester students did not venture beyond the offered opportunities, some used optional badge challenges to explore new areas, even if they never completed the work to receive a badge.

Assessment and Feedback

Rubrics were developed for each competency, and artifacts for each badge were evaluated by at least two instructors from different fields and a teaching assistant to offer more holistic multi-faceted feedback. Because of the open-ended nature of the projects and the focus on mastery, instructors found that they provided much more extensive feedback at every resubmission than they would have otherwise. The submission of the artifacts in support of badge attainment was based on soft deadlines or natural constraints, like the end of the semester. Unfortunately, this created a bottleneck with many concurrent submissions closer to the end of the experience, increasing the load on the faculty and stressing students because of a slower turn-around time for their feedback. Late submissions made it difficult to provide time for a meaningful feedback and revision loop, which is the foundation of gaining mastery.

Due to the nature of the competency-based program that focuses on mastery versus "seat time" for each class, students were encouraged to complete the required badges within the semester when the TDE was offered. However, many students did not complete all of the badges in time. An additional challenge faced by the TDE designers was the need to comply with the University requirements for grading and transcripts. Therefore, at the end of the course students were granted both badges and a traditional grade for the classes that comprised the transdisciplinary learning experiences. Those students who had not completed one or more required badges by the end of the semester were given an "Incomplete" and faculty continued receiving submissions and giving feedback well into the following semester, only granting the letter grade (an A) when all of the badges were awarded.

Evaluation

The process used to evaluate the overall program and the individual components was multi-faceted. The goal for this first year pilot was formative evaluation, allowing for continuous improvement of the program. An internal evaluation team observed, surveyed, and interviewed faculty and students at regular periods to monitor progress of the program and satisfaction with its features. The aggregate results were presented at multiple points throughout the semester to inform faculty decision-making. Additionally, the program design team, faculty, teaching assistants, and evaluation team participated in weekly reflection meetings where they could discuss current experiences and challenges, formal and informal program evaluation results, and anecdotal evidence, and make modifications as needed.

Overall, students achieved or nearly achieved expected learning outcomes. Even though almost half of the students (40 percent) were still working on their badges well into the new semester, ensuring that students actually attained mastery of each skill justified the delay.

The experiences and evaluation results for the pilot program have informed the redesign of our competency structure for the new Transdisciplinary Studies in Technology degree. Changes will include migrating away from low-level competency and badge development. The Seminar and Design Studio will be transformed into learning experiences that "connect the dots" between traditional courses and broader competencies and provide students with opportunities to engage in larger-scale, personally meaningful projects. Students may use all experiences (whether in Seminar, Design Studio, outside courses, internships, or extracurricular activities) as opportunities to grow competence and acquire broad, interdisciplinary competencies such as *Critical Thinking, Design Thinking,* and *Social Interaction and Teamwork.*

Conclusion

Challenges

Based on the results of the program evaluation, systemic and systematic challenges can be identified:

- ongoing support of faculty and students;
- responsiveness and flexibility of the badging system;
- translation of badges to credit hours used within the traditional systems of the University; and
- development of awareness about benefits of competency-based program and mastery-focused approach across internal and external stakeholders.

Thus, the focus on mastery rather than performance was rewarding for many students, although some found it very challenging. As several students shared, they would have preferred to get a poor grade and "be done" instead of going through artifact revisions. To help students think about this process as iterative, reduce the stress and perceived demotivation when a badge was rejected, students were encouraged to consult with an instructor or a teaching assistant at any time during or after regular sessions, or to seek informal feedback from peers on their projects prior to submission. We believe that this approach also helped students develop lifelong learning skills, appropriate help-seeking, and collaboration skills.

Some issues continued to be worked out on the instructor's end throughout the first semester. For example, it was sometimes a struggle to reach agreement on the level at which instructors would declare a competency was truly achieved. The high workload of mentorship and providing feedback on multiple revisions was a constraint on the instructors as well, and the group continues to explore what might be needed to allow this approach to scale up.

Though there is some scaffolding built into the badging system, both students and instructors faced technical challenges with Passport. One of the most significant ones was that all of the badges could only be listed individually and in a linear fashion, making the interface rather cumbersome. Although the faculty envisioned badges as building upon one another to some extent, there was no way to display a hierarchy, interconnection, or recommended sequence within the system.

Other issues only became apparent once the semester was underway. The badges created for the TDE required multiple artifacts to pass challenges within a badge. Because of the limitations of the system, all of the artifacts must be uploaded at one time. If any of the artifacts were missing or an instructor determined that one or more needed further work, the student would have to re-upload and resubmit everything, not just a missing component. Furthermore, if faculty provided feedback and students resubmitted, the earlier feedback was no longer visible. These behaviors created frustration among students and instructors. However, the rapport the TDE group formed with the IT department allowed for a continuous dialogue towards resolving these issues.

Another salient challenge was based on developing a mechanism through which understanding the use of badges as microcredentials could be aligned with the traditional system of credit hours, grades, and transcripts. One of the most significant differences encountered was providing customized learning experiences that allowed students to develop key competencies while tackling transdisciplinary themes and creating unique projects (e.g., Seminar) in place of the traditional courses being replaced (e.g., English, communication). Students also received holistic feedback and assessment for each badge, rather than numerical grades for each project. Because of the expectation that students would resubmit an artifact until instructors felt the competence was mastered, there was no option to receive partial credit; they must continue to resubmit until competence was demonstrated. In the end, students received badges (a binary designation of having demonstrated or not yet demonstrated) rather than grades. As a result, as mentioned above, concessions were made to align badges with traditional grading to meet the needs of both the registrar and bursar offices. However, the grades submitted did not look like those for a traditional class; 60 percent of students received all As the first semester, and 40 percent received incompletes. This was difficult for stakeholders across the university to understand and to fit into traditional systems (including advising, bursar's office and financial aid, and other university offices). In the long run, the expectation is that such alignment or translation of badges to credit hours will no longer be necessary, once the university and employers are ready to accept a competency-based portfolio model.

Finally, a major concern shared by students throughout the semester was how potential employers would perceive a badge-based "transcript," particularly in engineering, where expectations are believed to be highly specific. Although the faculty believe that in the future employers would prefer a system that offers real evidence of students' abilities and skills (such as the badge e-portfolio), they recognize that in the short-term, the burden is on us to educate students and employers about the benefits of competency-based learning. Despite all of these concerns, a number of departments within the university have gained interest in using the competency-based model in their program.

Badge Benefits

The program designers believe that the challenges experienced by students and faculty were outweighed by the benefits of using badges.

One of the main purposes for pursuing a competency-based system within this program was to create opportunities for more meaningful experiences and deeper learning by removing the concept that grades would be used to punish "wrong" answers. Students felt encouraged to explore new topics and take risks by stepping beyond their comfort zones. This also helped increase their innate interest and motivation to explore topics beyond the requirement. As became apparent in student interviews and focus groups as well as observations, personal investment in their learning resulted in the shift among many students towards becoming more independent and interdependent learners, who are more open to creative solutions developed in collaboration with peers and instructors.

The use of badges as a microcredentialing tool allowed students to explore beyond their fields of interest. More than half of the students explored at least some topics and completed challenges outside the required set of badges. In future years, students will be encouraged to explore outside learning opportunities or take courses from other departments, which can be credentialed with badges within our system.

Lessons Learned

Embedding badge-based credentialing as an integral part of the overall program required extensive upfront and ongoing planning and evaluation as well as significant collaboration and buy-in across a large number of stakeholders. Since such transdisciplinary learning experiences are created within a larger university, additional considerations should be made as to how to align competencies and badges with traditional coursework and grading. Internally, the program needs to have a solid scaffolding system to ensure the success of the students at each stage of their learning experience, including, but not limited to: alignment of competencies and badges; the hierarchy of badges and a suggested order to build on gained skills and experiences; and tools and strategies for students to effectively set their own learning goals, determine an appropriate learning path, and proceed with their learning in a timely manner.

References

Association for American Colleges & Universities (AAC&U) (n.d.). *Essential learning outcomes.* Retrieved from www.aacu.org/leap/essential-learning-outcomes.

Felder, R. (2006). *A whole new mind for a flat world.* Retrieved from www.che.ufl.edu/cee/.

Finkelstein, J., Knight, E., & Manning, S. (2013). The potential and value of using digital badges for adult learners. Draft for public comment. *American Institutes for Research.* Retrieved from https://lincs.ed.gov/publications/pdf/AIR_Digital_Badge_Report_508.pdf.

Litzinger, T., Lattuca, L., Hadgraft, R., & Newstetter, W. (2011). Engineering education and the development of expertise. *Journal of Engineering Education, 100*(1), 123–150.

Mili, F. (2014). *Three roadblocks to creating a competency-based program (part I).* Retrieved from www.evolllution.com/program_planning/roadblocks-creating-competency-based-program-part-1/.

Morell, L. (2010). *Engineering education in the 21st century: Roles, opportunities, and challenges.* Hewlett Packard Laboratories. Retrieved from http://luenymorell.files.wordpress.com/2010/12/morell-eng-edu-in-21st-cent-roles-opport-and-challenges.pdf.

National Academy of Engineering (NAE) (2004). *The engineer of 2020: Visions of engineering in the new century.* Washington, DC: National Academy of Engineering. Retrieved from www.nap.edu/openbook.php?record_id=10999&page=10.

Pearson Learning Solutions (n.d.). *Open badges for higher education.* Retrieved from www.pearsonlearningsolutions.com/blog/wp-content/uploads/2013/12/Open-Badges-for-Higher-Education.pdf.

Purdue Polytechnic (2014). *Daniels awards prize for competency-based degree to Purdue Polytechnic Institute.* Retrieved from www.purdue.edu/newsroom/releases/2014/Q3/daniels-awards-prize-for-competency-based-degree-to-purdue-polytechnic-institute.html.

Purdue Polytechnic (2015). *Educational research and development—2014–2015 annual report.* Retrieved from https://polytechnic.purdue.edu/incubator.

Purdue University (2012). *Digital badges show students' skills along with degree.* Retrieved from www.purdue.edu/newsroom/releases/2012/Q3/digital-badges-show-students-skills-along-with-degree.html.

Purdue University (2013). *Center for Digital Education picks Jetpack, Passport as top innovations for 2013.* Retrieved from www.itap.purdue.edu/newsroom/news/130920_Studio_DEAaward.html.

Purdue University (2014). *Passport.* Retrieved from www.itap.purdue.edu/studio/passport/.

Reigeluth, C. (2012). Instructional theory and teaching for the new paradigm of education. *Revista de Educacion a Distancia, 32.* Retrieved from www.um.es/ead/red/32/.

18

EVALUATING DESIGN FRAMEWORKS FOR BADGES

A Case Study and Comparison Analysis of Two Types of Digital Badging Systems

Rudy McDaniel and Joseph R. Fanfarelli

In 2013, U.S. Secretary of Education Arne Duncan stated that digital badges "hold the key to recognizing non-traditional learning and skills developed in information settings, empowering students and marking personal development" (McAndrew & Farrow, 2013, p. 71; see also Duncan, 2012). While the literature is steadily establishing guidelines for badge design in support of student learning (Blair, 2012; Charleer, Klerkx, Santos, & Duval, 2013; Denny, 2013), we know substantially less about the design of badges to support instructor goals. Designing badges that support factors such as student engagement or performance is a necessary pursuit that raises complex and interesting questions, but information design is an equally intriguing area of research that can be analyzed from multiple and interdisciplinary perspectives (Morville & Rosenfeld, 2007; Weinschenk, 2011). We know that pedagogy can be conceptualized as a transactional process between educator and student. While it is logical to research the aspects of badging that directly impact students, the ability of such a badging system to be integrated into a course structure, by an instructor, requires a well-designed system congruent with an instructor's course goals.

For instance, a badging system can be designed and developed from the ground up—a fully developed stand-alone system with seemingly endless possibilities for anyone who understands how to read and manipulate the underlying coding language. These systems are not constrained by the limits of an existing system; they can be reprogrammed to afford nearly any capability that can be imagined. However, the enabling mechanism of such a system can also be the limitation. For those who understand the code, the sky is the limit; for those who do not, the challenges are insurmountable. Little can be done to enhance the flexibility of a system without the prerequisite technical knowledge. Any desired modifications must be outsourced, leading to communication barriers between the instructors and developers, in addition to the extra costs and development time required by outside developers. Even then, there may be issues integrating the system with existing instructional systems. Furthermore, the issues of badge exchange and the development of interoperable standards with popular badging systems such as Mozilla's Open Badge Framework (Goligoski, 2012) become complicated.

A commercial badging solution, on the other hand, is built within an existing instructional system, requiring little additional design and development work. An example of this type is Canvabadges (Canvabadges, 2015), a plug-in module for the open-source Canvas learning management system (LMS). Such a system leverages the existing interface and communication infrastructure, often meaning that the transition from instruction to badging is more fluid. Additionally, such a system is simpler to develop with the pre-existing tools of the LMS. Instructors are already familiar with the course tools, enabling them to transfer that knowledge to the workings of the badging system, but the cost of ease and simplicity is flexibility. Since the system relies on someone else's code base that must also cooperate and work well with other modules, the possibilities of modification and expansion are limited by the constraints of LMS infrastructure.

Project Overview

This chapter introduces two brief case studies involving badging systems. Both were used in a higher education setting with university students as the primary stakeholders. Both attempted to improve student engagement and motivation in online courses and redirect problematic online behaviors to more appropriate types of activities. The two case studies are presented side by side to illustrate the differences between two different technological approaches to digital badging.

For our first case study, we discuss a custom-designed badging system, *Adventures in Emerging Media*, that was developed from the ground up using the so-called "LAMP stack" (Linux, Apache, MySQL, and PHP). Although such a system created enormous opportunity for designing a badging system exactly the way we wanted it, it also created a number of challenges that will be discussed in this chapter.

Our second case study profiles a different approach to badging in which we integrated a commercially designed system for digital badges into an existing LMS. In this case, we created a badging system for two sections each of two undergraduate courses, Graphic Design and Web Design, in the spring semester of 2014. These courses were taught using the Canvas online learning management system and badges were delivered using Credly. Within Canvas, a module was developed to add digital badging functionality to the existing software system. Fifteen badges were common to both courses, while additional badges were course specific to Web Design (4) and Graphic Design (3). The badging interface was integrated directly within the existing course management system, adding a link within the existing navigation menu in order to access the badge display page and instructor award controls.

Analysis

As our focus for these two case studies is primarily on technology and systems design, we will only briefly discuss analysis here and then evaluate the systems in more detail in terms of their design, development, and implementation. The technology chosen for badging significantly impacts the context of student learning in badging systems, so it is worthy of consideration. We analyze two technological methods and consider the strengths and limitations of each system in supporting the instructor's dual role of course facilitator and badge provider.

One note about analysis needs to be mentioned, however. In order to appropriately analyze the advantages or shortcomings of badge technologies, it is important to consider the various stages in which one interacts with badges in a typical learning scenario. For example, badging requirements change in phases, such as initial course setup, regular semester use, maintenance, and course evaluation and assessment. It is possible that a system that excels in one area of badging falls significantly short in another area, leading to unanticipated problems for instructors and learners alike.

Due to the consideration of two case studies within this chapter, we will consider the design, development, and implementation of each system in turn. Following that, we will present a combined evaluation of both systems following the overall review of each system. These areas further relate to analysis as each of these categories correlates to other important items to be considered by a potential user. For example, the ease with which a badge system can be configured during the design phase impacts the cost of that system, just as the ease of tracking data within a system during implementation impacts its potential use as a research tool.

Design, Development, and Implementation

Case Study 1: Customized Badges from the Ground Up

The first badge project we discuss provides ultimate flexibility for badge design, development, and implementation, but it also requires substantial overhead. In this particular case, the conditions allowing such an approach were enabled through the receipt of an internal university grant received by the project team. The grant was awarded as part of an initiative focused on improving undergraduate education through a series of pilot projects funded by the Office of the Provost at the University of Central Florida. One of those projects, titled *Adventures in Emerging Media (AEM)*, aspired to improve the online educational experience for digital media undergraduates. AEM was a choose-your-own-adventure course offered in a custom-built learning management system developed by the team (McDaniel, Lindgren, & Friskics, 2012; Lindgren & McDaniel, 2012). Rather than students proceeding through course content in a purely linear fashion, the AEM system allowed students to choose their own content during selected weeks of the course. Adaptive testing mechanisms then allowed the course instructor to customize assessments that would only require students to demonstrate knowledge about those course modules they had selected throughout the duration of the course.

AEM ran its inaugural pilot in the fall of 2010 and enrolled approximately 100 students. Although student feedback indicated that the students enjoyed the nonlinear aspects of the course, the instructor reported some anxiety about not having as much control over student decisions made within the course shell. To help address this issue, the design team spent the winter of 2010 developing a framework for a badging system to be integrated into the course. The central idea was that the instructor of the course could use badges to incentivize certain actions within the AEM system. Accordingly, the next offering of the course in the fall of 2011 included a beta system for badges. Figure 18.1 shows an example of one of the badges devised to incentivize preparedness and reduce the number of students taking the midterm and final exams at the last possible minute.

In addition to the custom badges designed around these instructor-identified course behaviors, *Adventures in Emerging Media* also included an interface for the instructor to use when awarding badges. Each individual badge was listed in a drop-down list within an instructor resource page. The instructor could then select a badge from that list and assign it to particular students in the course quickly and easily (Figure 18.2). Upon receipt, students would then see a pop-up window congratulating them on earning the badge when they next logged into the system. Additionally, there was a separate "achieve" section (Figure 18.3) that students could visit at any point to see their prior awards and compare their own badges to others in the course through a collective leaderboard. By providing an additional area for achievement and assigning that area within the same grouping priority as learning, creating, and discussing, we were able to visually and thematically endorse the importance of badges within our learning environment.

Providing precise control to the course instructor was a key design principle that the project team used to build the AEM badging components. We can better understand how a customized badging solution addresses precise control by considering the composition and function of badges in more detail. Research from achievements in video games helps in this regard. For example, consider the work of Hamari and Eranti (2011). After studying more than 1,000 hours of participant gameplay involving players attaining achievements in video games, these authors concluded that achievements are composed of signifiers, completion logics, and rewards. Badges, as visual indicators of achievement, can be considered within this same framework. The premier advantage of *Adventures in Emerging Media* is that

FIGURE 18.1 Sample badge for Adventures in Emerging Media.

it provided us with ultimate control in each of these areas. For example, we as designers could determine in precise detail how the badges would be signified, both in terms of the specific visual design of each badge as well as the overall aesthetic "look and feel" of the entire system. Relying on pre-designed badges does not always provide this ability, although some systems do allow for visual tweaking of badges. Additionally, we could specifically indicate the conditions in which badges were awarded, addressing the completion logics for each award. Finally, we could clearly specify how the rewards of attaining badges related to a student's work in the course. For example, as explained previously, in addition to relating the attainment of badges to student participation grades, we also developed a leaderboard and structured it exactly the way we wanted it.

Within the AEM system, Structured Query Language (SQL) statements further allowed us to communicate with our MySQL badge database and determine exactly how the data should be manipulated in its raw form. For example,

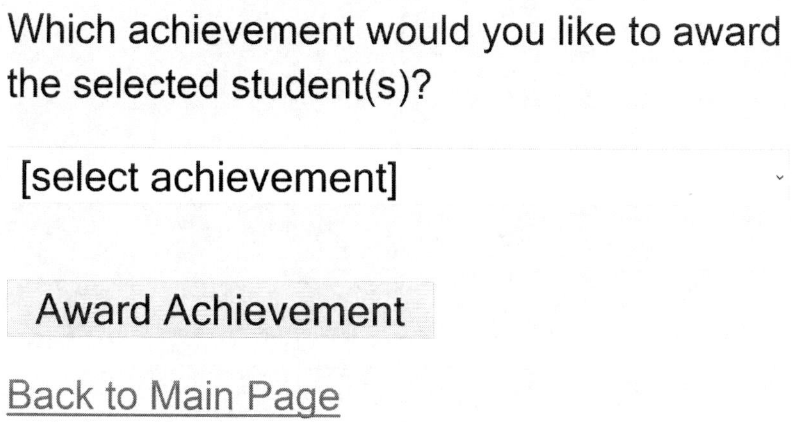

Which achievement would you like to award the selected student(s)?

[select achievement] ⌄

Award Achievement

Back to Main Page

FIGURE 18.2 Awarding badges in Adventures in Emerging Media (anonymized with names removed).

we specified the precise number of achievements to be shown for each student and outlined the exact number of students to be listed on the leaderboard. We also determined the various facets to be shown to the students on their profile. These included indicators such as total badges earned, last badge earned, earliest badge earned, and so forth. Without direct access to the database and the ability to manipulate SQL statements using programming scripts, this would not be possible and we would have to settle for the capabilities given to us by the developers of the system.

Case Study 2: Using Modular Design Frameworks

The second case we consider in this chapter was less flexible and provided less overall control in terms of design, development, and implementation, but it also required substantially less effort from the project team. The system was funded as a side project to a larger internal university grant study awarded to improve understanding of the effects of professional certifications on employability, job satisfaction, and other metrics related to career success. Students were offered four courses, two in graphic design and two in web design. One of each type of course included badges; the other did not. All courses were provided fully online via the *Canvas* (Canvas, 2015) learning management system, which hosted all of the courses' learning content and assessments, including assignment instructions and submissions, exams, and learning modules. These courses provided a fast-paced introduction to either Adobe Dreamweaver (web design) or Adobe

FIGURE 18.3 Navigation grouping for Adventures in Emerging Media.

Photoshop (graphic design) through an equal emphasis on timed examinations and project-based assignments. Badges were deployed through Credly.

While planning this project in its early stages, conversations with various faculty and staff revealed that an experimental badging system had already been created as an optional module for Canvas by the Course Development and Web Services (CDWS) division within the university. Since this badging system already existed, worked with our institutional LMS (Figure 18.4), and required no substantial development by the researchers, it seemed like a great choice for the study. The badges themselves were stored in Credly and the CDWS team had previously developed a web-scraping tool to harvest the Credly badges and display them natively within the instructional LMS so that the students could see them in their normal course home page when they logged in.

Additionally, original badge images and descriptions could be included, and badges could be awarded either manually by the instructor or through automated means if grade was the criterion for award. This system was chosen as the study's badging system due to these features.

However, a few tweaks were necessary. The system was originally meant to work in conjunction with an external badging website, and this study required

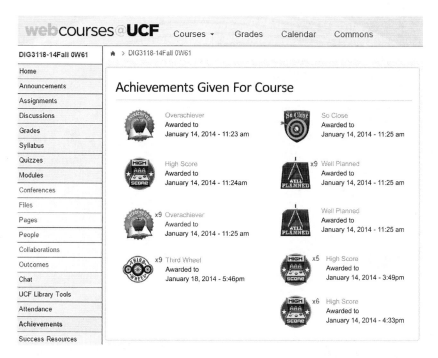

FIGURE 18.4 Component badge system integrated with Canvas LMS.
Used with permission from University of Central Florida. Images by M. Dunn.

that the system function 100 percent internally. The notification system for badge award communicated through an external website, which could have been confusing for students. The list of earned badges was also hosted on that website, but they needed to be hosted through the Canvas LMS. Additionally, several of the badges that were planned for inclusion required time-based assessments. Canvas enables time-based tests, and it would have been interesting to include badges that have both time and performance criteria (e.g., complete a quiz in 10 minutes and receive a 90 percent or better score). This sort of criteria combination may have influenced students to study more before taking the quiz so they could have answered the questions quickly and correctly—a desirable condition for any instructor.

However, not all of these were possible. The developers were notified and agreed to make the required modifications to the badging system, but the existing system had limited affordances. While removing the external notification system and hosting the list of earned badges within canvas were feasible (Figure 18.5), time-based criteria were not possible, and those badges had to be discarded and replaced with other badges, limiting the study's potential range of findings. These were regarded as acceptable limitations and the study continued.

Badges you own:

So Close
Awarded Manually

High Score
Awarded Manually

Third Wheel
Awarded Manually

FIGURE 18.5 List of earned badges integrated with the Canvas LMS.
Used with permission from University of Central Florida. Images by M. Dunn.

Overall, the effort went smoothly for the rest of the semester. The award interface was fairly intuitive (Figure 18.6) and students did not appear to encounter
any issues accessing or understanding the badges.

Having not developed the badging system, and not having a clear view of
how students interacted with the system, introduced some additional anxiety
for the instructor. For instance, since the indications that students were actually
receiving the badges were infrequent, there was no easy way to check in and
see who had earned what in the course. We did not have low-level access to the
web-scraping tool, so we had to rely on the built-in indicators on the course
home page. However, everything seemed to be in order when data was collected
at the end of the semester.

The project was continued for another semester, in much the same way as the
first, but with a few differences. On the development side, various updates were
made to the system for maintenance and improvement. On the practical side,
badges could now be awarded multiple times for satisfying the same criteria in
multiple assignments, and the courses without badges turned into courses with
hidden badges—the badges were still awarded by the instructor, but students did

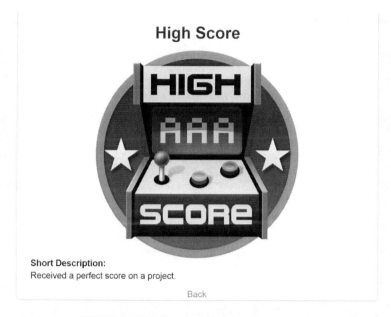

FIGURE 18.6 Awarding badges with the component system.
Used with permission from University of Central Florida. Images by M. Dunn.

not receive them or notifications of receipt. This was done so that the researchers could compare students who did and did not receive badges, while understanding who would have received badges if they were enabled for the non-badged courses.

The semester again proceeded smoothly, until about midway through. A student contacted the development team, asking to no longer be bothered by e-mails of badge awards. After further investigation, it was found that this student was not only receiving badges from the external system that was removed prior to the first semester of experimentation, but this student was also part of the non-badging course; in reality, no notifications should have been sent at all. The line was now blurred between badged and non-badged students and a major experimental confound was introduced, making the data unreliable for that semester. This is likely an issue that could have been avoided if the system was designed from the ground up and the instructor had more control and customization over the badging system and its notifications.

Evaluation

In this section, we evaluate and compare these two case studies by briefly outlining the advantages, disadvantages, and specific characteristics of commercial badge design systems versus customized systems such as the *Adventures in Emerging Media* badging system discussed in our first case study. Table 18.1 summarizes the major data points along these lines. As evidenced in this summary, customized badging systems offer benefits in that they are flexible, customizable, and great for customized data collection scenarios. On the other hand, they are also expensive and hard to maintain, while commercial frameworks have strengths in those areas.

Table 18.1 reveals that the two approaches to building badging systems have significantly different advantages and disadvantages. So, how do you choose the

TABLE 18.1 Comparison between badging systems

	Custom frameworks	*Commercial frameworks*
Form Factor	Completely flexible.	May be tied to particular LMSs.
Cost	Relatively expensive.	Relatively affordable.
Technologies	Varies by developer. Open source technologies such as Linux/Apache PHP/MySQL are common.	Varies by company. Some (e.g., OpenBadges) use an open technical standard, while others are commercial and proprietary. However, Open Badges could also be considered a customized badging system and it somewhat fits in both categories.
Maintenance	Relatively difficult.	Moderate to easy.
Customization	Very customizable.	Limited customization options.
Data Collection	Extensive data collection can be done internally, behind the scenes.	Limited internal data collection can be done.
Strengths	Completely customizable, good opportunities for custom research, easy to fine tune exactly as desired.	Much less expensive to develop and deploy, may be familiar to learners due to prior experiences, may have commercial support.
Weaknesses	Expensive to develop and maintain, may be difficult to convince IT to allow their deployment.	Limited customization and configuration regarding how research is collected and badges are configured and deployed.

most appropriate format for your own badge study? It is a complex question. In the next section, we provide an overall recommendation based on our own experiences using both types of systems.

Conclusions

Having considered both an open source badging system designed from scratch and another commercial badging system that integrates into an institutional learning management system, our final recommendation regarding the ideal format is not surprising. One must ultimately make one's own decision based on the idiosyncratic nature of the learning environment and the learners. Despite the convenience of definitive answers, there is no "one size fits all" solution for any given learning scenario. The particular solution that will work best for your situation will depend on available maintenance and development resources, the particular needs of your research program and data collection, if applicable, and any other factors that may be unique to your own organization.

If one has the financial and personnel resources to build and maintain a badging system, then that route is likely to provide the most customized feature set useful for your own learning scenario and data collection plans. On the other hand, while the supreme flexibility of a system designed specifically for your own research is enticing, institutional barriers to resources or IT may make that unfeasible. In that situation, if there is an existing badge development and deployment technology that already does what you need, there is no reason to reinvent the wheel unless it is severely lacking in one or more critical areas.

So, our ultimate recommendation based on these experiences is this: Before designing a study around badges or using badges to enhance the learning environment of a course or curriculum plan, the researcher or instructor must carefully outline his or her requirements for a badging system and any associated research questions and learning objectives that are tied to that system. This must be done before considering the type of system and will allow the selection of a badge framework that works best for the specific needs of the learning environment. If a middle ground solution is desired, such as a case where more customization is necessary than existing commercial solutions provide but resources are still scarce, it may be that a badge system that somewhat straddles both categories, such as Mozilla's Open Badges, will best suit the project.

References

Blair, L. (2012). The use of video game achievements to enhance player performance, self-efficacy, and motivation. Doctoral dissertation. University of Central Florida, 1–30.

Canvabadges (2015). Retrieved from www.canvabadges.org.

Canvas (2015). Retrieved from www.canvaslms.com.

Charleer, S., Klerkx, J., Santos, J. L., & Duval, E. (2013). Improving awareness and reflection through collaborative, interactive visualizations of badges. Proceedings of ARTEL '13, 69–81.

Denny, P. (2013). The effect of virtual achievements on student engagement. Proceedings of CHI 2013, 763–772.

Duncan, A. (2012). Digital badges for learning. *Remarks by Secretary Duncan at 4th Annual Launch of the MacArthur Foundation Digital Media and Lifelong Learning Competition.*

Goligoski, E. (2012). Motivating the learner: Mozilla's open badges program. *Access to Knowledge: A Course Journal, 4*(1).

Hamari, J., & Eranti, V. (2011). Framework for designing and evaluating game achievements. *Proc. DiGRA 2011: Think Design Play, 115*, 122–134.

Lindgren, R., & McDaniel, R. (2012). Transforming online learning through narrative and student agency. *Educational Technology & Society, 15*(4), 344–355.

McAndrew, P., & Farrow, R. (2013). From the practical to the theoretical. *Open Educational Resources: Innovation, Research and Practice, 65.*

McDaniel, R., Lindgren, R., & Friskics, J. (2012, October). Using badges for shaping interactions in online learning environments. In *Professional Communication Conference (IPCC), 2012 IEEE International* (pp. 1–4). IEEE.

Morville, P., & Rosenfeld, L. (2007). *Information architecture for the World Wide Web.* Sebastopol, CA: O'Reilly.

Weinschenk, S. (2011). *100 things every designer needs to know about people.* Pearson Education.

19

A CASE STUDY OF DIGITAL BADGES IN COMPOSITION COURSES

Alan J. Reid and Denise Paster

Coastal Composition Commons (CCC) is an online digital badge system created through a collaboration of English faculty members at Coastal Carolina University in Conway, South Carolina (undergraduate student population of approximately 10,000). The digital badge program was developed in response to institutional assessment findings that indicated students enrolled in the first-year composition program were not meeting the benchmarks established by the course outcomes, specifically in the areas of analysis, critique, and synthesis of sources. In an effort to provide consistency of instruction for all first-year writing students enrolled in *English 101: Composition* and *English 102: Composition and Critical Reading*, while still maintaining instructional flexibility in the individual classrooms, the CCC translates existing course outcomes into individual digital badges that students earn in order to certify and recognize specific composition-based skills.

Digital badges are being used creatively in academic settings. A badge is defined as a "validated indicator of accomplishment, skill, quality or interest that can be earned in many learning environments" (HASTAC, n.d.). Whereas some badge systems award digital badges for higher-order accomplishments such as degrees, certificates, or course completion, other systems recognize participatory or achievement-based activities, using badges as a gamification and motivational device. The CCC is unique in that it utilizes digital badges as part of a larger assessment model, certifying specific learning outcomes consistent with the mission of our first-year writing program. Each badge in the CCC translates to a specific skill in conversation with our student learning outcomes, such as the ability to quote, summarize, paraphrase, and synthesize texts. In essence, students demonstrate their writing competencies by earning these badges. Currently, there are eight digital badges required in English 101, six badges required in English 102, and five optional badges. Earning the digital badges accounts for

18 to 25 percent of the student's final course grade, depending on each professor's grade weighting.

The CCC was developed for composition courses in an effort to quantify students' acquisition of academic literacies. The digital badge format allows for instructional consistency across numerous course sections taught by full- and part-time instructors, but because the instructor chooses the sequencing of the badges and the pedagogical context in which badges are applied, we avoid the standardization of assessing writing skills through rote drill-and-practice methods. In its inaugural semester, Fall 2014, the badge program accommodated more than 2,300 undergraduates in 122 different sections of composition courses, taught by 63 different faculty members. More than 17,000 badge submissions were assessed, and approximately 11,000 badges were awarded by the end of the 16-week semester.

The CCC addresses the needs of students and faculty at Coastal Carolina University specifically, but its design is universally replicable. The customized website was built using a free WordPress theme ("Spun" by Caroline Moore) and is hosted on the university server. It utilizes a combination of the BadgeOS plugin and the Credly integration for WordPress. Each badge page embraces a multimodal approach to teaching a specific composition skill using a combination of text, videos, infographics, podcasts, and one-on-one video interviews with faculty members. The badges are meant to resemble chapters from a digital textbook and provide students with an explanation of the concept being taught, an expert's model that executes this concept, a practice exercise for implementation, and a writing assignment for assessment. The writing assignments are designed particularly for each badge; the submissions are reviewed by English faculty members and are either approved or denied based on their quality. This system has enabled uniformity without imposing assimilation and serves as the foundation for a measurable programmatic assessment model.

Analysis

As a first-year composition program, we are deeply invested in supporting our students' development as writers and readers. To investigate our effectiveness, each spring we conduct an assessment of our writing program by collecting three sample essays from each section of English 101 and 102, which a team of 8 to 10 instructors rank according to our students' learning outcomes. This process makes for an intense week of assessment training, reader norming, and focused readings; at the end of the process, those involved are left surprisingly energized by new assignment ideas and a renewed focus on our collective goals as writing teachers. Our assessment findings consistently suggest we need to provide students with more support as they learn to work with sources in sophisticated ways; namely, our assessments regularly suggest that students need to be taught how to weave other texts into their writing as they analyze, evaluate, and synthesize them.

In the fall of 2011 and spring of 2013, we responded to these findings by partnering with librarians who taught a one-credit research strategies course coupled with sections of English 101 to stress the collection, analysis, and evaluation of sources. After assessing this initiative, though, we realized that our writing program needed to focus more extensively on intertextual work by teaching students how to manipulate sources as they bring them into their writing. As a result, we decided to fold the additional credit hour back into English 101 and 102, making the four-credit courses. As we proposed the addition of this fourth credit hour to composition courses, we used our assessment findings to guide their development. From our annual assessments, we knew that we needed to do more to support our students' development of higher-order skills (including synthesis, analysis, and critique); we also knew that our writing program would benefit from a more explicit focus on our learning outcomes. In addition, we realized that we wanted to create a customized credit hour for our students' concerns and goals. We wanted to construct a platform for this initiative in house so we could invite input from our faculty and revise the program as our needs as a program evolved. Our goal was to design a digital delivery system that would help us respond to our findings.

Design

To stress our student learning outcomes in more systematic ways that would provide our writing students with a more uniform experience, we began exploring options for a multimodal approach to teaching composition. We began investigating existing program designs by first interviewing individuals from reputable institutions with successful multimodal composition programs, including Duke University, Purdue University, and The Ohio State University. Although these programs are lauded, they did not fit the specialized need for a highly targeted approach to reinforcing specific composition skills. Later, a conversation with instructional designers from Stanford University regarding the development of their OpenEdX program highlighted the potentials associated with using digital badges to assess and certify skills. After researching digital badge programs such as *Passport Studio* at Purdue, it was clear that digital badges could offer the multimodal approach to reinforcing composition skills in first-year writing students.

In the spring of 2013, construction of a prototype for a digital badge program was approved by the university administration. Three main priorities quickly emerged regarding the program's infrastructure: interface design, accessibility, and delivery. But also, what would the actual badges look like? The badge system needed to have high usability for faculty and students, be accessible in and out of the classroom setting (this included a mobile-friendly design), and enable smooth communication between students and faculty through an automated delivery process. In order to provide this level of customization, Dr. Reid designed a custom WordPress site that implemented the BadgeOS plugin, which afforded the hierarchical structure of awarding badges to users through a completion of steps. Several introductory badges were created and a small pilot test was conducted with one class of students.

Interface Design

The usability of the badge site was of utmost concern. If a site is disorienting, it is likely that the user will not persevere and complete the task. With this in mind, the CCC embraces a minimalistic graphical interface design. The main menu located in the upper right hand portion of the screen contains three links: Login, Badges, and Submissions. These three pages are the most common functions for students and faculty and are therefore the most prominently displayed.

Within each page, there is a set of subpages. Figure 19.1 represents the menu structure for the entire CCC site, where each page has a specific function. Under the Login page, the student can view *My Badge Profile*, which displays all of the badges he or she has earned to date. The *Student Support* and *Faculty Support* pages list frequently asked questions about the site and contain a contact form where students and faculty can submit a question or issue. This request is delivered directly to a support specialist who responds within 24 hours. The *Badges* page contains all of the available badges for English 101 and English 102 as well as an *Other Badges* page that contains supplementary awards, and a *Faculty Badges* page, where badges are awarded to faculty for advancements in professional development.

In the student view, the *Submissions* page lists pending, approved, and denied badge attempts for the student who is logged in. In the faculty view, all student submissions are presented to the faculty member who is logged in; this is also where submissions are either approved or denied by the faculty member.

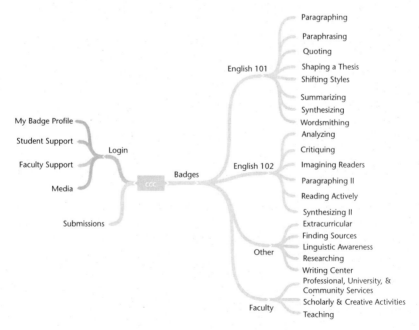

FIGURE 19.1 A visual representation of the CCC's menu structure.
Used with permission from Coastal Carolina University.

Accessibility

Another important design consideration was to maximize the accessibility of the digital badge site. In an effort to accommodate the increasing number of mobile devices being used on campus, the CCC was designed with mobile compatibility specifically in mind. A major advantage of the chosen WordPress theme is that it automatically converts the site into a readable format across any mobile device or platform (see Figure 19.2). Though it is not an ideal writing environment, the CCC does have full mobile functionality, and students are able to view, compose, and submit work using any mobile device with Internet connectivity. This was imperative given the increase in popularity of Bring-Your-Own-Device (BYOD) classroom initiatives and the mobile learner's expectations for just-in-time learning and universal access.

Delivery

The third design consideration was how to deliver the program to faculty and students. Although the university recognizes Moodle as its official learning management system (LMS), some faculty members choose other open source platforms, such as Canvas, or do not utilize an LMS whatsoever. Because of this, we decided to host the CCC on an independent WordPress site so that it may be

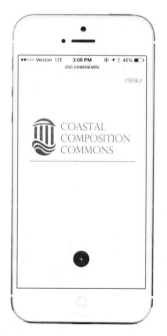

FIGURE 19.2   The CCC embraces a mobile-friendly design.
Used with permission from Coastal Carolina University.

delivered to all users via a single URL. In this sense, faculty can deliver the URL to students using a number of methods regardless of the LMS choice. The login process is authenticated using Lightweight Directory Access Protocol (LDAP), which enables students and faculty to log in to the site securely with their university-powered credentials. If the student user is currently enrolled, or if the faculty member is currently employed at Coastal Carolina University, he or she does not need to create a new account in order to log in to the site.

It was also critical to simplify the delivery process of awarding and denying digital badges. The BadgeOS plugin enables the badge delivery system, which communicates between the student user and the badge issuer. When a student submits an assignment for a particular badge, it remains pending until the faculty member chooses to view the submission and either approve or deny it. If approved, a digital badge containing metadata is delivered to the student user via university email. This badge also is represented on the student's badge profile page in the CCC. If the submission is denied by the faculty member, a notification email is sent automatically to the student, which also includes feedback from the faculty member if it was provided. The CCC has a streamlined delivery system, requiring only basic technological savvy for the student and faculty populations.

Badge Design

The initial digital badges were designed using the custom badge builder provided by Credly. Although this online tool allows for easy customization, early badges lacked consistency in graphical design and did not indicate the name of the issuer: Coastal Carolina University. To address these issues, a second design was produced, this time including a portion of the university's logo, but still lacking name recognition and design uniformity. The current design includes the university's insignia, the title of the badge program, and the name of the skill being certified. This design is produced by a graphic design team at Coastal Carolina University. Figure 19.3 shows the evolution of the badges.

FIGURE 19.3 The evolution of badge design (from left to right). The MLA Master badge, an early attempt, the Synthesizer, a mid-phase design, and the most recent Critiquing badge design.
Used with permission from Coastal Carolina University.

Development

The first-year composition committee comprises six English faculty members who serve three-year appointments. This group oversaw the development of the instructional content for each of the digital badges, but all English faculty members were encouraged to contribute. To foster collaboration, we created a shared Google Drive document for each badge, and during summer faculty workshop sessions, instructors revised the content. In total, eight digital badges were developed for the fall 2014 semester. The bulk of the material was created solely for this badge program.

To achieve design consistency, the template for all badges is the same. A badge homepage displays all available badges along with a short description of their specific objectives (see Figure 19.4). By clicking on the badge, the user is taken to a single page that contains the instructional content, an example, and an assignment. A rubric that explains the criteria for approving and denying the badge is attached to the bottom of each page. This design template was important to the flow of the site, given the numerous contributors.

Because the CCC takes a multimodal approach to teaching skills central to college composition, various media are embedded in the badge pages. This media includes text, infographics, narrated and animated videos, audio recordings, quizzes, surveys, and faculty interview videos. Particularly, our goal was to concretize our program's identity by creating our own instructional content rather than aggregating materials from external sources. In doing so, we were able to articulate our expectations for our student population, specifically, and retain authorship. To preserve accessibility, all of the media was designed to operate on a variety of platforms and devices so that no additional plugins or programs are necessary to view and interact with the content.

 *Quoting*

This badge certifies that students can effectively introduce, analyze, explain and frame quotations when integrating them into their own work.

FIGURE 19.4 Each badge clearly defines its objectives.
Used with permission from Coastal Carolina University.

Implementation

Faculty buy-in was critical to the success of the digital badge initiative. As such, we have encouraged and welcomed faculty participation in a range of workshops, presentations, and online surveys. Beginning in February 2014, we began offering faculty workshops ranging from one-hour to half-day sessions in which members of the English faculty received professional development credit to attend and were encouraged to create, contribute, and review the content on the CCC. At the time of this writing, we have hosted seven faculty workshops and have given five formal presentations within our institution. During the faculty workshops, we ask faculty to generate ideas and review badge content and then submit their responses in the CCC in order to earn a participation badge. This has been beneficial because it allows faculty to experience the CCC from a badge earner's perspective, and it enables us to formatively evaluate the CCC on a small scale.

Because the CCC continues to be shaped collaboratively, there is a sense of ownership among the faculty, and this has facilitated the program's implementation as the fourth credit hour. We understood the tricky balance of creating a multimodal composition program that offered instructional consistency across all course sections while still allowing for instructor freedom, flexibility, and autonomy. We also recognized that the success of the program relied (and still relies) on the faculty making an earnest attempt to maximize the program's potential. Realizing this, we attempted to gain faculty buy-in through transparency in developing and implementing the badge program and by encouraging input from the very beginning.

Evaluation

In fall 2014, the digital badge program served 122 sections of courses (2,326 students): 101 sections of English 101 (1,917 students) and 21 sections of English 102 (409 students). We evaluated the effectiveness of the digital badge program using quantitative and qualitative research methods. First, we collected and analyzed the data for all student users in regards to the number and types of badges being earned and when they were earned to gain an understanding of how instructors were implementing the badge program in their courses. Although instructors had the freedom to sequence the badges in any order, a natural progression emerged; the "Shifting Styles" and "Summarizing" badges were typically introduced at the beginning of the semester, whereas the more difficult skill of "Synthesizing" was taught later in the semester. Figure 19.5 illustrates the total number of earned badges by type and month. We also recorded and analyzed students' self-reported levels of intrinsic motivation and expectancy values. The findings have been submitted elsewhere for publication.

Badge Submissions

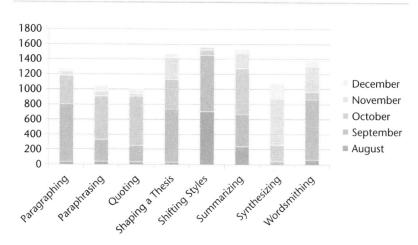

FIGURE 19.5   A breakdown of badge earnings by type and month.
Used with permission from Coastal Carolina University.

During fall 2014, students in the 122 sections of English 101 and English 102 produced 17,674 badge submissions, 10,976 of which were approved, yielding a badge approval rate of 72 percent. Faculty deemed this an appropriate level of acceptance. A major concern going into the semester was the potential for unevenness in badge approval standards. Awarding badges for low-quality student work would diminish the value of the badges, but making badges too difficult to earn would sabotage student grades and alienate them from the program.

At the conclusion of the Fall 2014 semester, we administered an online survey to students (n = 202) in order to gauge student attitudes towards the digital badge program. The survey (Appendix A) was derived from previous research on educational badges (Abramovich, Higashi, Hunkele, Schunn, & Shoop, 2011). Overall, the majority of students (51 percent) reported a positive experience with the digital badge program, 31.7 percent described a negative experience, and 17.3 percent gave a neutral response. It also was discovered that students had a more favorable view of the badge program as they earned more badges. Table 19.1 gives specific student responses to the open-ended survey question: Would you describe your experience with digital badges in this course as positive or negative?

The summative assessment at the conclusion of the semester prompted revisions to the program. Originally, several badges used color coding in the instructional content to identify certain parts of the text. This hindered students with colorblindness and was not ADA compliant. As a result, we removed

TABLE 19.1 Students' descriptions of their experiences with digital badges

Positive	Neutral	Negative
Positive because it related directly to what we were learning and will help me in my future experiences with writing.	I am in between with the badges because some of them helped, but a lot of them weren't really necessary and [required] too much reading.	This seems like a great idea for high school freshman, not college level.
I would describe it as positive as I learned different skills throughout them.	It was a neutral experience. I did not really enjoy doing them but it did help me.	The badges are a pain to do. If they were an in-class assignment, then they wouldn't be so bad.
Positive. It gave me a better understanding.	Neither. Just another assignment. Either you do it or you don't.	Negative. They seemed more like busy work.
Positive, the things we were working on in class matched up to what badges we had to do.	I would say neutral. Although they were not very hard for me to complete but they were often tedious.	My experiences with digital badges in this course were negative because I think the badges are a waste of time and they are frustrating.
Positive due to the fact it was different to me and allowed me to experience something new.	I would describe my experience with digital badges in this course as both positive and negative. Mostly positive, because now I am trying to apply what I learned to my other assignments in college.	Negative, because they were time consuming and I did not learn from the badges.
It was a positive experience because it went along with what we needed in the papers that we were writing at the time. The badges prepared me for these assignments in all.		I would describe my experience with these badges as a negative one because they were very difficult and caused stress.
I would say it is positive because the badge did help me overall. They helped me on the papers that were due in the course.		

all color-coding examples from the site and replaced them with interactive videos that explained the same concepts. This realization prompted a more formal evaluation of the site, using the free website testing tool, Nibbler, which evaluates the website in a number of different categories, including accessibility, user experience, technology, and server behavior, among many others. This evaluation rating is closely monitored any time changes are made to this site, and recommendations are always welcomed from the faculty and student users.

Another important revision involved the design of the badge assignments. Through numerous faculty workshops and online surveys, we received feedback that the texts and passages provided for the writing assignments seemed disconnected from the class. For instance, the "Synthesizing" badge formerly required students to read two provided sources related to climate change, identify common themes using a matrix table, and then compose a well-written response paragraph that synthesized the source information using summaries, quotes, and paraphrases. Now, all badge assignments have been redesigned to be more open-ended; instructors are encouraged to provide their own selected texts, but the assessment framework remains the same. This has helped establish a smoother integration of badges into courses.

Challenges

Prior to the official launch of the CCC for the Fall 2014 semester, we anticipated that there would be some unforeseeable hiccups. A major technical challenge was the issue of organizing students' submissions. The CCC is not parceled into courses, sections, or instructors. Instead, it operates as a giant pool, where all student badge submissions are collected. For each badge, there is a writing assignment that the student completes and then attaches as a document. In the original site design, the student was asked to include his or her professor's name in a text box along with the attached file. This made the submission searchable, which meant the professor only had to filter the submissions page by his or her name, and all of his or her students' submissions would populate. This quickly became problematic, though, because we falsely assumed that students: (1) would follow this specific direction, (2) knew the name of their professor, and (3) could spell the professor's name accurately. And while we thought this was a calculated risk, the issue proved to be nearly crippling for the program. A student's submission that failed to include the professor's name was rerouted to a virtual no-man's land of nameless submissions, rendering the filter search only partially useful. And because students are not able to resubmit until the initial submission has been approved or denied, this caused a major disruption for students and professors. Our solution was to add a dropdown box that requires the student to select a professor's name before being able to submit. The addition of this user-centered design feature, known as a force-function, has reduced the number of errant submissions almost entirely. We now only have to assume that the student can identify his or her instructor's name from the list (still, a calculated risk for some).

Another major technical concern was whether or not the site could sustain the influx of an undergraduate population of more than 2,300 students. Because students submit documents for badges, there is the issue of server storage space. Additionally, there is the question of how long student work should be retained on the server. These are issues we are still deliberating, but currently, we have ample storage space and we are recommending preserving student work for at least three years. However, these issues are not yet resolved and will need to be addressed in the future.

Conclusion

Currently, we are exploring many new and exciting possibilities with digital badges in our first-year writing program. The program now has a graduate assistantship position to troubleshoot student and faculty issues with the site. This person has the title of "badge-uate assistant," and is a key appointment. Other experimental ideas include a cross-grading model, where faculty members assess the badge submissions of students from other course sections, which possibly could promote a true consistency of evaluation, and a badge-training program that certifies students to serve as peer evaluators. The site also has begun to offer digital badges to recognize professional development of English faculty members.

Admittedly, there is still some opposition to the digital badge program at Coastal Carolina University, though this is to be expected with any programmatic change. Many still hold the sentiment that there is an inherent danger in using digital badges because they are merely extrinsic rewards. We agree. When offered as incentivizers, digital badges will most likely fail. As such, we believe that digital badges function best when used to recognize and certify learning that has already occurred as a result of the instruction and not as an enticement of receiving the digital badge. We propose that digital badges be viewed as assessment tools through a high-stakes learning process of providing feedback and self-reflection. As this case study has shown, badges can pave the way for an open assessment model, especially in composition courses, where faculty can define measurable expectations for writing, and where students can demonstrate their writing skills, one badge at a time.

Finally, and most importantly, the success of this digital badge initiative rests on the shoulders of many. The CCC is an ongoing commitment from administration, faculty, and students. We are truly grateful for our supportive university community, our innovative and progressive colleagues, and the open-minded and dedicated students at Coastal Carolina University who are not afraid of a challenge.

Open-Ended Questions

1. Did you treat the assignments with digital badges any differently than other course assignments? Explain why or why not.
2. Would you describe your experience with digital badges in this course as positive or negative? Please explain.
3. Would you recommend that other classes use digital badges? Why or why not?

References

Abramovich, S., Higashi, R., Hunkele, T., Schunn, C., & Shoop, R. (2011). *An achievement system to increase achievement motivation.* Paper presented at the Games Learning Society 7.0, Madison, WI.

CCC (n.d.). *Coastal Composition Commons.* Retrieved from http://ccc.coastal.edu/.

HASTAC (n.d.). *What is a digital badge?* Retrieved from www.hastac.org/digital-badges.

Appendix A
Badge Opinion Survey

1 = Strongly Disagree
2 = Disagree
3 = Somewhat Disagree
4 = Neutral
5 = Somewhat Agree
6 = Agree
7 = Strongly Agree

1. I understand why I earned all of my badges.
2. The badges were more important to me than learning.
3. I think the badges are a good addition to the course.
4. I knew what badges were before I started working in this course.
5. I wanted to earn more ENGL course badges.
6. I don't care about the ENGL course badges.
7. I like earning badges but not the ones in this ENGL course.
8. I wish the ENGL course badges were harder to earn.
9. I wish the ENGL course badges were easier to earn.
10. I want to earn badges in future ENGL courses.
11. I told others about my badges earned in this course.

12. The ENGL course badges made me want to keep working.
13. Compared to other assignments in this course, the digital badges motivated me to work harder.
14. I shared my digital badges on a social networking site.
15. The badges I earned represent what I learned in this class.
16. The badges were more important to me than my grades on my ENGL assignments.

20

A DELAYED BADGE IS A WORTHY BADGE

Designing Digital Badge Architectures Based on Academic Delay of Gratification

Răzvan Rughiniş and Ştefania Matei

Digital badges are often discussed in the context of gamification, since points, badges, and leaderboards are the most frequent game design elements used to assemble a gameplay layer for non-gaming applications (Deterding, Dixon, Khaled, & Nacke, 2011). Of course, badges in material form have been used since well before the advent of digital games (Halavais, 2011). However, digital badges depend heavily on games as a communication medium. It is thanks to games that an increasingly larger segment of the population, across all socio-demographic categories, has become familiar with this incentive and credentialing system. Digital badge architectures are somehow gameful; they are situated on a continuum between "use" and "play" (Casilli, 2012; Digital Youth Network, 2012), thus facing several challenges when introduced in educational contexts.

In current literature, badges are discussed from a functional perspective, pointing to their roles in sustaining commitment to collective activities through goal setting, instruction, reputation, status affirmation, and group identification (MacArthur Foundation, 2013). In an educational context, badges are discussed as a means to get students focused on valuable learning activities and outcomes (Rughiniş & Matei, 2013; Rughiniş, 2013a, 2013b). Badges can also be a topic for peer conversation—or, as Jarvinen phrases it, "concrete evidence for bragging rights" (Jarvinen, 2009).

In this chapter, we begin by discussing the principle of academic delay of gratification while introducing the distinction between cumulative and summative badging systems. Then, we present an example of summative badge architecture from the Cisco Networking Academy Center of the University Politehnica of Bucharest, Romania (SumUps CCNA.ro). We discuss the badge architecture that we designed and implemented in the spring semester of 2013, as well as the results of our evaluation research based on interviews with students and instructors. We conclude by pointing to the specific findings that can be used for improving the SumUps CCNA.ro badge architecture, and by identifying several typical risks and solutions that could emerge in similar contexts.

Academic Delay of Gratification and Digital Badges

Academic delay of gratification (ADOG) is used to describe a mode of conduct directed towards achieving advantages after a period of time, instead of pursuing immediate observable successes (Bembenutty, 2009). The concept is employed to designate a personality trait (Silverman, 2003), a student decision (Bembenutty, 2008), or, as is the case in our research, a principle for designing learning activities (Bembenutty & Karabenick, 1998, 2004). Accordingly, ADOG implies that recognition and rewards are postponed in order to stimulate engagement.

The main challenge of using digital badges in education lies in their contingent, situated effectiveness: Badge representation and acquisition patterns are socially and technologically dependent. Whether badges will actually work as planned depends on the interpretive work required to make sense of them (Rughiniş, 2013b). Badges are rendered ineffective in some circumstances, both when users do not share a common understanding and when badges do not manage to establish a rapport between users, or between users and technologies of distribution (Jarvinen, 2009).

Designers of badge architectures have many decisions to make in order to specify which learning and teaching events will be associated with badges. One important choice, on which we shall focus, refers to a broad distinction between what we term cumulative and summative badge systems (Table 20.1).

The introduction of summative digital badges in educational contexts implies a delay of gratification in acquiring rewards, thus creating various contingencies

TABLE 20.1 Cumulative and summative badge architectures

	Cumulative badges	*Summative badges*
Forms of attainment	Intermediary	Final
Type of learning goals rewarded	Minor (intermediary) and major (final)	Major (final)
User-experience of gratification	Instant	Delayed
Relevance for self-presentation	Internal to the community of learners	Internal and external (as credentials)
Organization of the awarding event	Casual	Memorable

in user experiences that influence effectiveness. Summative badges are used to award final and widely acknowledged learning achievements. Cumulative badges are more playful; they reward events here-and-now and focus especially on the learning community and internal appreciation, whereas summative badges lean towards the serious pole of the continuum and aim to offer credentials that are meaningful for outsider observers (such as employers).

The ADOG principle raises specific challenges for badge architectures: While the meaning of other rewards (financial, material, and even grade points) is relatively stable across situations, the meaning of badges is heavily dependent on developing mechanisms to bring them to the attention of potential recipients (Rughiniş & Matei, 2013). A summative (delayed) badge may gain significance as a valuable indicator of skill, or it may be thought of as a useless technical feature with no relevance. As badges are more frequently used, there is also the risk of "badge fatigue": Users who are already accustomed to this type of reward system may not feel intrigued by badges or eager to earn them.

The meaning of badges is locally constructed, through interactions and through learning *vocabularies of motive* (Mills, 1940) that offer users accounts of why these badges are valuable. It is expected that a delay in the summative allocation of badges would obstruct interaction—since it is easier to talk about and assign significance to a badge that one has earned, rather than to a badge that one may earn in the future. A badge architecture that is summative and thus uses delayed allocation is especially dependent on instructors' active promotion of the badge system in their discussions with students. Alternatively, the interactional presence of future badges may be supported through online display technologies, making them visible on the learning platform at all times.

SumUps CCNA.ro Design

The Cisco Networking Academy Center of the University Politehnica of Bucharest (CCNA.ro) is a training center for computer networking that recruits learners among University students, as well as professional engineers. The focus of our analysis is the SumUps CCNA.ro digital badge system, which was designed to symbolically reward students for fulfilling a set of learning goals: final GPA over 75 percent (Bronze Medal); final GPA over 85 percent (Silver Medal); final GPA over 95 percent (Gold Medal); completion of all laboratories (Technical Stamina); participation with more than three contributions on forum (Community Catalyst); involvement in over 50 percent of class discussions (Inquisitive Mind); and all test scores over 90 percent (Perfectionist). Each medal is displayed on the student's personal profile and can be seen by others.

The badge typology was designed to reward final, not intermediary, contributions, aiming to create a classroom culture that supports academic delay of gratification. A second goal was to sustain long-term student involvement by developing overall activity goals. We decided to translate formal evaluation

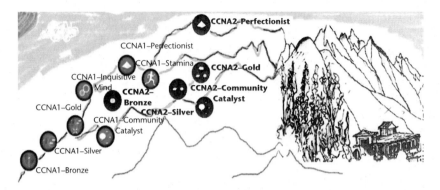

FIGURE 20.1 A map-type representation of digital badges in SumUps CCNA.ro.
Used with permission from Cisco Networking Academy CCNA.ro, University POLITEHNICA of Bucharest.

(test grades) into symbolic measures (digital badges), instead of introducing new criteria of informal evaluation. Ultimately, through the badge architecture, we organized learning as a summative activity, rather than a cumulative process (see Figure 20.1): Badges were designed to represent a culmination of multiple learning events to assess overall engagement.

The SumUps CCNA.ro badge architecture is meant to support students' academic involvement through a community of practice (Wenger, 1998). The SumUps CCNA.ro badge architecture aims to stimulate learner sociability by facilitating students' conversations with instructors (there is a dedicated badge for course involvement) and colleagues (unlike grades, badges are legitimate topics of peer conversation). Since these courses provide valuable credentials that employers appreciate, badges are visible on learners' public profiles as credentials after course completion.

A badge architecture may combine intermediate, immediate gratification badges as well as final, delayed gratification badges (Digital Youth Network, 2012); still, there is no neutral solution for combining cumulative and summative design principles. The introduction of intermediate badges has interactional consequences— for example, it encourages competition between learners, and it makes the badge architecture more playful. Based on these anticipated advantages and disadvantages of cumulative and summative badges, we have opted for a completely summative system. Also, because CCNA.ro courses offer professional training and are important for career development, the badge architecture was meant to generate credentials that are relevant to students, instructors, and potential employers.

SumUps CCNA.ro Implementation

The SumUps CCNA.ro badge architecture was implemented at Cisco Networking Academy, a training center affiliated to the University Politehnica of Bucharest and supported by Cisco, a worldwide provider of IT&C solutions. Cisco Networking Academy is part of an international IT skills building program developed by Cisco in partnership with local learning institutions. Cisco Networking Academy offers training and certification for people interested in developing a professional career, improving their IT&C competencies and qualifications.

The courses are organized in four modules (CCNA 1 [CCNET], CCNA2 [CCDA], CCNA 3 [CCDP] and CCNA 4 [CCDE]) with different degrees of difficulty and specialization (entry level, associate, professional, and expert). The modules follow an international curriculum covering various aspects of computer networks, such as architecture, security, and performance. Activities are organized as instructor-led classes (lectures and laboratories) in which students have to complete various assignments: They practice their skills by using both real equipment and Cisco Packet Tracer (a simulation tool used to visualize and operate a virtual computer network).

The SumUps CCNA.ro badge architecture was implemented in the spring semester of 2013, engaging 22 instructors and up to 250 students. Among them, 90 percent received the Bronze Medal (final GPA over 75 percent), 40 percent received the Silver Medal (final GPA over 85 percent), 14 percent received the Gold Medal (final GPA over 95 percent), 62 percent received the Technical Stamina badge (completion of all laboratories), 34 percent received the Community Catalyst badge (participation with more than three contributions on forum), 80 percent received the Inquisitive Mind badge (meaningful involvement in class discussions), and 6 percent received the Perfectionist badge (all test scores over 90 percent).

Evaluating Summative Badge Architecture

In our evaluation of SumUps CCNA.ro badge system, we focused on two broad functions of badge architectures: guidance, that is, highlighting valuable learning events and focusing students' attention on specific actions; and resource for self-presentation, through users' public profiles and various instances of interaction in which they become visible.

Methodology

The evaluation of SumUps CCNA.ro badge system is based on 10 semi-structured interviews with students and instructors who volunteered to participate in the study. The interviews were designed as a discussion in which participants were asked to describe their overall learning experience in order to improve next year's courses. The interviews give us access to the participants' vocabularies of motive (Mills, 1940) that sustain or inhibit the value of badges in the particular context of CCNA.ro. The value of badges is not given, but depends on the social interaction in which they can become significant; therefore, interviews are particularly useful for highlighting types of discourses that make badges intelligible to participants.

In interviews, we aimed to gain insight into the following issues:

1. *Badges and learning activities:* We analyzed students' and instructors' descriptions of their personal learning experience in terms of motivation, interest, strategies, attention, difficulties, failure, and success.
2. *Badges and social interaction:* Because learning is not an individual process, but it occurs through social interaction, we examine how badges are integrated into classroom activity. Accordingly, we studied badges as potential facilitators of various relationships: student–student, student–instructor, and instructor–instructor. Also, we tried to explore how other academic or professional communities are included as referents in respondents' discourse. We tried to explore the group dynamics by taking into consideration the emergence of reputations, social statuses and inequalities, power relations, and conflicts.

Findings

Summative badges and learning goals. CCNA.ro students and instructors integrate summative badges using a vocabulary that favors a unitary and synoptic approach to the learning process (Table 20.2). Summative badges are understood as a symbolic reformulation of the course objectives, supporting students' commitment to some ultimate goals. Hence, summative badges are described as a means of directing attention towards learning requirements (LP1, Table 20.2) while defining standards of performance in an academic community (LP2, Table 20.2). However, compared to cumulative badges, which we expect to sustain accounts of

TABLE 20.2 Interview extracts exemplifying the guidance function of summative badges (English translation)

Interviewees' responses

LP1. It is difficult to appraise each presentation or lab separately. You realize that you really have learnt something at the end of the module. Then you look back and you see how all assignments you completed come together into a whole. I just love badges because they tell you that everything went well. That's the whole point! (Student 6)

LP2. You receive badges at the end of a class. This is when you know if you've done well. They show how well you performed during the training when the only criterion to confirm your merits is the smile of your instructor. Well, you also have some assignments in the form of tests, and a mid-term exam, but they don't say much about your overall performance (Student 1).

LP3. Do you know that saying? Appetite comes with eating. This is exactly the case with our classes. When freshmen enroll in our course they know nothing about networking, about the purpose of the course and they don't know where to go. Badges help them adapt to the situation, they tell students that they can follow something until they become more familiar with the subject and able to set their own priorities (Instructor 3).

intermediate task completion, summative badges support accounts of prospective completion, thus upholding a definition of learning as a continuous, engaging, and long-term process (LP3, Table 20.2).

Summative badges and self-presentation devices. By relying on a summative system of rewards, we started from the premise that displaying knowledge is a function of peer-group organization: displaying skill that supports identities and reputations. Badges can be seen by peers, instructors, or other professionals, thus functioning as a persistent device for prestige formation (Table 20.3). Indeed, badges also appear in interviews as discursive instruments meant to foster interaction and to create valuable identities for students: e.g., the self-portrayal of students as "sociable" or "perfectionist" persons (SP1, SP2, Table 20.3).

Summative badges emerge as a symbol of recognition not only for students, but also for instructors. Badges are used as instruments that allow instructors to assess their pedagogical competence by showing the effort they put into students' preparation and professional success (SP3, Table 20.3). Therefore, by encouraging

TABLE 20.3 Interview extracts exemplifying summative badges as self-presentation devices (English translation)

Interviewees' responses
SP1: You have to overcome some critical moments [in order to receive a badge]. You don't receive a badge straight away … and you cannot go through those critical moments unless you collaborate with others. You help others and you ask others for help. This is how you receive a badge. It does not mean that you help others just to get a badge, but you cannot get a badge without the others' help because this is how things work. Handbooks cannot teach you everything, so you ask instructors for extra assignments and explanations, and your closest colleagues for clarification (Student 7).
SP2: If you receive a bronze or a silver medal, you feel that something is missing and that's why you want the gold (Student 3).
SP3: When one of your students gets a badge, it's like you get one yourself. If you notice that none of your students ever managed to get a badge, then the problem does not lie with the students, but with the instructors who did not manage to make themselves understood when teaching. In our academia we have high standards and we have never come across such a situation because we develop mentoring relationships. (…). I verify the badges received by my students because I care about them, and I want my students to have good results because I evaluate myself based on their results (Instructor 3).
SP4: One strategy to receive a badge is to learn from (your) mistakes. This is my learning principle and I have been using it since high school. And it works with badges, too. I always try to find someone better than me, someone who can show me why and when I am wrong. That's because when you realize that you are wrong, it is easier for you to improve yourself. And if you are wrong once, I bet you won't make the same mistake again. You learn something that you remember for the rest of your life (Student 4).

mutual awareness between students and instructors, summative badges appear not only as an output of individual learning (which usually is the case with popular cumulative badges), but also as an opportunity to represent and make visible a collective outcome of learning.

Both cumulative and summative badges offer visualizations of the history of students' activities, becoming traces of achievement. While a collection of cumulative badges represents such a history, a single summative badge contains in itself a history. A cumulative badge is related to a single event characterized by a high degree of specificity, while a summative badge provides clues about a longer period of engagement. The architecture of rewards developed in our application supports the creation of narratives of personal experience. By comparing SumUps CCNA. ro with other badging systems encountered in academic or non-academic contexts, respondents claim that what we term as summative badges are more likely than cumulative badges to enter as a reference in students' stories of achievement (SP4, Table 20.3) because of their focus on the entire process of learning. Specific forms of involvement in the course setting or problems faced in the context of independent study are invoked by students to describe their path to success. We consider that these narratives of self-development are less encouraged by awarding cumulative badges, because their acquisition does not foster the aggregation of many situational details in order to sustain a coherent storyline.

Contrasting accounts of summative badges. During the interviews, students and instructors shared a wide range of views regarding the significance of badges. Respondents made implicit comparisons between badges and other previously encountered systems to assess the significance of badges (Table 20.4). On the one hand, in interviews, badges are presented as an attraction that does not detract from fulfilling the learning goals (VR1a, VR2a, Table 20.4). On the other hand, results show that deferral is likely to make final rewards irrelevant to guiding students' behavior. In this case, summative badges are described as superfluous formal evaluation (VR1b, VR2b, Table 20.4).

Co-authored accounts of summative badges. Students offered inconsistent or even contradictory accounts of their experiences with summative badges, not only across interviews, but also within the same interview (Table 20.5). As we can observe from the differences found between the three conversational sequences, one important problem raised by using a summative system of allocation is the difficulty of creating a vocabulary of owning a badge (describing "how it is to have a badge"). Since the badge acquisition is delayed, students do not have an actual and continuous experience of ownership, which could make those rewards relevant to peer interaction. In describing badges as a learning component, however, students rehearse a vocabulary acquired from discussions with instructors, even if this vocabulary is not always introduced as an active part of their own experience. Since this architecture is in its first year of functioning, potentially encouraging discussions about badges with senior colleagues are not yet available.

TABLE 20.4 Interview extracts presenting multiple accounts of summative badges (English translation)

Code	Interviewees' responses
VR1a:	Badges do not expire. Badges are always available and you can receive them even if you had a bad day. If you can't keep up with others, you can catch up by working harder. You set your own pace without being afraid that you are going to lose a badge (Student 6).
VR1b:	Badges, what about them? I don't know, they need to be visible from the beginning. They [Academy's coordinators] told us that we [the instructors] should make them visible by referring to them and by directing students to them in classes, but I am adamantly against this view. They [badges] should be made visible from the beginning. If a student waits until mid-semester to get a badge, then the whole potential and the significance of badges as learning tools go down the drain (Instructor 2).
VR2a:	Yeah, well you know, there are some badges, I can show you, but you cannot take them now, you take them later.... I don't know, there is something like "you take a badge if you do well on the final exam, and you do well on the exam" ... and it's good to do well on the exam and for that you get something extra. It is not redundant. It is not like you learn just for the sake of getting a degree ... a badge is something more than a degree. It's not like you learn for the sake of getting a badge, which could make you an eager collector. You learn for the sake of learning and those badges stimulate students. They show students what they have to do and why they are here (Instructor 1).
VR2b:	To have badges is a good idea, but the medals we have are useless because a medal is just another way to represent your grade on the final exam. A gold medal for course completion actually doesn't reveal anything extra about you, it is like having a virtual report card with icons instead of having a report card in which grades are represented by linguistic characters (Student 5).

TABLE 20.5 Interview extracts presenting co-authored accounts of summative badges (English translation)

Code	Interviewees' responses
C1a	Interviewer (I): But what can you tell me about the badge system? I have heard that you have a badge system in the Academia and ... Interviewee (L): Yeah. What about them? I don't know. I: What is it like to have one of them? L. It's like ... you don't have one of them now. You get them later. [...]

(continued)

TABLE 20.5 (*continued*)

Code	Interviewees' responses
C1b	I: Do you think it's fun to have a badge? L: It's fun to get a badge, but there is also something serious about them. They show you that you are skilled in many areas. There are badges in games, the so-called achievements, but they are designed to show how maniacally you are playing that game. SumUps CCNA badges are different, they are perfect for our university. You enroll and know that you work in a professional environment with certified instructors. Badges are fun, but they are not ludicrous. [...]
C1c	I. What do you think about them? Do you think they are meant for one particular type of student? L: I noticed that most guys my age are like "yeah, we receive badges, just like in the games we play, it's awesome," but there are some colleagues who are much older, they have wives, children, they work and badges don't motivate them. Badges are definitely not for them (Student 7).
C2a	Interviewer (I): What do you think about the badges you receive? Do you find them efficient for learning? Interviewee (L): That's a good question because I don't see any efficiency since they are non-existent. [...]
C2b	I: But why do you think they were created? L: It is good for us to receive badges. They motivate us throughout the learning process to give our best, to improve our skills. Everyone wants to do well, or at least this is what I think. I want to be better than others, others want to be better than me and so on. [...]
C2c	I: Do you think that badges could make students learn just for the sake of receiving a badge? L: There are achievement hunters, but the badges we have are different. Achievements are good when people know each other, when they compete with one another and when they interact daily. Medals are good when a group is not already created, they can help create a group, build a team because there is no competition involved and everybody is on an equal footing (Student 1).

Conclusion

Our evaluation of the SumUps CCNA.ro badges indicates that summative architectures have specific merits and risks. We have observed that learners' and instructors' accounts vary hugely. For some, badges are utterly irrelevant, while for others, they offer highly valuable support for performance and reputations. The meaning of badges, in any learning situation, is not given, but discursively constructed through vocabularies of motive (Mills, 1940), which may turn them into effective motivators or inconsequential signs. These vocabularies, in turn, develop through student-instructor interaction throughout the semester. Instructors play a key role in constantly re-defining the meaning and worth of a summative badge system. Instructors and students alike are not naïve observers but, as a rule, have previous experience with badges, from game achievements or other online platforms. The value of a badge architecture is not generic, but specific: It is constructed as the value of "our" badge system, in contrast to other systems. Course designers and instructors should therefore pay close attention not only to the technical and instructional design of a badge architecture, but also to the vocabularies used to describe this architecture and to account for its relevance and value—or lack thereof.

Our approach shows that interviews are especially useful for diagnosing and improving the implementation of summative badges from one semester to the next, taking into account the meaning of summative digital badges as it appears in students' and instructors' discourse. Interview analysis is useful to assemble a list of topics that instructors should address in their discussions with students about the badge architecture, such as the role of badges in the organization and planning of individual and personalized learning processes, their role in self-presentation as indicators of competence for employers and other community members, their serious character despite their playful appearance, their significance for maintaining a continuous learning path, their relevance besides official diplomas, etc. Carefully composed accounts can also be communicated via the online platform in order to increase badge visibility.

The ADOG principle in badge design supports the guidance function while hindering their self-presentation role, since the delay of allocation creates a time frame when badges are present in discourse, but not as objects that students own. The experience of possession and the value of summative badges as conversation topics could be increased by introducing one badge for valuable achievements at the beginning or midway through a course. Also, summative digital badges could be accompanied by material objects (pins, prizes, custom and symbolic diplomas), or they could be awarded in a ceremonial context, or both. We expect the interactional disadvantage of delayed allocation to be relieved for architectures that span multiple generations of learners. Junior students can see the badges of senior colleagues and be inspired by them. The specific challenges of longer-term architectures are, therefore, a valuable topic for further research.

Acknowledgment

This article has been supported by the research project "Sociological imagination and disciplinary orientation in applied social research," with the financial support of ANCS/UEFISCDI with grant no. PN-II-RU-TE-2011-3-0143, contract 14/28.10.2011.

References

Bembenutty, H. (2008). Academic delay of gratification and expectancy-value. *Personality and Individual Differences, 44*, 193–202.

Bembenutty, H. (2009). Teaching effectiveness, course evaluation, and academic performance: The role of academic delay of gratification. *Journal of Advanced Academics, 20*, 326–355.

Bembenutty, H., & Karabenick, S. A. (1998). Academic delay of gratification. *Learning and Individual Differences, 10*, 329–346.

Bembenutty, H., & Karabenick, S. A. (2004). Inherent association between academic delay of gratification, future time perspective, and self-regulated learning. *Educational Psychology Review, 16*, 35–57.

Casilli, C. (2012). Mozilla Open Badges: The ecosystem begins to take shape. *Persona*. Retrieved from https://carlacasilli.wordpress.com/2012/07/31/mozilla-open-badges-the-ecosystem-begins-to-take-shape/.

Deterding, S., Dixon, D., Khaled, R., & Nacke, L. (2011). From game design elements to gamefulness. In ACM (Ed.), *Envisioning future media environments*. Paper presented at the 15th International Academic MindTrek Conference, Tampere, Finland, 28–30 September (pp. 9–15). New York, NY: ACM Press.

Digital Youth Network (2012). Badges for learning: A design framework. *Open Badges: 10 Million Better Futures*. Retrieved from http://10mbetterfutures.org/wp-content/uploads/2013/11/BadgeFramework_v3.pdf.

Halavais, A. M. C. (2011). A genealogy of badges. *Information Communication Society, 15*, 1–20.

Jarvinen, A. (2009). Psychology of achievements & trophies. *Gamasutra*. Retrieved from www.gamasutra.com.

MacArthur Foundation (2013). Digital media learning badges competition. *Hastac. Digital Media + Learning Competitions*. Retrieved from www.hastac.org/competition/digital-media-learning-competition-1.

Mills, C. (1940). Situated actions and vocabularies of motive. *American Sociological Review, 5(6)*, 904–913.

Rughiniş, R. (2013a). Badge architectures in engineering education. Blueprints and challenges. In Foley, O., Restivo, M. T., Uhomoibhi, J. and Helfert, M. (Eds.), *Proceedings of the 5th International Conference on Computer Supported Education (Volume 1)*. Paper presented at the 5th International Conference on Computer Supported Education, Aachen, Germany, 6–8 May (pp. 548–554), SciTePress.

Rughiniş, R. (2013b). Talkative objects in need of interpretation. Re-thinking digital badges in education. In ACM (Ed.), *CHI '13 Extended Abstracts on Human Factors in Computing Systems*. Paper presented at ACM SIGCHI Conference on Human Factors in Computing Systems: Changing Perspectives, Paris, France, 27 April–2 May (pp. 2099–2108). New York, NY: ACM.

Rughiniş, R., & Matei, S. (2013). Digital badges: Signposts and claims of achievement. In Stephanidis, C. (Ed.), *Communications in Computer and Information Science (Volume 374)*. Paper presented at the 15th International Conference on Human-Computer Interaction, Las Vegas, NV, 21–26 July (pp. 84–88), Berlin, Heidelberg: Springer.

Silverman, I. W. (2003). Gender differences in delay of gratification: A meta-analysis. *Sex Roles, 49*, 451–463.

Wenger, E. (1998). *Communities of practice. Learning, meaning and identity*. Cambridge, UK: Cambridge University Press.

21

TEACHER LEARNING JOURNEYS

A Design Case Study of a Learner-Centered STEM Digital Badging System

Chris Gamrat and Heather Toomey Zimmerman

Case Overview

Penn State University developed the digital badging system, Teacher Learning Journeys (TLJ), in partnership with the National Aeronautics and Space Administration (NASA) and the National Science Teachers Association (NSTA) to support science, technology, engineering, and math (STEM) professional learning for educators. The partners' goal for TLJ was to support educators' STEM learning by enriching educators' engagement with their pupils in school, university, and museum environments.

Travel Metaphor Guiding the TLJ Design

The research and development team used a travel metaphor to design TLJ. This travel metaphor emphasized the idea of educators engaging in personalized learning journeys (Kearney, Schuck, Burden, & Aubusson, 2012) where they were empowered to make and record personally relevant choices (Borko, 2004). Consequently, the badging system features were designed using travel symbolism: (a) the educators created an itinerary when badging activities were added to a queue for future investigation; (b) the lower level badge resembled passport stamps given to travelers upon entry into a country (Figure 21.1, left); (c) the higher-level badge resembled a sewn souvenir patch (Figure 21.1, right); and (d) the reflective written submissions used as evidence of content mastery for each stamp or badge were referred to as logs.

FIGURE 21.1   A TLJ stamp (left) and TLJ badge (right).

Learner Experience in Teacher Learning Journeys

The learner experience in TLJ started with educators setting up accounts and then drafting goal statements. In the goal statements, educators were asked to articulate how they hoped to grow personally and professionally after completing the TLJ badge activities. Educators next selected and added badging activities to their itinerary from the TLJ badging library. In Year 1, 54 badging activities, related to STEM content in three areas (solar system, engineering, and weather and climate), were options in the TLJ library. In Year 2, 80 badging activities related to five STEM content areas in the TLJ library were available to educators: solar system, engineering, and weather and climate from Year 1, plus physics and earth science. Educators could preview each badging activity to determine if the activity met their needs and was appropriate to their teaching before adding it to an itinerary (Figure 21.2).

After their itineraries were created, educators worked on the required criteria for a given badging activity. Badging activities included attending and reflecting on webinars, reviewing online materials, and engaging in participatory science activities. Badges were not awarded to learners for participating in events because previously published research has suggested that is not good for maintaining learners' motivation (Abramovich, Schunn, & Higashi, 2013). Instead, to earn badges in TLJ, learners provided evidence that they understood and could apply the STEM content in classrooms, museums, training sessions, or other educational settings. The educators had a choice of assessment in the TLJ badging system—educators choose the depth in which they were assessed by selecting to earn a stamp, badge, or both. To earn a stamp and/or badge, educators submitted reflective logs to their respective NASA mentors who evaluated the materials and determined whether the educators had demonstrated competency in the activity. The mentors provided feedback, and if needed, suggested additions

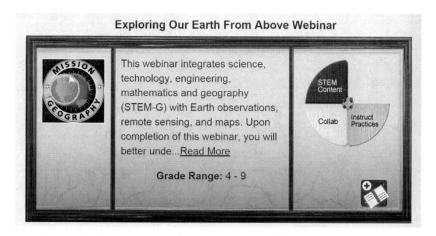

FIGURE 21.2   The Exploring Our Earth From Above badging activity within the physics topic area.

for educators to resubmit their materials. Finally, upon positive review by the mentors, educators were provided with a stamp or a badge. Recognition could be consolidated to printable certificates and downloadable reports of educator effort that could be used to demonstrate professional learning to supervisors, institutional administrators, and others.

Analysis

We based the development of TLJ on theoretical and research considerations and on an evaluation of how to improve the TLJ partners' current efforts to provide educators with STEM learning opportunities. Prior to TLJ, Penn State engaged in a collaborative effort with NASA to support and conduct STEM educator professional development (PD). In this prior PD effort, face-to-face workshops or similar events provided educators with professional learning experiences in real time. In this face-to-face approach, educators were limited by their ability to attend real-time events in person. The chief consideration in the development of TLJ was the ability of educators to personalize their experiences (Gamrat, Zimmerman, Dudek, & Peck, 2014; Gamrat & Zimmerman, 2015) in terms of variety of content, flexible availability of activities, leveled assessment, reflections as evidence, and mentored assessment.

Diverse Badging Activities to Meet Learners' Expertise and Interests

An important consideration in TLJ was to provide a variety of STEM badging activities to meet educators' diverse expertise and interests in learning about STEM. Initially, we offered badging activities related to three topics: engineering, solar system, and weather and climate. Then, based on educators' feedback, we added physics and earth science badging activities in Year 2, which brought the total areas of study to five STEM domains.

These five topics were selected because of their popularity in face-to-face PD events offered by NASA, the quality of available activities for the topic, and the requests of members in a NASA educator online learning community. This topical variety offered learners the ability to learn broadly across STEM domains or to specialize by gaining deep expertise in a particular area of content.

In addition to having five topic options, TLJ learners were offered a range of content in multiple badging activities providing the opportunity to further specialize. Novice educators strengthened their understanding of core STEM concepts and experienced educators explored new content and pedagogical approaches. Importantly, this allowed educators who were responsible for only one STEM domain or who taught in a specialized science or STEM magnet or charter school to develop deep specialization.

Providing Badging Activities with Flexible Time Offerings

To make STEM learning available to multiple educators, a key consideration was to provide badging activities with flexible availability of offerings. To support educators nationwide, badging activities were designed to offer both synchronous and asynchronous learning experiences.

We provided content for several badging activities via live webinars; the webinars were scheduled at two different times on a given day and also on multiple days to meet various scheduling needs and address time zone issues. In addition, many badging activities included the archived webinar for greater flexibility.

Several badges were designed to have only asynchronous communication requirements. These asynchronous communication badges were particularly popular with the participants who reported that they often did not have time for professional development until the evening when their children were in bed. Educators with children valued these as unique experiences not offered by traditional PD. By designing badging activities to allow time flexibility, learners were able to decide when they were best able to participate in their PD (Gamrat, Zimmerman, Dudek, & Peck, 2014), and learners with a variety of needs (e.g., parents) were accommodated.

Assessment Levels

Our design of TLJ presumed that the educators engaging in professional STEM learning would value multiple learning outcomes. Consequently in TLJ, two levels of assessment were offered, as stated earlier: stamps and badges. Both stamps and badges captured more than just educator participation in an activity because educators were asked to reflect upon their learning experience.

Stamps marked the lowest level of achievement. Stamps offered educators the ability to receive recognition for experiences after demonstrating reflective thinking and cursory application of STEM content in their workplace. Offering a stamp as a lower-level achievement benefited many educators who wanted the exposure to the STEM content but were less interested in meeting the higher-level requirement of an in-depth reflection.

To earn a TLJ badge, educators were asked to focus their reflections on practice-changing considerations (i.e., how to incorporate the learned STEM content into their teaching). Offering a badge as a higher-level achievement offered educators the opportunity to develop lessons, reflect on their pedagogy, and consider how new STEM content resources might be utilized in K-12, higher education, or museum classrooms.

From our own research (Gamrat, Zimmerman, Dudek, & Peck, 2014; Gamrat & Zimmerman, 2015), we found that both levels of assessment provided educators with a means to demonstrate evidence of learning and capture their experiences and thoughts with the ability to decide how much they wanted to explore a STEM activity. This suggestion also aligns with the recommendation by Hickey et al. (2014) to use leveled badge systems.

Personal Reflections as Evidence

Given that our goal was to create active, engaging STEM learning for the educators, we designed TLJ to include logs of educators' reflections of how to use the TLJ badging STEM content in their schools, universities, or museum classrooms. In Year 1 of TLJ, educators were given general guidance on the reflections that were required for a log; they were simply asked to reflect on their experience, which resulted in a wide range in terms of both focus and length. In Year 2, the instructions for logs were redesigned with an implementation focus, rather than open-ended general reflections, to better support the educators as they completed badges and stamps. Using the concept of "channeling" (Pea, 2004, p. 432), educators were guided to create the types of reflection necessary for either a stamp or badge, but still were given considerable freedom in their responses. These added suggestions for reflective logs offered learners the ability to focus on specific questions addressing adoption rather than deciding what, of many things, should be the focus of the reflection.

Mentored Assessment

In Year 1, based on enrollment in webinars and badging activities, NASA education experts took turns mentoring the educators who were using TLJ. In Year 2, we assigned each TLJ participant a mentor who stayed the same for that year. To maximize the mentors' familiarity with the education standards and current events of their learner's local area, mentor assignments were based on geographic proximity. Year 2 mentors provided feedback that included both nationally and regionally relevant information. The use of mentors as badge evaluators supports the badge design recommendation of Hickey et al. to "enhance validity with expert judgment" (2014, p. 3). The goal of having mentors was to provide specific feedback for each badge or stamp completed by an educator and to develop an educator-mentor relationship over time. However, only a few educators used TLJ enough to develop this intended relationship. In future iterations, we intend to increase this mentorship by offering educators more opportunities to interact with their mentors.

Design

The TLJ system and badges were developed over two consecutive summers. At the start of the process, strategic discussion, design options, and conversations occurred between the representatives of NASA, NSTA, and Penn State. We established a shared vision of the project's initial setup and development over time.

Year 1 Initial Badges and Badging System Design

Several working groups of NASA education experts developed the badges, with each group focusing on a different topic. The topics most requested by the participants in a NASA online learning community were used along with topic-related activities selected by the NASA education experts, which were based on their experience and understanding of a broad library of educational materials. The first author oversaw platform development, which the project's principal investigator, developer, and graphic designer helped to further drive via weekly discussions.

Year 2 Badges and Badging System Refinement

The Year 2 design considerations focused on the feedback garnered from interviews and surveys of Year 1 learners. Ensuring clear and thorough explanation of the TLJ system and the requirements for a given activity was the project's most important design improvement. Since all of the participants were engaging with TLJ from a distance, it was necessary to have clear steps for the activity, the criteria required for recognition, and the process necessary to be awarded a badge. When TLJ was launched, learners asked many questions that sought clarification about the system. Their concerns were quickly addressed to support the remote users.

The second key design improvement was that all of the badges were updated with clearer instructions and stronger ties to pupil learning outcomes; we accomplished this by adding an educator who had both classroom and online teaching experience to the team. More support was designed and implemented for educators' reflections at the end of activities to encourage critical thinking about the activities. Additionally, we had an editor review the badge activities to help provide consistency and clarity for the entire badge family.

The TLJ system design also faced the challenge of improving metadata for each badge and stamp. While nearly all of the activity development team members had significant experience in curriculum design, the concepts of badges, badging, and metadata were new to them. During each iteration, the activity development team also considered what metadata were to be associated with each badge to communicate learners' accomplishments as well as to be used by mentors and learners to better support learning within TLJ.

Development

We developed the TLJ system in PHP and went through several development iterations. To provide the desired flexibility and personalization in TLJ, the development approach included the basic structure for badging system functionality: create an account, select badge activities to complete, submit a log to earn a badge or stamp, receive feedback from an assigned mentor, resubmit the log as needed, and access badges in a personal archive. While we intended to integrate with Open Badges (through the Mozilla Open Badges Backpack program), the grant cycle ended before this work was completed.

Agile Development Model

The system designer, badge developer, and graphic artist used the Agile model to develop TLJ. The initial focus of the development was split into two areas: content and system. The content, with a group of activities per topic area, was developed through the support of NASA education experts. The activities were developed iteratively to help focus the content and to present it in a form that also made sense for a professional learning badge. Features and bugs were identified weekly for development and improvement. The Year 1 development focused on the creation of a system that offered a specific set of core functionality. The Year 2 development attempted to enhance the features that were most popular, update the interface, and add suggestions for missing functionality from the Year 1 feedback.

Redevelopment from Year 1 to Year 2

Survey feedback from Year 1 educators (described in the Evaluation section below) showed that educators were confused about how to earn a stamp or badge. In response, we redesigned each badging activity to include a thorough explanation of how to complete and submit the log to meet the criteria for the activity. Relatedly, in Year 2, we developed an orientation badging activity; the orientation provided information to support educators earning recognitions within TLJ. To encourage educators to sign up for this badging activity, the orientation badging activity was displayed at the top of every search list.

Implementation

Educators were invited to use TLJ through contacts of the NASA education experts. To participate, they had to volunteer as research participants who were testing a new tool for STEM education over the summer in Years 1 and 2. Each summer's group of participants was intended to be small in scope ($n = 78$) in order to ensure necessary functionality before a larger scale project was attempted.

Overview of Teacher Learning Journeys Educators

The TLJ participants were primarily from the United States, and most of them were elementary and middle school educators. Preservice teachers and high school, college, and informal (museum) educators also participated. Over the first two years of the TLJ, 78 educators completed 315 badges and stamps. Stamps (lower level) were the most popular form of assessment in both years, comprising nearly 86.98 percent of all recognitions earned.

There was a wide range in the number of badges completed by each educator with an average of four badges per person. One-third of the participants completed five or more stamps and badges across the two years of the pilot. Several participants each completed over a dozen activities (Table 21.1 and Figure 21.3). From our summative surveys and badge activity logs, the educators responded favorably to TLJ. Overall, the request that came from the badging participants was to further increase the external recognition of badges with school administrators so that badges could be part of the required recertification effort.

The biggest TLJ success was that educators reported that while they appreciated receiving recognition through badges and stamps, they were driven to use TLJ because of the available STEM content. During the two years, 174 activity survey responses were collected. An analysis of the survey showed that 94 percent agreed (or strongly agreed) that the activity they had completed was of high quality; 94 percent of the respondents agreed or strongly agreed that the "activity was relevant to their teaching." While most of the educators found TLJ to be a valuable learning experience, only 49 percent of the educators responded that their supervisor would count the TLJ badges in lieu of in-house professional development.

Evaluation

Multiple evaluative tools were used in TLJ and outside of TLJ to understand learning and the learners' experience with badging. These evaluative tools included learner-submitted *bug reports*, interviews with focal educators, activity-based surveys, summative surveys at the end of each development cycle, analyses of learners' logs and reflective statements, and system log files.

TABLE 21.1 Awarded badges and stamps during TLJ's first two years

	Project year		
Award	1	2	Total
Badges	21	20	41
Stamps	131	143	274
Total	152	163	315

Please note that participants have permissions to delete account data. All data is as of November 25, 2015.

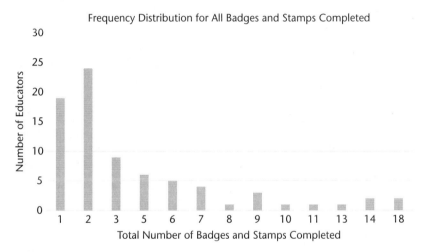

FIGURE 21.3 Frequency for all badges and stamps completed.

Ongoing Formative Assessment

We conducted formative system assessment in Years 1 and 2 through the use of a learner feedback system called bug reporting. A bug report feature was made available on every page of TLJ badging system. With the bug reports system, all learners had the option to immediately identify and report any problems they experienced. To ensure that the bugs were understood, the first author corresponded with the educators who submitted bug reports. He also confirmed with these educators that an update was made or explained how their suggestions were to be addressed in the upcoming development cycles.

Research on Teacher Learning Journeys

We completed a summative assessment of the educators' TLJ experience through case study analyses based on interviews, learner-created artifacts, and surveys. The TLJ research team (Gamrat, Zimmerman, Dudek, & Peck, 2014) selected eight focal educators for interviews, which were completed with educators who represented a range of both years of teaching experience and grade level. This analysis offered an in-depth understanding of why educators signed up for TLJ, what their experience was like, and what they wanted to see in future iterations. A second analysis (Gamrat & Zimmerman, 2015) investigated TLJ more broadly ($n = 36$) by examining Year 1 educators' activity logs, reflective statements, activity surveys, and summative surveys.

Through the summative survey on the first year, the TLJ participants ($n = 29$, 80.5 percent of total) answered questions regarding their overall impressions of the user experience and future iterations of design. When asked "If we continued to add and enhance the content, would you be likely to continue using the TLJ system?" 92 percent said they either might or definitely would continue. Also, 96 percent of respondents agreed with the statement "I would recommend Teacher Learning Journeys to other educators."

From our analysis, we determined that a number of revisions could improve the overall TLJ program, including creating additional content for learners, developing an easier search feature for users, adding stronger learning analytics capabilities for researchers and administrators, providing learners the ability to follow others to create a stronger community, and integrating the project's badges with Open Badges and backpack systems. When asked about social components to TLJ, 72 percent of Year 1 survey educators asked to be able to see resources and badge activities that other educators recommended. This supports educator professional learning by presenting more opportunities to identify learning activities through available metadata.

Conclusions

In this chapter, we presented the case of TLJ as providing and recognizing professional STEM learning via digital badges for K-12 teachers, university educators, and informal museum educators. From the experiences of the educators in TLJ, we assert the importance of (a) collecting multiple forms of feedback from participants as formative and summative evaluation; (b) including multiple choices in the types of content available for the development of expertise and the support of interest; (c) including at least two levels of badging assessment; (d) providing clear instructions and orienting materials; and (e) developing strong mentoring relationships between the badge assessors and the learners.

Acknowledgments

The development of the TLJ system and its research were partially supported by the NASA Aerospace Education Services Project and the Center for Online Innovation in Learning at Penn State University. We acknowledge team members Kyle Peck and Jaclyn Dudek for their contributions to the broader TLJ research project.

References

Abramovich, S., Schunn, C., & Higashi, R. M. (2013). Are badges useful in education?: It depends upon the type of badge and expertise of learner. *Educational Technology Research and Development, 61*(2), 217–232.

Borko, H. (2004). Professional development and teacher learning: Mapping the terrain. *Educational Researcher, 33*(8), 3–15. doi:10.3102/0013189X033008003.

Gamrat, C., & Zimmerman, H. (2015). An online badging system supporting educators' STEM learning. In D. Hickey, J. Jovanović, S. Lonn, & J. E. Willis (Eds.), *Proceedings of the 2nd International Workshop on Open Badges in Education co-located with the 5th International Learning Analytics and Knowledge Conference (LAK 2015)* (pp. 12–23). Poughkeepsie: CEUR Workshop Proceedings. Retrieved from http://ceur-ws.org/Vol-1358/.

Gamrat, C., Zimmerman, H. T., Dudek, J., & Peck, K. (2014). Personalized workplace learning: An exploratory study on digital badging within a teacher professional development program. *British Journal of Educational Technology, 45*(6), 1136–1148. doi:10.1111/bjet.12200.

Hickey, D. T., Otto, N., Itow, R., Schenke, K., Tran, C., & Chow, C. (2014). *Interim report. Badges design principles documentation project.* Bloomington, IN: Indiana University Center for Research on Learning and Technology.

Kearney, M., Schuck, S., Burden, K., & Aubusson, P. (2012). Viewing mobile learning from a pedagogical perspective. *Research in Learning Technology, 20.* doi:http://dx.doi.org/10.3402/rlt.v20i0.14406.

Pea, R. D. (2004). The social and technological dimensions of scaffolding and related theoretical concepts for learning, education, and human activity. *The Journal of the Learning Sciences, 13*(3), 423–451.

22

VIF INTERNATIONAL EDUCATION

Global-Ready Teacher Badging

Julie Keane, Mark Otter, Tamara Oxley, and Leslie Lipscomb

Project Overview

VIF International Education was founded in 1987 in Chapel Hill, North Carolina, as Visiting International Faculty, a family business that sought to promote the value of international perspectives in education by providing universities with international faculty recruitment, relocation, and support services. The organization shifted its focus to K-12 education in 1989 when state departments of education began requiring world language learning for K-12 students. From the start, our turnkey process provided school administrators access to recruitment at a global level and enabled them to effectively host visiting teachers.

Throughout the 1990s, VIF placed thousands of K-12 teachers and was designated (and continues to be) a U.S. Department of State Exchange Visitor Program sponsor. Teacher placements expanded to all subjects, including math, science, and special education. In the early 2000s, we began to leverage our expertise in international teacher recruitment and placement to develop accessible and scalable global education programs, and we rebranded as VIF International Education. VIF's continued commitment to supporting international teachers' success in the classroom and our established belief in the importance of exposing students to intercultural experiences at the K-12 level are the foundations for VIF global education programs and services.

Today, VIF provides schools and districts with cultural exchange teachers, comprehensive frameworks, and support services to develop and maintain global and cultural literacy programs, and Spanish and Mandarin dual language programs through which students become bilingual and biliterate. Our clients are distinguished by school-wide commitments to building global competence and language acquisition in teachers, students, and administrators, and they endeavor to integrate technology, cultural literacy, and other twenty-first-century skills into everyday classroom instruction.

All VIF programs are rooted by teacher professional development (PD) and curricular resources offered through our online PD platform (VIF, 2015). VIF's PD and curricular resources are designed to support teachers in developing critical, cultural frameworks for engaging students in cross-disciplinary, inquiry-based approaches in all academic subjects. VIF's PD platform offers specific PD pathways for integrating global content into dual language immersion, English as a second language (ESL), and standard classroom instruction.

The majority of teachers accessing and participating in VIF's PD are doing so as a result of district and/or school initiatives to integrate global education as a component of transformation and innovation. The online platform that houses VIF's PD and resources also supports interaction between users so that teachers from rural, suburban, and urban districts in the U.S. are able to collaborate with peers from all around the world and with VIF staff.

In the fall of 2011, when the MacArthur Foundation announced the fourth Digital Media and Learning Competition to spur the development of digital badging for open learning, we were working with several districts through a Moodle Learning Management System (LMS) to support a diverse group of international and domestic teachers. The Moodle LMS we were using (essentially, the earliest version of our PD platform) was built to address the lack of transparency our instructional designers saw in migrating predominantly face-to-face workshops and synchronous webinars to blended learning approaches that rely on online platforms to enable continuous and progressive professional development. A primary challenge for VIF was the portability of professional learning accomplishments for our international exchange teachers. While exchange teachers were receiving continuing education credits for completing Moodle-based PD modules, there was no effective vehicle for teachers to share those accomplishments when they returned to their home countries.

Digital badging offered an ideal solution for acknowledging the PD our exchange teachers were completing and provided all of the teachers we were supporting an easy way to demonstrate and share their growing global expertise with professional and social networks. VIF designed a proposal to develop a badging system and to formalize our PD platform for the 2011 Digital Media and Learning Competition. We were a finalist in the competition but were not awarded a grant—however, we moved forward with establishing the platform and worked closely with the Mozilla Open Badge Initiative as we iteratively developed our digital badging approach.

Currently, advancement through VIF professional development is represented through the awarding of digital badges, which recognizes teachers' professional learning achievements. Each VIF PD module equates to 10 hours of professional development or continued education, which can be easily shared and acknowledged by districts and states. Teachers receive a digital badge for successful completion of each PD module and receive year-end badges upon completion of four successive modules. Year-end badges recognize teachers' gradual progression toward global competence.

A critical consideration for job-embedded PD programs geared toward educators is the need to balance the everyday demands that teachers face in their classrooms with the perpetual expectation for them to develop expertise across content, pedagogy, and new learning technologies. Learning to integrate global and cross-cultural concepts into classroom instruction often requires teachers to adapt their attitudes, skills, and knowledge—it almost always requires their willingness to be open minded. An open-minded approach is also critical for teachers' ability to collaborate with diverse peers, and to actively seek out opportunities to experiment with and incorporate new ideas and tools into their classrooms.

Analysis

VIF supports a unique community of international teachers who we recruit and place, and U.S. teachers who are participating in our school- and district-based programs. Consequently, in developing a comprehensive PD platform and educator community, we were determined to support teachers who are invariably at various stages in their global competence development. Our purpose, therefore, was to create an environment that would cultivate teachers' ability to extend and build on their existing proficiencies.

The attitudes, skills, and knowledge needed for global competence drive all of VIF's curriculum design and product development decisions. Student engagement in explorations of the world around them is nurtured when teachers expose them to open-ended inquiries in which they ask questions, initiate investigations, and are provided multiple avenues to create and innovate using tools that support content synthesis and hands-on production. VIF's PD and curricular resources consistently support teachers in implementing project-based inquiry approaches in their classrooms.

VIF has observed U.S. teachers moving away from project- and inquiry-based pedagogical strategies and toward basic skills approaches because of accountability pressures. Our initial task then was to design PD resources that would engage teachers in project- and inquiry-based learning activities and would also support increased student achievement. We believe that teachers have to experience inquiry as learners themselves in order to successfully scaffold inquiry into their classrooms, so we structured each PD module using the inquiry stages (ask, investigate, synthesize/create, and reflect/revise). All modules and inquiry stages are designed to help teachers:

- Build knowledge—Teachers review module content, engage in primary investigations, watch videos, read relevant articles, contribute to wikis, etc.

- Engage with ideas—Within modules, teachers experiment with, play, utilize, and share various tools and simulations with one another and with students.
- Collaborate online—Teachers use different tech tools and social media applications, such as Skype or blogging, to collaborate with international classrooms and with other educators in the VIF community.
- Plan with grade-level teams—Peer collaboration is inherent to VIF's PD approach as team planning encourages teacher expertise to be shared and builds community across grade levels.
- Demonstrate new knowledge—Teachers create original, global lesson plans based on module learning and demonstrate implementation of original lessons, new techniques, and global knowledge in their classrooms by submitting evidence, such as student learning products.
- Reflect and share—Teachers post reflections based on lesson implementation, initiate and participate in themed discussions, and share their original lessons with other educators in the VIF community.

Design

As mentioned earlier, in 2011 VIF was working through a Moodle LMS to support our community of international and domestic teachers. Our online portal enabled us to deliver ongoing professional development, but we still lacked an effective vehicle for our exchange teachers to share PD accomplishments with potential employers when they returned to their home countries. In addition, the growth of our teacher community and our desire for increased interaction among teachers had begun to outpace what could easily be managed through the Moodle LMS.

To better support our increasing community of educators, we decided to move away from Moodle because it limited peer collaboration and severely constrained the sharing of content created by both teachers and VIF curriculum designers. Moodle's LMS seems to best fit a higher education model in which students engage with designated content, participate in discussion forum with peers, and then submit work for a grade. As a tool, it was not ideal for teachers who, as learners, needed access to one another above all else. In addition, school districts were increasingly seeking out ways to support global education and innovation initiatives in their schools, and we were motivated to position VIF as a strong resource for those efforts.

After two years of implementing online professional development using Moodle, it was clear that we needed an open platform that would support our main goals:

- Foster participation in a vibrant, online community that incorporates the sharing elements of social media platforms such as Facebook and Twitter.

- Continuously enhance our professional development resources to support mastery in inquiry-based instructional design among adult learners and promote collaboration among professional peers.
- Provide access to a resource library that houses dynamic global content created by both VIF curriculum designers and teachers we support.
- Create an online platform robust enough to support a rapidly growing community of educators.

In the spring of 2013, VIF's product development and curriculum design teams were considering open-source resources such as Wordpress and Drupal for the new platform. However, VIF's expertise remained in global education and professional development—we simply were not a technology company. To successfully develop a new platform, we needed a resource that was accessible to and usable by many non-technical content developers. Though Drupal offered the most dynamic set of tools, we decided to use Joomla, which allowed for rapid development and design through its Jomsocial plug-ins. Joomla also fit our desired open-source criteria and was the most approachable option for our non-technical team members. Our badging system, which we had initially envisioned for a Moodle LMS, was instead designed for Joomla.

VIF's Professional Development Curriculum and Digital Badging

The aim of VIF's professional development curriculum is to support teachers in developing expertise in interdisciplinary and inquiry-based classroom instruction that continuously incorporates relevant and age-appropriate global concepts. Through VIF's PD modules, teachers build knowledge around specific content areas and instructional practices—individually and/or with their grade-level teams—and then share applications of new knowledge with other educators through the online community.

Tailored PD pathways have been designed for dual language immersion, ESL, and traditional teachers at every grade level; all of the pathways include extensive opportunities for peer collaborations, and all of the resources help gradually build teachers' global competence. Four successive modules make up a "year" of a professional learning progression with up to four years offered for each PD pathway. For example, Figure 22.1 outlines modules and badges for Years 1 and 2 of PD for traditional K-5 teachers.

VIF's badging system was deliberately designed to represent teachers' progress through their PD pathways and to reflect the ongoing nature of developing global competence. Every PD module includes multiple steps, so successful completion of a module requires a teacher to study module content, participate in a focused discussion with peers working on the same module, create an original inquiry-based global lesson plan that incorporates new learning, implement the

K–5 Year 1

///

Module 1: Globalizing Your Classroom

Globalizing Your Classroom explores opportunities to develop citizenship and global competence among students. Globalizing strategies combine with inquiry-based instructional approaches to enhance teaching along curricular standards.

Module 2: Culture in the Classroom

Culture in Your Classroom reveals that expectations in a school differ from those of international peers. Teachers will understand the role of culture in classroom relationships to leverage diversity of grade-level teams and students.

Module 3: Beyond Your Classroom

Beyond Your Classroom expands familiarity with technology use in class, including development of competencies around specific technical resources such as synchronous video chat (e.g., Skype).

Module 4: Blogging in Your Classroom

Blogging in Your Classroom continues the focus on digital training by sharing the instructional impact of classroom blogs and specific uses for blogs in classroom settings.

K–5 Year 2

///

Module 1: Intercultural Competence Inquiry

Intercultural Competence Inquiry focuses on three important components of intercultural competence: attitudes, knowledge and skills. Teachers develop intercultural competence and explore how it can be woven into curriculum.

Module 2: Global Interdependence Inquiry

In this module, you will explore how global trends and challenges have an impact on your local community. The module also references global trends, issues, and international organizations that provide institutional structures for engaging global challenges.

Module 3: Internet and Society

Internet and Society highlights the importance of critical thinking in relation to the Internet and the benefits of the Internet as a global phenomenon with significant socio-cultural impacts.

Module 4: Mapping the Local and the Global

Mapping the Local and the Global encourages critical approaches to data how it may affect students' world views. Teachers investigate online mapping tools while using international trends to enhance data skills and learning.

FIGURE 22.1   VIF modules and badges for Years 1 and 2 of PD for traditional K-5 teachers.

original lesson plan in the classroom, provide evidence of classroom implementation, and reflect on and revise the lesson created. The final product of every PD module is a tested, global lesson plan that articulates learning objectives, activities, assessments, and resources for each stage of inquiry. Upon completion, teachers may publish their finalized lessons in the VIF resource library where they can be accessed by other educators.

Completion of each PD module equates to 10 hours of professional development for which teachers receive a digital badge. Digital badges accumulate in educators' online profiles, can be shared via social media, and are easily acknowledged by districts and states. Upon completion of four successive modules, teachers receive year-end badges that signal their growing expertise as global educators and provide evidence of their participation in PD to cultivate skills for teaching with global perspectives and using twenty-first-century tools (see Figure 22.2). By Year 4, teachers are required to complete action research projects and will have completed 160 hours of inquiry-based PD in order to receive the Global-Ready Distinguished Teacher badge.

We are currently designing advanced Year 5 modules (and associated badges) that will provide opportunities for our most experienced educators to build and

Year-end badge progression toward global competence

Year 1: Global-Ready Developing Teacher

Teachers demonstrate basic knowledge, skills and abilities required to integrate globalizing strategies and inquiry instructional approaches in the classroom.

Year 2: Global-Ready Proficient Teacher

Teachers demonstrate growth in their competence to integrate global learning into their classrooms and to have meaningful conversations around sensitive cultural and global issues with their students.

Year 3: Global-Ready Accomplished Teacher

Teachers demonstrate strong competence in efficiently integrating inquiry-based, student-led global investigations into classroom learning. Teachers' instructional practices include skillfully guided conversations around intercultural competence, global interdependence and local-global interconnections, all in the context of standards-based teaching.

Year 4: Global-Ready Distinguished Teacher

Teachers demonstrate strong competence in designing and implementing Action Research Projects based on critical reflections of their own global education teaching practices. Teachers exhibit important skills and knowledge of strategies for collecting, analyzing, summarizing their data, as well as communicating their findings with larger education communities.

FIGURE 22.2 In progressing through VIF PD, educators cultivate skills for teaching with global perspectives and earn year-end badges for completing sequential modules.

share their expertise through global education leader training in the areas of research, policy, mentorship and training, and curriculum design.

Development

After our decision to build out the VIF PD platform using Joomla, the development team set to work developing a badging process that would support our inquiry model, fulfill design requirements of the Mozilla Open Badges Infrastructure (OBI) and, most importantly, function during the school year that was approaching. Our development team sat in on every Mozilla OBI community call, brainstormed with developers from other learning organizations, and considered badging platforms such as BadgeStack.

Things began falling into place when we realized that we could trigger badges directly from the forms we had embedded into PD modules for lesson plan creation and revision (see Figure 22.3). Teacher-created lesson plans are designed using a Joomla Component called BreezingForms. BreezingForms allows for PHP code to be inserted into the body of a form, within each form field, and before and after a form loads.

For our purposes, the end-product is a lesson plan created in the Joomla Component called K2, which can be published by a teacher from his or her profile. In addition to a K2 item, submission of a lesson plan form also creates a BreezingForm archive record, a reference record, and a badge assertion. The lesson plan form for each module contains a set of data fields. Some of these fields are visible to teachers and some are hidden. Visible fields capture data entered by teachers (e.g., lesson descriptions, grade levels, regions of study) and hidden fields either hold pre-set, hard-coded values or capture dynamic values based on MySQL queries.

Before each lesson plan form loads, a PHP code snippet runs to retrieve values for specific hidden form fields. After a teacher has completed a lesson plan form and clicks on the submit button, two additional code snippets run to make an update to the database and to check to see if the teacher has successfully earned a badge. Immediately following submission of each lesson plan, several "Integrators" also run (see Figure 22.4). Integrators are configured to insert or update specific database tables, with data contained in the form.

One of our main design and product delivery challenges was, and continues to be, that teachers using VIF's platform are actively completing PD modules throughout the school year, which is nine months of the year. Consequently, we only have about three months a year when teachers are somewhat inactive on the platform. Our rapid prototype process focuses on enhancing features and we deploy a monthly sprint cycle to update, add, remove, and/or change features. Larger structural changes and updates are made incrementally and completed on a 10-month cycle.

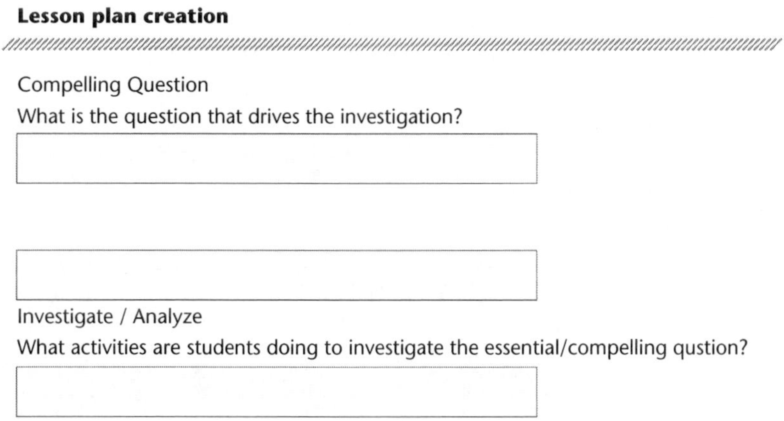

Lesson plan creation

Compelling Question
What is the question that drives the investigation?

Investigate / Analyze
What activities are students doing to investigate the essential/compelling qustion?

FIGURE 22.3 Embedded forms guide teachers through lesson plan creation and revision within VIF PD modules.

Lesson plan creation – badging process

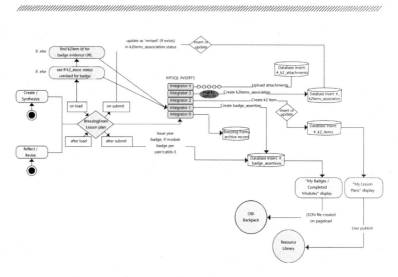

FIGURE 22.4   Following submission of each lesson plan, integrators configured to insert or update specific database tables are run.

Implementation

To prepare our educator community for the badging system we were developing, we created and disseminated an array of synchronous and asynchronous training content. All participating teachers were offered multiple ways to gain more information on what was coming, including through webinars, instructional videos, informal Google Hangout and/or Skype meetings and, in some cases, face-to-face training sessions. VIF's badging system became fully functional in January 2014. As of September 2015, 6,781 module badges and more than 2,100 year-end badges have been earned by teachers in the VIF platform.

As mentioned earlier, badges are triggered only after teachers have implemented their original lessons, attached artifacts of student learning, and revised lessons based on their classroom implementation experiences. While they are useful demonstrations of teacher learning and classroom implementation, lesson plans are generally a pretty narrow view of the work teachers do to impart information to students. And, of course, some teachers are excellent curriculum writers, while some include only basic details in their lesson plans. Our badging process is currently not designed to distinguish between the variations in lesson detail and quality inherent to a large population of teachers. That said, VIF's goal as a PD provider is not to mold teachers into curriculum writers; rather, it is to support them as they continue developing their instructional practices and build their global competence. We are currently working to differentiate products created as a result of doing our PD so that teachers have a choice in how they present knowledge and expertise gained through our modules.

A report published by the Badges Design Principles Documentation Project at Indiana University's Center for Research on Learning and Technology describes four design principles for badging systems: recognizing, assessing, motivating, and studying learning (Hickey et al., 2014, p. 5). So far, the most successful feature of our badging system has been the recognition and validation it has received from participating school districts. Each module badge is equivalent to 10 hours of professional development, which equates to one continuing education credit in most districts. We find that district and school administrators embrace digital badging because it provides visibility into their teachers' professional development activities.

In addition, North Carolina launched the first statewide recognition for global-ready teachers, the Global Educator Digital Badge, due in part to policy initiatives driven by VIF. This state-recognized micro-credential acknowledges the accomplishments of teachers committed to global competence, and PD completed through VIF's platform qualifies teachers for the recognition. Efforts to formalize the importance of global education at district and state levels are growing. The Houston Independent School District is creating an initiative to offer every student in Houston access to dual language immersion and/or global education programs. District leaders are collaborating with VIF to establish a digital badging system that will support the teacher training aspect of the initiative, trigger additional professional opportunities, and support career advancement based on demonstrated global expertise in the classroom.

Evaluation

In the spring of 2014, we conducted ongoing formative evaluations of the VIF platform, its PD resources, and badging process that included online surveys, focus groups, and classroom observations. According to the evaluations, teachers were starting to see the value of digital badges, but were still unsure of their professional applications (see Figure 22.5). It was clear that the overall lack of familiarity with digital badging was affecting teachers' use of badges outside of the platform and their immediate school contexts. Specifically, teachers were not utilizing access to Mozilla Backpack, which enables sharing of digital credentials across multiple sites. We realized that digital badging presumes a level of self-promotion in which few teachers regularly engage.

The timing of our rollout of the new badging system created some automatic challenges. January is the middle of the school year, and introducing the concept of badging and working with teachers to make it relevant to their PD pathways at that time essentially felt like creating more work for them. We know from experience that teacher schedules are often constrained, so their attention to additional training on top of what they were already doing for PD was limited. Improved communication and implementation approaches, and clearer district initiatives, were put in place for the 2014–15 school year to address these challenges. As a result, teachers started their school year with a better understanding of the

Professional application of badges

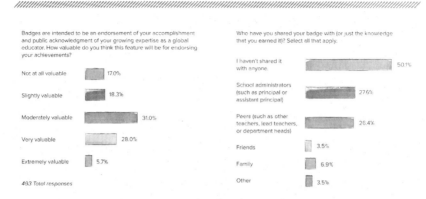

Badges are intended to be an endorsement of your accomplishment and public acknowledgment of your growing expertise as a global educator. How valuable do you think this feature will be for endorsing your achievements?

Not at all valuable — 17.0%

Slightly valuable — 18.3%

Moderately valuable — 31.0%

Very valuable — 28.0%

Extremely valuable — 5.7%

493 Total responses

Who have you shared your badge with (or just the knowledge that you earned it)? Select all that apply.

I haven't shared it with anyone. — 50.1%

School administrators (such as principal or assistant principal) — 27.6%

Peers (such as other teachers, lead teachers, or department heads) — 26.4%

Friends — 3.5%

Family — 6.9%

Other — 3.5%

FIGURE 22.5 Evaluation data shows that teachers were starting to see the value of digital badges but were still unsure of their professional applications.

benefits of digital badges in signaling PD completion, which directly translates into continuing education credit from their districts.

VIF's digital badging system has received overwhelming support from school and district administrators who track badges as evidence of teacher progress through PD. As we created our badging system, we maintained attention to the interoperability between our platform and data systems, which allowed us to take advantage of the increased analytics that digital badging provides. We enabled a sync between Joomla and Salesforce (the customer relationship management system that maintains all of our teacher and partner data) that provides valuable insights into how and whether teachers engage in VIF's PD or online community and allows us to produce tailored reports on PD progress for teachers and school and district administrators.

However, we want to be vigilant to protect our badging system from serving as a punitive accountability system used against teachers. While we were successful in creating buy-in for digital badging, we now need to make the process more dynamic than just serving as a metric for PD completion. We aim for VIF's badging system to drive the learning process for educators and not just celebrate the PD products they create.

Conclusion

Our digital badging system has become a critical component of VIF's PD platform. Designing a successful badging system forced our team—comprising program developers, curriculum writers, researchers and teacher educators—to identify, explore, discuss, argue about, create, and build value for a new approach to recognizing professional learning among educators. Our badging system also strengthened the infrastructure and effectiveness of our entire PD platform because it forced us to examine how inquiry could be scaffolded online and how teachers could be engaged in open-ended investigations.

Our badging system's biggest success has been its recognition for validating teachers' learning achievements by school districts and state boards of education. This success has also raised interesting questions and challenges. On one hand, it reflects our unique relationships with K-12 institutions and the effectiveness of our PD resources in supporting the goals of our partner schools and districts. On the other hand, it has the potential to create a tension between teachers' desire to become globally competent and districts' demand for the completion of PD. As explained by the Badges Design Principles Documentation Project, "the broader ecosystem constrains the learning that badges can be used to recognize. Recognition practices, in turn, constrain assessment practices; recognition and assessment practices together serve to impact motivation" (Hickey et al., 2014, p. 6).

PD for educators who represent and are trying to build understanding of diverse cultural contexts requires opportunities that build skills, provide support for experimentation and creation, and utilize social media technologies to position knowledge building as a social and cultural practice. We see our PD platform as an evolving environment that supports personalized and differentiated PD pathways while simultaneously providing a trusted, professional learning community that enables the sharing of ideas and practices.

We believe digital badging can be an important component of participatory PD that serves as a "model of knowledge circulation" to encourage teachers to share and build expertise with peers (Reilly & Literat, 2012). Celebrating expertise developed through inventive and flexible learning communities may foster teachers' ownership of their professional pathways. To further operationalize tailored professional pathways for teachers, our next stage of development will focus on building a peer-review system that incorporates robust peer and formative feedback cycles into the PD process to fully harness the powerful, collective intelligence of our international educator community. The success we've had with digital badging has motivated us to leverage existing educational systems to innovate and change approaches to professional learning for educators.

References

Hickey, D., Otto, N., Itow, R., Schenke, K., Tran, C., & Chow, C. (2014). Interim report. *Badges design principles documentation project.* Center for Research on Learning and Technology: Indiana University.

Reilly, E., & Literat, I. (2012). *Designing with teachers: Participatory approaches to professional development in education.* Annenberg Innovation Lab: University of Southern California. Retrieved from http://tinyurl.com/mh9x2fl.

VIF International Education (2015). *VIF's learning center.* Retrieved from www.viflearn.com.

23

DIGITAL BADGES AS A MOTIVATOR IN MOOCS

The Carpe Diem MOOC Experience

Kulari Lokuge Dona, Janet Gregory, and Ekaterina Pechenkina

Case Overview

This case study discusses the design and implementation of digital badges in the Carpe Diem Massive Open Online Course (CD MOOC) offered by Swinburne University of Technology, Melbourne, in March and April of 2014. Digital badges were integrated into the CD MOOC to enhance participants' motivation and engagement with the material and learning processes by offering rewards linked to the key milestones in the MOOC. Badges also assisted in streamlining the knowledge verification process as participants had to complete assessment tasks and earn intermediary badges to qualify for the completion award—a Mozilla Open Badge.

Our study adds to the body of research dedicated to online learning, specifically in MOOCs aimed at specialized learner cohorts. As the CD MOOC was focused on learning design, it was likely that participants would be predominantly educators interested in online learning design. Hence, digital badges in the CD MOOC acted both as an extrinsic motivator and as a tool that participants could explore from a student's perspective and potentially apply in their own practice. Our research demonstrates that many participants became motivated by badges, even if they were initially skeptical of the value of badging. This attitudinal shift in participants' perception of badges demonstrated the value of educators experiencing badging from a student's perspective.

The CD MOOC introduced participants to the Carpe Diem learning design process (Salmon, 2013), which consists of six stages: write a blueprint, make a storyboard, build a prototype online, check reality, review and adjust, and plan your next steps (Salmon & Wright, 2014). As the Carpe Diem learning design process is usually conducted in a face-to-face environment, one of our key challenges was to design and deliver this team-based model in a MOOC environment. We focused on ways to encourage participants to stay motivated and work together in completing the stages in the Carpe Diem learning design process. The importance of keeping students motivated (Brown, Armstrong, & Thompson, 2014; Clark, Howard, & Early, 2006; De Castella, Byrne, & Covington, 2013) becomes more salient in MOOCs where individualized student support is not feasible due to mass participation and limited staff resources. With MOOCs having a low entry barrier and no dropout penalties, it becomes easier for students to decide to leave (Yang, Sinha, Adamson, & Rose, 2013), as typical MOOC completion statistics show (Clow, 2013; Jordan, 2014; Kolowich, 2013). Research into student participation in MOOCs further argues that MOOCs are unlikely to "provide the kind of social environment that is conducive to sustained communities" (Yang, Sinha, Adamson, & Rose, 2013, p. 1); hence, aspects such as students' personal attributes, readiness levels, and prior academic experiences may dictate how students' participation trajectories unfold.

Digital badges can be utilized to incentivize desired student behaviors, especially when linked to concrete achievements (Gibson, Ostashewki, Flintoff, Grant, & Knight, 2013; McDaniel, Lindgren, & Friskics, 2012). As well as motivating learners, badges can inspire competitiveness (Glover, 2013), recognize achievement (Frederiksen, 2013), and act as credentials and digital currency (Bowen & Thomas, 2014; Gibson et al., 2013). There are also reported successes with badging used to motivate cohorts of mature-age students (Banner, Caldwell, & Monroe, 2014; Finkelstein, Knight, & Manning, 2013, July), and in professional development MOOCs aimed at educators (Gamrat, Zimmerman, Dudek, & Peck, 2014; Schmidt-Crawford, Thompson, & Lindstrom, 2014)—successes that we hoped to build on in the CD MOOC.

We expected the CD MOOC to attract large numbers of educators and learning designers. Consequently, our design efforts in relation to the badges in the CD MOOC were shaped by this expectation. We intended for the badges to enhance participants' extrinsic motivation, help them track their progress, reward them for mastering the key stages of the Carpe Diem learning design process, and encourage them to gain digital credentials as evidence of what they had learned. Due to the specific composition of the CD MOOC cohort, we also had an opportunity to observe how educators engaged with badges, and whether they were inspired to use badges in their own teaching practice.

Badges were awarded each week, with the exception of the first week, for the completion of specific activities. Each week's activities were aligned with the stages of the Carpe Diem learning design process (Figure 23.1).

Badges for Weeks 2, 3, and 6 were awarded for submission of completed work with no evaluation of content. For the more complex tasks covered in Weeks 4 and 5, submitted work was assessed by the CD MOOC facilitators, who were responsible for deeming the work competent prior to awarding the badge. The final Mozilla Open Badge was only awarded to participants who had earned the previous five badges, therefore acting as an equivalent to a certificate of

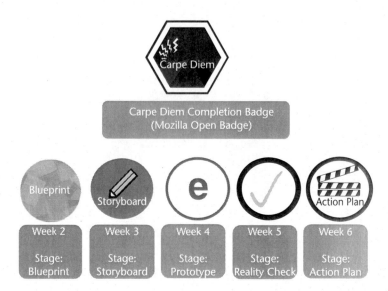

FIGURE 23.1 Carpe Diem MOOC badge design.

completion. It could be immediately displayed in a wide range of participants' online spaces, such as LinkedIn and blogs.

Free online materials and expert advice (Knight & The Mozilla Foundation, 2012; The Mozilla Foundation, Peer 2 Peer University, & The MacArthur Foundation, 2012) offered via Badge Alliance, CourseSites, and Mozilla Open Badge websites, among others, helped us consider the pros and cons of badging prior to introducing badges into the CD MOOC. In developing the badges, we also utilized the resources and workshops provided by HASTAC (2015), the Badge Alliance (2014), Mozilla Open Badges (2015), and MacArthur Foundation (2013).

For the CD MOOC badges, we considered three badge issuing platforms: Credly, Open Badge Designer, and Blackboard. The choice of a system for implementing the CD MOOC digital badges was guided by our preference for a platform that would allow us to create customized badges representative of the key stages in the Carpe Diem learning design process. Another consideration was for a system allowing the use of internal awards as well as integration of an Open Badge. While designing the CD MOOC, Blackboard's free Learning Management System (LMS) CourseSites began offering an internal badge system compatible with the Mozilla Open Badge platform. This enabled a seamless process for issuing badges, preventing the manual entry of badge-related data. The compatibility of the CourseSites' internal badge system with the Mozilla Open Badge platform was a key benefit for us as it allowed participants to export the CD MOOC completion badge to Mozilla Backpack (backpack .openbadges.org).

Analysis

The Carpe Diem learning design process has been successfully utilized with educators for more than 10 years (Salmon, 2013; Salmon, Jones, & Armellini, 2008; Salmon & Wright, 2014), providing us with a well-developed model to tailor for our MOOC cohort. Based on the pedagogical principles of scaffolding of knowledge and learning in groups, the Carpe Diem learning design process at the core of the CD MOOC translated into the experience of learning in teams online. Embedded into the CD MOOC's learning design, digital badges served as an effective formative assessment process and also an extrinsic motivator for participants.

Some of the important considerations for us were the composition of the CD MOOC cohort and their motivations for completing the CD MOOC. As our earlier research (Salmon, Gregory, Lokuge Dona, & Ross, 2015) demonstrates, the primary reasons for doing the CD MOOC were professional development and acquisition of new skills in online education. However, in line with the typical issues of high dropout rates and disengaged learners, known as "lurkers" (Cao, 2014; Hew & Cheung, 2014), we also expected that many CD MOOC participants would not engage with the material and tasks at the same level as in a certified course. We hoped badges would enhance participants' existing motivation to learn about the Carpe Diem learning design process and ultimately improve completion outcomes.

Design

The ability to award internal badges and easily export them into Mozilla Backpack was a key factor in choosing the CourseSites LMS for the CD MOOC. Furthermore, being able to upload pre-designed badge graphics into CourseSites enabled the badges to visually represent the six stages of the Carpe Diem learning design process. The customized badges were designed using Photoshop and Adobe InDesign.

To facilitate badge design, development, and implementation, we adopted the Rapid Application Development (RAD) process (Beynon-Davies & Holmes, 2002) and agile management techniques (Boyle et al., 2006; Conforto & Capaldo Amaral, 2010). This included agile walls, meetings, workflows, boards, and resources allocation. To test the methods and assumptions of the design and implementation of the CD MOOC badges within CourseSites, feedback was sought from colleagues with relevant expertise. This feedback demonstrated the need to clearly explain the concept and value of badges to both MOOC facilitators and participants. It also highlighted the importance of providing clear instructions for submitting assignments to gain badges. Once the CD MOOC badges were implemented in the LMS, we established badge award criteria within CourseSites. The final Mozilla Open Badge was offered by Swinburne without an expiration date.

Development

The badges were tested in several rapid development cycles. During the initial iteration, one badge (Prototype activity) was created by the MOOC designers before it was presented to the CD MOOC team for feedback. Based on this feedback, the rest of the badges were designed and offered to Swinburne staff within our unit to review. Staff were asked to comment on the look and feel of the badges and report on how they perceived these badges. In its next iteration, the CD MOOC badges were presented for feedback to a team that consisted of learning designers, Carpe Diem experts, and other education specialists both within and external to Swinburne. In its final iteration, the badges were reviewed by the technologists supporting the MOOC. The technologists conducted a final review of the design, achievement criteria, meta-data component of the final badge, and other critical aspects of the badging process. At this stage, we also developed resources on how to earn and export badges into Mozilla Backpack to familiarize CD MOOC participants with badging.

The iterations suggested several areas for improvement. For instance, in relation to the badges' "look and feel," pilot participants identified some color schemes as more attractive and engaging than others. In particular, the color green was preferred to purple and yellow, a finding supported by literature locating cold colors (such as green) as more calming and comfortable compared to warm colors (AL-Ayash, Kane, Smith, & Green-Armytage, 2015). To accommodate this feedback, two of the CD MOOC badges (awarded for completion of Prototype and Reality Check activities, respectively) were designed in green. Furthermore, in line with research correlating streamlined round shapes with positive emotions (Plass, Heidig, Hayward, Homer, & Um, 2013), all of the badges were designed as circles with the exception of the final Mozilla Open Badge, which was a hexagon.

Finally, badge metadata and award criteria were identified as areas in need of clarification. To address this issue, we included information about the badge issuing authority (Swinburne) and badge award criteria and requirements into the badge metadata.

Implementation

After the RAD iterations, the CD MOOC badges were implemented in CourseSites, and resources on how to earn badges were created and linked to the course. The CD MOOC team comprised seven facilitators and two technical support staff. Most facilitators participated in the pilot and had a good understanding of the badges prior to the CD MOOC commencing. By the time the

CD MOOC started, the facilitators' key role in regards to badging was to raise awareness and encourage participants to earn badges.

As stated, the majority of the CD MOOC participants were educators and most of them had prior experience using an LMS, such as Blackboard or Moodle, and many had prior MOOC experience. Nearly half (45 percent) of the interviewees in our research had participated in a MOOC prior to the CD MOOC, and 27.6 percent had either designed or conducted a MOOC themselves. However, our research suggested that participants' experience with digital badging was limited. To address this knowledge gap, participants were directed to the *Earn a Badge* section of the CourseSites CD MOOC. Despite the instructions, many participants had difficulties exporting badges into Mozilla Backpack as this required a higher level of technical knowledge; therefore, additional instructions and support were provided through a virtual classroom, Blackboard Collaborate.

Technical challenges encountered during the implementation process included working around the changes in Mozilla's Application Programing Interface (API), which hindered our ability to use Blackboard's own Open Badges. Alternative solutions were developed, and after working closely with the CourseSites team, who were made aware of our badging requirements, the necessary changes were introduced, enabling us to offer Mozilla Open Badges through CourseSites.

Evaluation

The CD MOOC commenced with 1,029 participants, with 31 percent of those earning the first badge offered and 17 percent earning all badges, including the final Mozilla Open Badge. Research was conducted to evaluate various aspects of the CD MOOC (Lokuge Dona, Gregory, Salmon, & Pechenkina, 2014; Salmon et al., 2015), with 155 participants completing an online questionnaire and 29 of these participating in a phone interview. Participants' responses demonstrated the overall interest that the CD MOOC badges generated, with 74 percent of questionnaire respondents reporting that they either strongly agreed or agreed with the statement "I enjoyed being able to earn badges," with only 7 percent disagreeing.

Our evaluation research demonstrated that the weekly badges acted as an additional motivator to achieve the weekly tasks for some of the CD MOOC participants. By earning badges, participants not only engaged with the CD MOOC content and materials, but also became more invested in learning and applying what they learned. This would not have been as easily achieved by simply offering a final badge for completion, and excluding intermediary rewards along the way (Ahn, Pellicone, & Butler, 2014).

An important reason the badges worked well in the CD MOOC was that they were designed as part of the CD MOOC's learning design process and were linked to the mastery of the Carpe Diem learning design process stages, so their purpose was clear to participants. However, it is the shift in participants' attitudes towards the badges, as data evidences, that is of particular interest to us. By experiencing digital badges firsthand as online students, some CD MOOC participants became interested in badges to the point of competitiveness, even if they initially were skeptical. One interview participant who was at first "rather skeptical about badges" then "noticed that [badges] had motivated [him] to study." Another interview participant was also "a bit skeptical about badges but [...] was really pleased to be picking them up," and even admitted to feeling "very anxious" thinking he was not going to get the final badge. He found his own response unexpected as his initial reaction to badges was that they were "a bit of a laugh," but over the course of the CD MOOC, he found "something motivating about them." In addition to motivation, some stressed the competitive aspect of earning the badges. As one interview participant stated:

> I think we all have this kind of competitive streak in us, and also ... we want to be rewarded—it is a basic psychological need, and there is a satisfaction in the knowledge that you are actually going well [*sic*] and that's a confirmation of that.

Participants also appreciated badges as a means of keeping track of completed and submitted work. An interesting and unexpected outcome was that participants contacted the facilitators to inquire when they would receive their badges for the evaluated activities in Weeks 4 and 5. As these submissions required assessment, badges were not issued immediately, leaving some participants concerned. This was another indicator of participants' interest in achieving badges.

The acquisition of badges in the CD MOOC was an individual pursuit; however, a number of interview participants felt that a "Group Badge" awarded specifically for group participation would be appropriate in future iterations of the CD MOOC. One interview participant suggested that a group badge "might have kept us a bit closer together ... It might have given us some focus if we thought we were working towards something as a team."

The finding that the majority of the questionnaire respondents (72 percent) would use badges in their teaching practice further strengthens the point that when used holistically within the learning design process, badges have a capacity to work not only as a personal motivator, but also as a technique educators can apply in practice. A participant who was ambivalent about badges stated that, to him, traditional rewards like physical copies of certificates were more attractive than digital badges. However, he felt that his students would be more appreciative of badges, which he explained as a generational gap, believing that a young generation of learners might feel differently about badges. Generally, participants were of the view that for the badges to work, and work well, they had to be attached to a reward system that was integrated with the learning design of the course.

As our evaluation process confirmed, the nature of the CD MOOC participants as educators themselves drove their special interest in the Carpe Diem learning design process and in badging. Badges, hence, were perceived not only as personal motivators, but also as a technique to apply in one's own practice. Some participants were surprised at how motivated they became by the possibility of earning badges, while others were interested in badges as a practical tool to use with their own students (Lokuge Dona et al., 2014). This attitude shift is of importance as it demonstrates how participants are affected by experiential learning (Gregory & Salmon, 2013), that is, by experiencing the role of a student firsthand and having an opportunity to consider the implications of this experience for their own practice.

In alignment with our future research into the Carpe Diem learning design process and the pedagogical frameworks guiding its delivery to academics, we intend to use our badging experience to improve future iterations of the CD MOOC. A group badge is one consideration, as it might improve collaboration outcomes and encourage group work. Future linking of the CD MOOC badges with badges being introduced into the Graduate Certificate of Learning and Teaching—Higher Education (GCLT-HE) offered by Swinburne will further enhance the existing badge ecology we have developed. This will also link the CD MOOC with the GCLT-HE and overall strengthen the professional development aspect of the process.

Conclusions

Aligning the badges with the stages of the Carpe Diem learning design process resulted in predominantly positive responses by participants, as well as interest in adopting badges in their teaching practice. Presenting the participants with a chance to experience badging and the online learning process as students meant they could gain a student's perspective and critically reflect on their own teaching practices. To successfully deploy badges in a MOOC, it is imperative to consider who the participants will be, their professional level, and motivations for participating.

Approximately half of the interviewed CD MOOC participants felt motivated, or at least intrigued, by the badges, while the other half maintained a level of skepticism, mostly citing their age and professional experience as reasons they felt badges did not influence their decision of whether to continue with the CD MOOC or not. However, all of the participants were interested in the concept of badges as something they could apply in their own teaching practice. Even those who were skeptical of badges admitted they might consider badging as credentialing and a motivating technique in their teaching practice.

The CD MOOC experience confirmed our view that badges need to be embedded as part of the learning design process and not added as an afterthought. It also demonstrated the value of providing opportunity for educators to experience badges as a tool to use in their own practice to motivate learners.

References

Ahn, J., Pellicone, A., & Butler, B. S. (2014). Open badges for education: What are the implications at the intersection of open systems and badging? *Research in Learning Technology, 22.* doi:http://dx.doi.org/10.3402/rlt.v22.23563.

AL-Ayash, A., Kane, R. T., Smith, D., & Green-Armytage, P. (2015). The influence of color on student emotion, heart rate, and performance in learning environments. *Color Research and Application.* doi: 10.1002/col.21949.

Badge Alliance (2014). Working Groups. Retrieved from www.badgealliance.org/.

Banner, D., Caldwell, K., & Monroe, L. (2014). Digital badging: A promising distance education trend. Retrieved from www.dianebanner.com/uploads/4/0/0/8/40085297/643-final_dbing_paper_-banner_caldwell_monroe5_12_14.pdf.

Beynon-Davies, P., & Holmes, S. (2002). Design breakdowns, scenarios and rapid application development. *Information and Software Technology, 44*(10), 579–592. doi: 10.1016/S0950-5849(02)00078-2.

Bowen, K., & Thomas, A. (2014). Badges: A common currency for learning. *Change: The Magazine of Higher Learning, 46*(1), 21–25. doi: 10.1080/00091383.2014.867206.

Boyle, T., Cook, J., Windle, R., Wharrad, H., Leeder, D., & Alton, R. (2006, December). *An agile method for developing learning objects.* Paper presented at the Twenty-third Ascilite Conference, Sydney, Australia.

Brown, S., Armstrong, S., & Thompson, G. (Eds.). (2014). *Motivating students.* Abingdon, London: Routledge.

Cao, M. (2014). *Understanding learners' experience in MOOCs: A review of literature.* Doctoral dissertation. The University of Texas Digital Repository.

Clark, R. E., Howard, K., & Early, S. (2006). Motivational challenges experience in highly complex learning environments. In J. Elen & R. E. Clark (Eds.), *Handling complexity in learning environments: Theory and research* (pp. 27–43). Oxford: Elsevier.

Clow, D. (2013). MOOCs and the funnel of participation. *Proceedings of the Third International Conference on Learning Analytics and Knowledge,* Belgium, 185–189. doi: 10.1145/2460296.2460332.

Conforto, E. C., & Capaldo Amaral, D. (2010). Evaluating an agile method for planning and controlling innovative project. *Project Management Journal, 41*(2), 73–80. doi: 10.1002/pmj.2008.

De Castella, K., Byrne, D., & Covington, M. (2013). Unmotivated or motivated to fail? A cross-cultural study of achievement motivation, fear of failure, and student disengagement. *Journal of Educational Psychology, 105*(3), 861–880. doi: 10.1037/a0032464.

Finkelstein, J., Knight, E., & Manning, S. (2013, July). Digital badges for adult learners: The potential and value of using digital badges for adult learners: Draft for public comment. Retrieved from https://lincs.ed.gov/publications/pdf/AIR_Digital_Badge_Report_508.pdf.

Frederiksen, L. (2013). Digital badges. *Public Services Quarterly, 9*(4), 321–325. doi: 10.1080/15228959.2013.842414.

Gamrat, C., Zimmerman, T. H., Dudek, J., & Peck, K. (2014). Personalized workplace learning: An exploratory study on digital badging within a teacher professional development program. *British Journal of Educational Technology, 45*(6), 1136–1148. doi: 10.1111/bjet.12200.

Gibson, D., Ostashewski, N., Flintoff, K., Grant, S., & Knight, E. (2013). Digital badges in education. *Education and Information Technologies.* doi: 10.1007/s10639-013-9291-7.

Glover, I. (2013). Play as you learn: Gamification as a technique for motivating learners. In J. Herrington, A. Couros, & V. Irvine (Eds.), *Proceedings of World Conference on Educational Multimedia, Hypermedia and Telecommunications 2013*. Chesapeake, VA, (pp. 1999–2008). Retrieved from http://shura.shu.ac.uk/7172/.

Gregory, J., & Salmon, G. (2013). Professional development for online university teaching. *Distance Education, 34*(3), 256–270. doi:10.1080/01587919.2013.835771.

HASTAC (2015). Digital badges. Humanities, HASTAC—Arts, Science, and Technology Alliance and Collaboratory. Retrieved from www.hastac.org/digital-badges.

Hew, K. F., & Cheung, W. S. (2014). Students' and instructors' use of massive open online courses (MOOCs): Motivation and challenges. *Educational Research Review, 12*, 45–58. doi:10.1016/j.edurev.2014.05.001.

Jordan, K. (2014). Initial trends in enrolment and completion of massive open online courses. *The International Review of Research in Open and Distance Learning, 15*(1), 133–160.

Knight, E., & The Mozilla Foundation (2012). RFC: An open, distributed system for badge validation (Working Paper). Retrieved from https://docs.google.com/file/d/0BwJ_PQhV0lJTSnYtQzV5Q0FxNDA/edit.

Kolowich, S. (2013). Coursera takes a nuances view of MOOC dropout rates. *The Chronicle of Higher Education*. Retrieved from http://chronicle.com/blogs/wiredcampus/coursera-takes-a-nuanced-view-of-mooc-dropout-rates/43341.

Lokuge Dona, K., Gregory, J., Salmon, G., & Pechenkina, E. (2014). Badges in the Carpe Diem MOOC. In B. Hegarty, J. McDonald, & S.-K. Loke (Eds.), *Rhetoric and reality: Critical perspectives on educational technology. Proceedings ascilite Dunedin 2014* (pp. 120–128).

MacArthur Foundation (2013). Digital badges. Retrieved from www.macarthur.org/programs/digital-badges/.

McDaniel, R., Lindgren, R., & Friskics, J. (2012). *Using badges for shaping interactions in online learning environments.* Paper presented at the Professional Communication Conference (IPCC), 2012 IEEE International, Orlando, FL.

The Mozilla Foundation, Peer 2 Peer University, & The MacArthur Foundation (2012). Open badges for lifelong learning: Exploring an open badge ecosystem to support skill development and lifelong learning for real results such as jobs and advancement (Working Paper). Retrieved from https://wiki.mozilla.org/images/5/59/OpenBadges-Working-Paper_012312.pdf.

Mozilla Open Badges (2015). Get started issuing open badges. Retrieved from http://openbadges.org/issue/.

Plass, J. L., Heidig, S., Hayward, E. O., Homer, B. D., & Um, E. (2013). Emotional design in multimedia learning: Effects of shape and color on affect and learning. *Learning and Instruction*, 1–13. doi: http://dx.doi.org/10.1016/j.learninstruc.2013.02.006.

Salmon, G. (2013). *E-tivities: The key to active online learning* (2nd ed.). New York, NY: Routledge.

Salmon, G., Gregory, J., Lokuge Dona, K., & Ross, B. (2015). Experiential online development for educators: The example of the Carpe Diem MOOC. *British Journal of Educational Technology*. doi:10.1111/bjet.12256.

Salmon, G., Jones, S., & Armellini, A. (2008). Building institutional capability in e-learning design. *Research in Learning Technology, 16*(2), 95–109. doi: 10.1080/09687760802315978.

Salmon, G., & Wright, P. (2014). Transforming future teaching through "Carpe Diem" learning design. *Education Sciences, 4*(1), 52–63. doi:10.3390/educsci4010052.

Schmidt-Crawford, D., Thompson, A. D., & Lindstrom, D. (2014). Leveling up: Modeling digital badging for preservice teachers. *Journal of Digital Learning in Teacher Education, 30*(4), 111. doi:10.1080/21532974.2014.928180.

Yang, D., Sinha, T., Adamson, D., & Rose, C. P. (2013, December). Turn on, tune in, drop out: Anticipating student dropouts in massive open online courses. *Proceedings of the 2013 NIPS Data-Driven Education Workshop.* Retrieved from http://lytics.stanford.edu/datadriveneducation/papers/yangetal.pdf.

24

LEARNING TECHNOLOGIES BADGES FOR FACULTY PROFESSIONAL DEVELOPMENT

A Case Study

David A. Goodrum, Serdar Abaci, and Anastasia S. Morrone

Universities invest considerable resources in learning technologies in support of the core mission of teaching and learning. They depend on their faculty members to use this technology appropriately to engage with students in academic pursuits. Indiana University (IU), a large public research institution with more than 110,000 students enrolled at eight campuses throughout the state of Indiana, has adopted action items in its latest strategic information technology plan to leverage faculty professional development regarding the effective use of technology for teaching and learning (Empowering People, 2009). Current campus workshops and online training opportunities—though valuable for faculty professional development—generally do not provide convincing evidence of faculty development beyond documenting attendance or completion.

Learning Technologies (LT) badges are offered by University Information Technology Services, in collaboration with IU's teaching academy, the Faculty Colloquium on Excellence in Teaching (FACET). LT badges aspire to provide IU faculty and instructors an improved way of documenting LT competencies that are valued by students, administrators, and higher education. Each digital badge is meant to signify knowledge or expertise around a particular topic at basic, proficient, or advanced levels, with the goal of incrementally bringing faculty to the advanced level. The three levels are presented visually as bronze, silver, and gold digital badges, respectively. Currently in its pilot phase, the LT/FACET Badges program offers faculty digital badges or micro-credentials for three topics: eTexts, Accessibility, and Online Presence. Figure 24.1 shows the three levels of each badge topic.

	Basic (Bronze)	Proficient (Silver)	Advanced (Gold)
eText			
Accessibility			
Online Presence			

FIGURE 24.1 Learning technologies badges are offered at three levels.
© The Trustees of Indiana University.

Badges are awarded upon the successful completion of milestone activities, documented through an evidence-based rubric with emphasis on:

- Furthering best practices of teaching;
- Using available campus resources for teaching and learning;
- Planning and making considerations for implementing a badge topic in an actual course;
- Documenting the results of implementation and refining methods before further course implementation;
- Sharing findings within and beyond the IU community; and
- Conducting a FACET peer review for advanced level badges.

The biggest challenge we have faced is gaining clarity on the intended outcomes—and working back from them to designate specific activities, as well as ways to document them and provide overall support. The technology actually has fewer challenges. So far, we have used both Purdue University's Passport and Accreditrust's BadgeSafe™ to deliver the LT/FACET Badges within Canvas (IU's learning management system), but we continue to evaluate other standards-based badge systems, including new capabilities being added to CourseNetworking. Once added to the site, participating faculty can view the criteria to earn a badge for a given topic, submit materials, track their progress, and publish their earned badges. All platforms under consideration comply with Mozilla Open Badges Infrastructure (OBI) standards, allowing the badge earners to publish badges in Mozilla Backpack. Since badge artifacts are submitted as Microsoft Word documents, faculty can use them for their annual reports and dossiers for tenure and promotion purposes.

Analysis

Regardless of the teaching mode—online, face-to-face, or hybrid—technology is part of the fabric of today's university education. At the very least, universities use a learning management system (LMS). According to a 2013 nationwide survey, all but 4 percent of US higher education institutions have a single, campus-wide LMS, and 62 percent of higher education classes use an LMS to some degree (Green, 2013). IU Bloomington's strategic plan and IT strategic plan both include action items focused on using technology effectively in education (Empowering People, 2009; Campus Strategic Plan, 2014). In order to achieve this goal, IU strives to support incorporation of various learning technologies and best instructional practices in courses.

Generally speaking, most faculty have not had formal training in teaching and often shape their teaching based on their collegiate experiences. Therefore, it is critical to provide visible and usable support to faculty for improving teaching—leveraging academic resources, mentors, or services available. At IU, campus centers for teaching and learning (CTLs) support teaching excellence and faculty professional development. The centers offer workshops, self-paced online modules, one-on-one consultations, learning communities, and grants and initiatives to encourage and equip the faculty with technology skills and instructional strategies. Most faculty users of CTLs attend workshops or use self-paced resources, while a smaller number seek one-on-one consultations. Even fewer faculty participate in learning communities or receive grants, which typically culminate in presentations or publications about changes in their teaching strategies or pedagogies. On the whole, there is a lost opportunity to document and share the professional development activities of most faculty.

Regardless of their position—tenured, tenure-track, lecturer, or adjunct—all teaching faculty at IU must submit reports such as the *Faculty Annual Report* to document their teaching activities each year. In these reports, they include courses taught, student evaluations, and professional development activities such as workshops, faculty learning communities, and so on. However, faculty are left to their own devices in documenting these activities.

The original impetus behind the LT/FACET Badges was that faculty could potentially benefit from a framework that guides them from planning to reflecting to sharing the results of implementing a learning technology and pedagogy designed to enhance student engagement and learning. In choosing initial badge topics, we looked at recent LT initiatives to promote and encourage innovative teaching, such as engaging in online learning, using electronic textbooks (eTexts), and increasing accessibility of courses for all learners. These factors came together in our attempt to offer faculty a systematic way to improve their teaching practice, document their efforts, share their experiences, and gain recognition.

Design

To identify the components of a rigorous digital badge program for faculty professional development, in summer 2013, LT formed a task force that comprised professionals from the campus CTLs, IT training unit, and online learning design and development unit. The task force focused on four design considerations as the project unfolded: (1) evidence for badge completion; (2) hierarchy of badges; (3) badge topics; and (4) rigor of the program.

Evidence for Badge Completion

As with many digital badges for professional development, initial thoughts for the LT Badges program primarily focused on tracking faculty attendance at workshops on teaching with technology. However, upon further reflection, it became clear that our LT badge program should go beyond tracking in order to gain rigor and impact. To model effective pedagogy based on learning theory, we need to support faculty as they learn about and implement these technologies to improve their teaching. At the same time, completing badge requirements should feel natural to the faculty since taking time for professional development is already a struggle with their busy teaching and research schedule.

We designed the evidence for badge completion to document the activities that more naturally occur in professional development for faculty. Teaching a course inherently involves planning, designing and developing materials, instructing during the course, and reflecting on future improvements during and after the course. For teaching-related professional development, faculty may review resources, attend workshops, consult with instructional support centers (e.g., CTLs), share practices and results with colleagues, and submit their course development for teaching awards and publications. With the LT Badges program, we wanted to support participating faculty as they develop and refine their teaching skills while also helping them document these efforts.

Hierarchy of Badges

We designed a three-level badge system to break down the badge completion requirements into sequences that could be completed in a semester or an academic year: basic, proficient, and advanced. The goal of the program is to bring all participants to the advanced level; however, completing all the requirements to earn a single badge might take several semesters. Therefore, a three-level system offers attainable goals along the way and acknowledgment of incremental accomplishments, which is intended to motivate faculty to complete all three levels.

With each level culminating in a key activity, the multiple-badge approach is designed for faculty to both track their progress and to make their work available to colleagues. Badge topics vary, and each badge is associated with topic-specific outcomes. However, the badges share a common framework in terms of expectations for completion of three levels:

- Basic Level (Bronze Badge): Faculty become familiar with the essentials of the topic and how it is supported at IU. They plan to implement it in their teaching, and they receive consultation and formative feedback from campus CTLs on their implementation plans.
- Proficient Level (Silver Badge): Faculty implement the badge topic within an actual course, and then reflect upon and share their experiences and results with their colleagues.
- Advanced Level (Gold Badge): Faculty continue to refine their implementation of the badge topic across multiple courses or multiple offerings of a particular course, share their experiences beyond the IU community, and submit their work for a FACET peer review.

Although the three levels are cumulative, the program allows faculty to apply directly for the advanced level if they already meet the requirements of the basic and proficient levels.

Badge Topics

For the initial launch of the program, we decided on three topics based upon current initiatives: eTexts, online presence, and accessibility. IU's eText initiative aims to reduce textbook costs while also providing new tools for student engagement via faculty and peer notes and highlights within the text (IU eTexts, 2015). IU's Online Learning initiative aims to provide a quality, engaging experience for students across Indiana and beyond, who are taking online courses (IU Online, 2015). Accessibility of IU teaching and learning materials and technology systems is a stated priority that supports learning for all IU students. Beginning with these three topics further encourages the adoption of these technologies and high-quality pedagogical practices regarding their use. Nevertheless, these are only the beginning, with additional topics related to digital education and student engagement planned for future implementation.

Rigor of the Program

The LT/FACET Badges program is intended for all levels of teaching faculty at IU, including tenure-track and tenured faculty, as well as part-time and full-time lecturers. It is critical that the program be rigorous, so badges and accompanying evidence are recognized among peers and by university administration as having value for reporting and potentially for promotion purposes. Early discussion about the project focused on completion of faculty development activities and assessing understanding by quizzing participants about the topic content and concepts. As we moved from thinking about the badge as documenting completion to documenting impact, we wanted to leverage the natural accountability that occurs in and out of the classroom. Faculty are wary of coming across as unprepared and ineffective when trying a new pedagogy or a learning technology in the classroom. Furthermore, faculty hold each other accountable in informal settings such as workshop presentations and showcases of their experience and results, which are central to both the proficient and advanced badge levels. Ultimately, at the advanced level, accountability is even more rigorous with the expectation of presenting or publishing outside of IU and undergoing a faculty peer review conducted by FACET. For some faculty, this peer review would be a valuable addition to their teaching dossier for promotion and tenure. The goal is to provide rigorous micro-credentialing, which will have value for faculty regardless of their level, career stage, and department or school.

A breakthrough in increasing rigor occurred when the task force approached FACET to obtain their review of the entire badge framework process and to gauge their interest in conducting evaluations for the advanced level badges. FACET liked our framework and agreed to oversee peer review for the advanced level badges. Peer review is a well-regarded academic system for establishing rigor in teaching and research efforts. In addition, FACET is an academy of accomplished teachers, recognized for teaching excellence by all levels of the university administration on all IU campuses. Therefore, this review could increase the appeal to all faculty regardless of their tenure status. Details of the peer review process are explained in the evaluation section.

Development

The LT/FACET Badges program started in summer 2014 and, as of summer 2015, continues as a pilot program. As described in the design section, we developed a three-level badge system for each badge topic. Although we selected three topics for the initial launch of the project, we plan to expand our badge offerings, potentially to teaching pedagogy topics beyond learning technologies. Therefore, we sought a framework that could be replicated for any professional development topic related to teaching. We initially developed this framework by taking "online presence" as a sandbox topic. Through an agile development process, we applied the framework to the other two badges to test its generalizability. After several iterations, we created a final framework based on the following criteria: knowledge building, planning and implementation, reflection on practice, sharing with the community, and peer review (Table 24.1).

After applying the three-level badge framework, we presented the eText and Online Presence badges to two faculty members for feedback. These faculty have

TABLE 24.1 Criteria for three-level badge system

	Basic (Bronze)	Proficient (Silver)	Advanced (Gold)
Knowledge Building	Review concept areas (articles, online videos, and other resources)	Meet requirements of Bronze level badge Review additional concept areas	Meet requirements for Silver level badge
Planning and Implementation	Consult with campus CTL on Learning Technology utilization	Implement LT materials/strategies in a real course	Refine your materials/strategies and implement in the same or additional course
Reflection on Practice	Reflect on your planning for utilizing the LT	Reflect on course results Consult with CTL to discuss the implementation of LT in one or more courses	Reflect on experience and results over time
Sharing with the Community		Share at IU	Share beyond IU
Peer Review			FACET peer review

been involved in the related LT initiatives outside of the badging program. Based on their feedback, we created *challenges*, which are activities that faculty need to complete in order to earn a badge at any of the three levels. These challenges mostly involve submitting structured documents that are reflective in nature. Challenges for each badge level are presented in Table 24.2.

The resources for the first two badge levels include topic-relevant resources (e.g., articles, online videos, guidelines, and frameworks) that faculty can opt to review. Most of these resources, including self-paced online modules, were already available and offered to the faculty who consult with the CTLs. There is a close alignment between badge topics and online faculty development modules related to aspects of digital education such as teaching online, hybrid, and flipped courses. The growing list of modules has received a positive reception from faculty and helps us plan future badges beyond the initial three topics.

The majority of the challenges require participants to complete structured documents, including a series of questions to help faculty document and reflect on their planning and implementation of badge topics in their courses. We created these materials as Microsoft Word documents, so faculty can both submit

TABLE 24.2 Challenges for each badge level

Basic (Bronze)	Proficient (Silver)	Advanced (Gold)
• Review resources • Consultation document • Reflection document • Planning document • Samples of course materials (planning)	• Samples of course material (implementation) • Implementation results (course outcomes, reflections) • Consultation document • Evidence of sharing the results within IU	• Refinement document • Further implementation results • Evidence of sharing the results beyond IU • FACET peer review results

them as attachments within the badge system and use them in their teaching reports. In addition, as campus CTLs play a significant role in the badge program, we prepared a guide to help CTL staff consult more effectively with participating faculty.

Badging Technology

We decided to use existing badging systems instead of creating our own. We had several criteria for selecting a digital badge system. First, the system should be compatible with OBI standards. Second, it should be something we could realistically support and maintain. Finally, it should integrate with IU's LMS because:

• Teaching faculty already spend considerable time in the LMS and are familiar with it.
• The LMS is a viable system for developing and presenting content.
• The LMS is a wider academic context in which to develop badges for students related to curricular, cross-curricular, and extra-curricular activities and accomplishments.

Few options satisfied our criteria at the time of our initial explorations of badge systems. Purdue University's Passport was an evolving badging system that met our criteria, and Purdue was seeking partners to test the new product. Passport is an e-portfolio system that demonstrates a user's competencies and achievements through digital badges, which can be shared publicly in Mozilla Backpack, LinkedIn, and Facebook (Passport, 2015). Passport can be used to view a rubric, submit evidence, document progress, receive feedback, and display a badge in supporting platforms. Given our established partnership with Purdue University, we acquired a license for Passport for the pilot phase of the LT/ FACET Badges program.

During the development of the badge framework in Passport, we were able to analyze our needs regarding integration with the LMS. Using the Learning Tools Interoperability (LTI) standard, Passport stores the information in the badging system and passes outcomes such as quiz scores or submission status back to the LMS; we realized in our analysis that we would prefer that the LMS handle information storage and testing when needed and pass this information to the badging system. For this reason, we are alternatively implementing LT/FACET Badges with Accreditrust's BadgeSafe™, an application specially designed for Canvas that also supports exporting badges to Mozilla Backpack for public sharing. We continue to explore other systems as well, including new capabilities in CourseNetworking, an online learning and collaboration environment.

Implementation

We communicate with IU faculty about LT/FACET Badges through email lists and the IU Badges website. This project website provides information about the program objectives, the types of badges offered, and how to participate in the program (Badges@IU, 2015). We ask interested faculty to contact their campus CTL to be added to the program. Once added, the faculty log in to the Passport platform through the Badges project website and can start completing challenges for the topic and badge level they aim to complete. Alternatively, faculty can be added to the LT/FACET Badges site in Canvas to use BadgeSafe™.

In the LT/FACET Badges program, campus CTLs play a key role in supporting faculty as they complete challenges by providing initial consultations and formative feedback for submissions. In their regular work with faculty, CTL consultants establish strong working relationships, which we intend to leverage in the badge program.

Terminology

A question that has arisen during implementation is whether the term "badge" will prove acceptable to faculty or whether some other nomenclature around micro-credentialing is needed. Even though feedback from faculty during the development phase was positive and there is growing recognition of micro-credentials, some faculty react negatively to the term "badge" and may not find the program worthwhile because of its name (Hart, 2015), which points to the need for more research on faculty attitudes towards badging.

Participation

Content modules related to the three badge topics—as well as other topics, such as teaching online, hybrid and flipped courses—have generated considerable interest among faculty. This interest constitutes a first step for faculty in evaluating how far they wish to pursue and document their professional development. More than 225 faculty have requested access to these modules. Interestingly, the strongest initial interest in the LT/FACET Badges has come at the program level. The Gateway Teaching Academy at Indiana University-Purdue University Indianapolis (IUPUI) is a prime example. With a goal of recognizing faculty for their efforts in teaching and professional development, this academy offers three-level advancement (bronze, silver, and gold) and helps more than 400 part-time associate instructors with their promotion applications. As the two programs share goals and a similar framework, the Gateway Academy is very interested in integrating LT/FACET Badges into their program. This integration creates direct incentives for faculty participation. The IUPUI Physical Education & Tourism Management Program, Social Work Program, and School of Health and Rehabilitation Sciences are also interested in encouraging their faculty to participate in the LT/FACET Badges program.

Evaluation

Evaluation of the LT/FACET Badges program includes evaluation of faculty submissions for badge completion at each level, and assessment of the program itself in terms of sustainability and impact for faculty professional development.

Evaluation of Badge Submissions

As explained in the previous section, CTL staff consult with faculty and provide formative feedback on reflections and plans. The centers are also a likely place for faculty to share their experiences and results via workshop presentations, showcases, and informal writing such as blogs. As long as faculty complete the expected documents and activities for the first two levels, they receive a badge.

FACET conducts a peer review evaluation for the completion of the advanced level badge. When participating faculty are ready for the FACET peer review, they make a formal request using the FACET online form. Once FACET assigns a peer reviewer, the faculty participant submits all completed badge materials, a copy of their CV, and a copy of the syllabus for each course in which they implemented the badge topic. After reviewing the materials submitted, the assigned peer reviewer writes a report and shares it with the faculty member. In the report, the peer reviewer ranks the quality of the submitted badge materials as *Excellent*, *Satisfactory*, or *Unsatisfactory*. Learning Technologies then grants the advanced badge for applications with excellent and satisfactory rankings. Unsatisfactory applications are not awarded the gold badge, but faculty can resubmit their applications for FACET peer review after addressing the issues detailed in the report. Peer review usually takes at least six weeks to complete.

Evaluation of the LT Badges Program Success

As we do not yet have any fully completed participation in our pilot program, we are unable to evaluate the success of the LT/FACET Badges program. However, we believe that the program can be considered successful when it:

- Fosters a sense of community and accomplishment among participants;
- Leads to local and national recognition for IU faculty teaching with technology;
- Leverages CTL staff support for faculty teaching with technology;
- Creates a model for other faculty and staff development; and
- Becomes a valued part of faculty incentives and promotion.

Conclusion

The LT/FACET Badges are offered as a means to help IU faculty document their professional development efforts and accomplishments in teaching. Faculty can use the digital badges and evidence they produce in their annual reports, which may also aid their promotion, tenure, and recognition at both the university and national levels. They can also share badges they have earned through digital platforms beyond IU. We recognize that the impact of this program on faculty promotion depends on academic unit (i.e., school and department) buy-in and support. We also recognize that this program may provide different incentives for tenured and adjunct faculty.

The biggest challenges in developing a badge program for faculty development are aligning the program with the university culture, identifying the areas of interest for faculty, supporting university initiatives, and creating a process that fits naturally with faculty activities. We accomplished alignment by framing the badge activities around the process of teaching a course—planning, implementation, reflection, sharing, and documentation.

With LT, the CTLs, and FACET already committed to faculty professional development, the LT/FACET Badge project has provided us a starting place for understanding badging and badge systems. It has also acted as a catalyst for discussions with academic units interested in badging for students within and beyond courses, and with other units interested in the professional development of their staff. All of these interests collectively share a common goal of helping to document, in substantive ways that are sharable within and beyond the university, the tangible accomplishments and abilities of people in the IU community.

Acknowledgments

We thank Jeani Young and Sarah Engel for their helpful suggestions on an earlier draft of this chapter.

References

Badges@IU (2015, January 20). Retrieved from http://badges.iu.edu.

Campus Strategic Plan (2014). *Bicentennial strategic plan for Indiana University Bloomington.* Retrieved from https://strategicplan.iu.edu/.

Empowering People (2009). *Empowering people: Indiana University's strategic plan for information technology.* Retrieved from http://ep.iu.edu/.

Green, K. C. (2013). *Campus computing survey 2013.* Encino, CA: Campus Computing Project. Retrieved May 7, 2014 from www.campuscomputing.net/sites/www.campuscomputing.net/files/CampusComputing2013.pdf.

Hart, M. (2015). Badges: A new measure for professional development. *Campus Technology*, January/February issue. Retrieved from http://campustechnology.com/articles/2015/01/14/badges-a-new-measure-of-professional-development.aspx.

IU eTexts (2015, January 20). Retrieved from http://etexts.iu.edu/.

IU Online (2015, January 20). Retrieved from http://online.iu.edu/.

Passport (2015, February 5). *What is Passport?* Retrieved from www.itap.purdue.edu/studio/passport/.

25

DIGITAL BADGES FOR CONTINUING EDUCATION AT COLORADO STATE UNIVERSITY

Michael Paul Macklin

Project Overview

Program Development

In 2012, Colorado State University (CSU) started investigating the emerging trend of digital badges and committed to piloting a digital badge program that would allow online, non-credit programming to reach a broader audience with a focus on quality instructional design, modality, access, and affordability. CSU's digital badge strategy is rooted in its land-grant mission of providing access to world-class education and research even for those not at the physical campus. Addressing this call, CSU OnlinePlus[1] (the division of continuing education) worked with CSU Extension (one of the University's outreach arms), both of which are divisions of the Office of Engagement, to convert the face-to-face, semester-based curriculum of the Colorado Master Gardener Program[SM] to the online CSU Extension Certified Gardener Program (ECG) (CSU Extension Certified Gardener, 2015).

CSU redefined this online delivery by unbundling the curriculum of the ECG program, and ensured that the curriculum was on-demand, competency-based, and mastery-driven. At its core, the ECG program is designed to expose learners to the latest gardening techniques, such that they become authorities for sharing their gardening expertise. By reimagining its delivery, the ECG program is now differentiated and more responsive to the learners' needs. In this structure students are able to take individual courses, bundle courses, or complete the full program, all while earning digital badges to signal their skill development and achievements. The ECG program and badge strategy around it was also designed to expand the Extension's offerings to a new population of users and customers. A primary goal of the Extension education model is to provide greater access to high-quality programming and curriculum. However, due to geographic and capacity constraints, particularly in a state like Colorado with a significant geographic diversity of mountain passes and remote rural areas, it sometimes becomes difficult for prospective learners to fully engage with and benefit from the traditional Extension structure. Digital badges allowed CSU to address multiple concerns including: providing relevant information regardless of location, time, or place; providing content in digestible modularized courses; and constructing a pricing structure where learners pay for only the information they want to learn versus what is prescribed to them.

Product Development

While CSU was well positioned to develop and implement a badging pilot program, this effort was not without challenges. First, in order to scale-up the digital badge initiative, CSU had to develop a common language and understanding around digital badges. Absent a defining framework, badges, like any emerging market, would invite numerous interpretations and variations of implementation, which could threaten the sustainability and portability of badges. While Mozilla's Open Badge Infrastructure (OBI) provided strong technical guidelines for application, it lacked a standardized framework for how a badge was earned and awarded (Mozilla OpenBadges, 2015). In order to create this needed scaffolding for its badge program, CSU focused on developing standards and hierarchical structures for badges. This structure clarified how badges were earned and awarded, all while promoting student choice and self-directed advancement through the curriculum. Furthermore, this approach ensured credibility through strong assessment and evaluation. Figure 25.1 represents the adopted hierarchy and nomenclature for digital badges. This hierarchy allows for multiple levels of subject exploration.

Additionally, CSU did not feel that existing badge management platforms were robust enough or allowed for the flexibility needed to meet its long-term vision for badges. Ultimately, CSU intends to support the widespread use and application of badges beyond the immediate function of higher education programming. CSU sees tri-sector (public, private, social) applications and future opportunities in badges. After researching options for badge management, CSU forged a partnership with RelevanceLogic, Inc., a Colorado-based company specializing in business intelligence and big data analytics and interpretation, to help develop the CSULogic badge management suite. Figure 25.2 shows the log-in screen to CSULogic that administrators and learners use to gain access to their appropriate functions within the system.

CSU Digital Badge Hierarchy

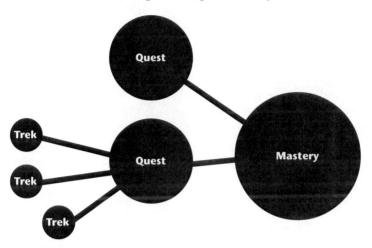

FIGURE 25.1 Illustration of digital badge hierarchy developed at CSU.

FIGURE 25.2 CSULogic login screen branded for the Extension Certified Gardener.

Analysis

Considerations and Challenges

After researching available options and defining needs to execute the badge strategy, CSU prioritized the following steps: developing University-wide standards for digital badges while maintaining compliance with Mozilla's OBI for all of the badges we issue; inventing and developing a one-of-a-kind software application that leverages private big-data analytics, badge management, and social networks; and partnering with The Institute for Learning and Teaching (TILT) at CSU to ensure pedagogical soundness and the development of practical but meaningful learning objectives that are tied to the assessments within the course (TILT Course Design and Development, 2015). Assessments include optional pre-/post-tests, guided discussion boards, lab assignments (to be completed in the field and most often requiring a hands-on component), quizzes, and a mastery exam. These assessments were modified, adapted, and created based on activities that would have traditionally taken place in a face-to-face workshop or course.

One of the largest considerations CSU recognized was that in order to make a granular and unbundled version of a traditional course work, there had to be intentional instructional design alterations. Digital badge courses needed to allow for access to curriculum that was not place or date bound, provided an opportunity for learners to gain mastery of a subject through assessment and evaluation, and increased learner engagement in the online classroom with peers and instructors. Courses in the program range from one to three weeks in length with the expectation that learners spend a minimum of five hours per week engaging with the content, assessments, peers, and instructors.

Ensuring Credibility

To lend credibility to the earning of a badge, a student must receive 80 percent or higher on all assessments to be issued the badge. CSU's badge strategy reflects a critical distinction from some badge initiatives. Trek, quest, and mastery badges are earned by demonstrating a firm grasp of the subject matter. CSU's badges are awarded for students' content mastery and demonstrable change in knowledge. Digital badges in the current iteration are designed to be portable and digestible to allow learners to tool and retool quickly as employers and personal edification dictate while requiring a relatively high level of proficiency. TILT's team of instruction and technology designers collaborated with faculty to develop courses in a way that allowed learners to interact with the curriculum at their own pace while incentivizing progression by only allowing badges to be issued if assessment requirements were achieved. This approach of high-quality and rigorous course material, along with a sound badging ecosystem, shaped the overall badge strategy at CSU and ultimately will help frame the direction of future work. Upcoming projects will require that course material with a potentially large audience of learners be developed with well-articulated learning objectives that are tied directly to assessment and activities.

Design

Badge Ecosystem Design

Once the project was defined, and initial objectives and goals were outlined, it became obvious that an existing solution was not going to provide what CSU needed. Since this was the first badge initiative at the University, we needed to develop the majority of the ecosystem from scratch. The only constant was that we knew we would issue Mozilla OBI compliant badges.

Step 1 – Hierarchy. One of the first objectives CSU tackled in the digital badge program strategy was developing a standard nomenclature and hierarchy for badge programs. Badges and their granular nature are exploratory by design, leading to the creation of Trek, Quest, and Mastery badges.

- *Trek Badges* – Building blocks for Quest badges. They are the most granular level of badge. They can be earned individually, or grouped together to earn a Quest badge.
- *Quest Badges* – Building blocks for Mastery badges. They can be earned individually, or grouped together to earn a Mastery badge.
- *Mastery Badge* – The Mastery badge is earned when the entire program's curriculum has been completed.

Step 2 – Curriculum Map. Working with the content/subject matter expert, we were able to unbundle the existing curriculum into distinct modules. These distinct modules were cross-referenced with search engines, environmental scanning that allowed CSU to build a map of possible progressions and student options. Figure 25.3 shows one version of the ECG curriculum map.

Step 3 – Badge Graphics. Figure 25.4 shows how the badge hierarchy was visually built into the graphic design of the badge. Stars and ribbons show progression in quests and the mastery badge. These small visual cues are intended to provide a game-type feel to leveling-up in the understanding of a subject.

Step 4 – Software Development Design. CSU and RelevanceLogic adopted an iteration of an Agile Development Process (ADP) to improve the business quality of CSULogic by closely aligning the platform development with the required business processes (Sutherland, Viktorov, Blount, & Puntikov, 2007). This ADP approach created frequent deliverables that verified the alignment of work efforts and required process support. It was decided that the first version

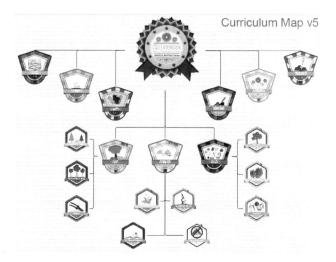

FIGURE 25.3 Expanded curriculum map with badge hierarchy and imagery for Extension Certified Gardener.

FIGURE 25.4 Badge hierarchy with treks leading to quests, leading to a portion of the mastery badge.

of the software would be a web-based application with multiple environments for testing, demonstrations, and new client deployments. Software development design requirements and goals included:

- Focus on end product versus development around existing process;
- Allowance for flexibility and a level of nimbleness that was critical for an evolving product;

- Flexible design based on CSU's badge ecosystem requirements;
- Product development driven by constant feedback between partners looking not only at current need, but also potential future roadmap; and
- Short release cycles.

Development

CSULogic – Badge Management Suite

This software allows for automation of badge delivery and integration with existing CSU systems and is agnostic to learning management systems and student information systems, allowing for deployment across sectors and industries outside of higher education as a licensable product. The platform leverages proprietary big-data analysis tools and social network integration that will allow CSU to keep the curriculum relevant and responsive to learner needs, and to continually evaluate and refine the existing curriculum. This step has been one of the most innovative elements of CSU's digital badge work and is critical to the long-term sustainability of badges. More importantly, CSULogic will support an expanded reach and propel badges into other networks and applications.

Phase 1 – Intelligent Content. This particular element of the strategy is arguably the most innovative. Using a proprietary connection engine, CSU is able to pull data from social sources, courses, and badge interactions, which allows CSU to evaluate and modify courses along with increasing their ability to build courses relevant to potential learner needs. The ConnectionEngine™ is a tool designed to analyze large amounts of unstructured data, and in the case of badges, couple that data with the META data included in badges to help make decisions on future curriculum development. CSU can use content analysis of social media and other sources to find areas for development or enhancement of courses.

Phase 2 – Badge Management Solution. The badge management solution has three core functions: badge development, badge awarding, and badge communications. Badge development is designed for system administrators to develop badges, manage users, and associate relationships between the two. Badge awarding and communications help learners know where they are in the process of earning a badge and provide multiple avenues for interacting with badges that they have earned or are in the process of earning. Figure 25.5 shows the learner portal of the CSULogic system where students can share their badges though social platforms.

Phase 3 – Future Development. Utilizing and expanding on existing social media (e.g., Facebook), we will create a private social learning community (accessible only to parties approved by CSU) that will allow select badge users to contribute, find, and share content. The interaction with this environment will help drive the intelligent content engine, which in turn will provide opportunities for course modification and new course development.

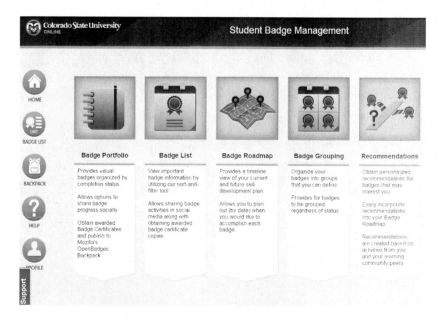

FIGURE 25.5 CSULogic student home page that allows students to interact with badges, go to Mozilla Backpack or request support.

Implementation

Controlled Pilot

In the summer 2014 semester, CSU went into a controlled release of the ECG courses and the beta release of the CSULogic badge management solution. This pilot was intended to provide insight into course quality, process verification, and bug testing of the software solution. This summer 2014 soft-launch had a limited number of registrations allowed, provided many opportunities for feedback, and helped position the program for a successful fall 2014 launch. In summer 2014, CSU allowed a maximum of 10 students per course. Students could register for multiple courses independently, through bundles, or for the full package. In the pilot, there were 13 students who registered for 66 badges associated with the 16 courses. The pilot was also date-based with each course running for a specific length of time and being offered once a semester. In the controlled pilot the instructor provided grade reports to an administrator for verification before issuing a badge, ensuring issuing integrity.

CSULogic Beta. While the students were working their way through the first round of courses, CSU launched a private beta test of CSULogic. This allowed staff and administrators to test all functionality of the system with real data. With confidence from the private beta test, CSU launched the production version of CSULogic, allowing students to login for the first time. E-mail correspondence was personally sent out to each learner letting them know the credentials for the system, functionality of the system, and opportunities for feedback as bugs or technical issues arose. Anecdotally, we noticed that learners in the pilot were primarily interested in the course content and secondarily interested in the badge itself.

Challenges and Modification

Through feedback from learners, users, and administrators, there was opportunity to make some modifications and changes prior to the start of the fall 2014 semester. The first modification was based on student feedback that the date-based course offerings were not conducive to one-to-three week courses. In fall 2014, all courses were modified for on-demand delivery. Learners now receive access to their course within 24 hours of registering and paying. This did require some changes in instruction, which included modification from an instructor-led model to an instructor-facilitated model.

Evaluation

Assessment

The ECG program provides both formative and summative assessments as a part of each course. Formative assessments in the courses include optional discussion board postings where students identify the main points of a video recording or reading. There are also options for students to participate in "test their knowledge" pre- and post-tests to help both learners and teachers understand where there may be issues with the way content is being provided, or with learner deficiencies. Finally, students were allowed options to participate in the "virtual coffee shop" and pursue readings and assessments "beyond the basics." Though valuable for both the learner and the instructor, the true value of the formative assessment allows CSU to continually review and evaluate course content and curriculum for enhancement or modification. The summative assessments are the most tangible for student achievement in the course as these assessments drive the issuing of digital badges. Again, students must achieve a cumulative 80 percent or higher on all summative assessments to earn their badge. These assessments are developed to ensure that students are meeting learning objectives within a particular course. The learning objectives also correlate directly to the criteria to earn the badge. In other terms, badge criteria are defined by learning objectives that are proven through summative assessment.

Program Outcomes

Since the launch in the summer of 2014 to February 15, 2015, CSU has awarded more than 130 digital badges to over 50 learners from across the United States.

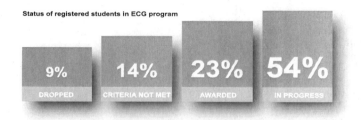

FIGURE 25.6 Current status of students in the Extension Certified Gardener program from May 2014 to December 2014.

The primary location of learners is in the state of Colorado, but interest in the program spans beyond the geographical boundaries of Colorado. Learners have various motivations for enrolling—from pure edification with no desire to earn a badge to green industry professionals being required to take it by their employers. Completion rates of badges at CSU are greater than massively open online courses (MOOC's). MOOC completion rates range from 0.9 percent to 36.1 percent, with completion rates of 5 percent being typical (Jordan, 2014). Interaction with badges upon completion also varies. Some students will share badges on social media in the form of a Facebook post or Tweet. Others utilize CSULogic's baked badges to publish to Mozilla's Badge Backpack. CSU is also working with green industry professionals and organizations to foster the conversation of the ECD badge to the standard for training in the industry and a consumer-recognized symbol of knowledge and expertise.

Figure 25.6 shows the current status of students in the ECG program from May 2014 to December 2014.

The figure highlights that even though learners are registering and paying for courses, not all of them are completing the required assessments to earn the badges. In a traditional course structure, it would be concerning if only 23 percent of students completed the course. However, in the badging structure, this is less alarming. The purpose of the badge model is to allow students to self-select into the information and learning they want and need instead of providing more information than they require. The first semester of data, as reflected in Figure 25.3, was for the courses being offered on a date-specific schedule, while the remaining data was for on-demand offerings; while the completion rate did not dramatically change, the number of registrations greatly increased.

Conclusions

It is generally difficult to move into any emerging market. That said, it can be an extremely rewarding experience knowing that the badge initiative at CSU is helping to advance educational opportunity by lowering cost, increasing access to high-quality content, and providing learners with options to manage their credentials and portfolio. Utilizing digital badges, CSU has a way to connect learning objectives, skills, and competencies into educational pathways in P-12, post-secondary learning, and on the job learning on a shared platform. With a project that encompasses multiple sectors and many partners, it is important to focus on coalition and consensus building. Success of digital badges lies in the ability of those involved in projects like these to set aside institutional differences and focus on the larger good of providing access to education in new ways to address changes in learners and generations to come.

With less than one year's data and a continually changing environment, the ECG program can be considered an emerging success. Enrollments continue to trend upward and badges as a whole are increasing in adoption (based on the interaction with badges in CSULogic summer 2014 versus fall 2014). Next steps in the strategy include expanding the portfolio of offerings and building partnerships with P-12 and higher education institutions, private industry, and government agencies to increase educational opportunities. Utilizing the CSULogic platform, we feel that there's an opportunity to scale-up operations and facilitate large numbers of learners from across the world, providing them with just-in-time education from a multitude of educational providers.

Note

1 Since the time of submission, Colorado State University OnlinePlus has been renamed to Colorado State University Online.

References

CSU Extension Certified Gardener (2015). Retrieved July 14, 2015 from Colorado State University Online, CSU Extension Certified Gardener website, www.online.colostate .edu/badges/certified-gardener/.

Jordan, K. (2014). Initial trends in enrolment and completion of massive open online courses. *The International Review of Research in Open and Distributed Learning*, 15(1). Retrieved from www.irrodl.org/index.php/irrodl/article/view/1651/2774.

Mozilla OpenBadges (2015). Retrieved July 14, 2015 from Mozilla Foundation, OpenBadges About website, http://openbadges.org/about/.

Sutherland, J., Viktorov, A., Blount, J., & Puntikov, N. (2007, January). Distributed Scrum: Agile Project Management with Outsourced Development Teams. In IEEE HICSS 40th Annual Hawaii International Conference on System Systems, 2007 (p. 274a). doi: 10.1109/HICSS.2007.180.

TILT Course Design and Development (2015). Retrieved July 14, 2015 from The Institute for Learning and Teaching, TILT Course Design and Development website, http://tilt.colostate.edu/courseDD/.

ABOUT THE AUTHORS

Serdar Abaci is the Educational Research and Evaluation Specialist for the Learning Technologies division of University Information Technology Services at Indiana University. Dr. Abaci conducts research on and evaluation of teaching and learning technologies. His research interests include feedback, online learning, program evaluation, and teaching and learning technologies in higher education. Dr. Abaci received his PhD in Instructional Systems Technology from Indiana University.

Samuel Abramovich is Assistant Professor of Education Informatics in the Graduate School of Education at the University at Buffalo—SUNY. Dr. Abramovich uses the learning sciences to unpack how emerging technology can be best used for students in both formal and informal learning. He has also circumnavigated the earth.

Iryna Ashby is a doctoral student in the Learning Design and Technology program in the College of Education at Purdue University (West Lafayette, IN). She is part of the evaluation team for the Transdisciplinary Experience. Her research interests focus on competency-based learning and learning culture.

Zane L. Berge is Professor in the Training Systems graduate programs at the University of Maryland, Baltimore County campus. He teaches graduate courses involving training in the workplace and distance education. Prior to UMBC, Dr. Berge was founder and director of the Center for Teaching and Technology, Georgetown University, Washington, DC, where he first combined his background in business with educational technology working in the areas of online scholarly journals and discussion lists, and online education and training. Today, he specializes in distance education and online learning.

Melissa L. Biles is an adjunct professor in the Educational Communication and Technology programs at New York University and a doctoral student researcher based out of the CREATE Consortium for Research and Evaluation of Advanced Technology in Education. Her research focuses on the design and evaluation of cognitive and socio-emotional aspects of digital media and learning games through the use of tools such as biometrics, learning analytics, and data mining.

Brett Bixler (PhD, Instructional Systems) has more than 30 years of experience in the instructional design field. He is the Lead Instructional Designer with Training Services, part of Information Technology Services (ITS) at Penn State. In his current position, Brett is working with the latest educational technologies and learning theories to produce learner-centered active and collaborative learning environments. Brett is actively investigating the use of games, simulations, and virtual worlds for educational purposes. He created the Educational Gaming Commons (see http://gaming.psu.edu) to support collaboration and initiatives in these areas throughout Penn State.

Rhonda D. Blackburn is VP, Instructional Services and Chief Academic Officer at LoudCloud and an adjunct faculty in the Masters of Distance Education and E-Learning at University of Maryland University College. Dr. Blackburn's professional portfolio includes Competency-Based Education and e-Learning initiatives.

Lucas Blair is a game designer and co-founder of Little Bird Games, a serious game development company. He received an MS in Instructional Technology from Bloomsburg University and a PhD in Modeling and Simulation from the University of Central Florida. His doctoral research explored the use of video game achievements to enhance player performance, self-efficacy, and motivation.

Kyle Bowen is the Director of Education Technology Services at Penn State University where he provides leadership for developing and cultivating innovative uses of technology to advance teaching and learning. A regular speaker on educational technology and the use of digital badges, Kyle's work on the topic has appeared in the *New York Times*, *U.S. News & World Report*, and the *Chronicle of Higher Education*.

Gi Woong Choi is a PhD candidate in Learning, Design, and Technology and a graduate research assistant in Education Technology Services at the Pennsylvania State University. His research interests include informal learning, mobile learning, learning technologies, and HCI in education.

Christine Chow is a consultant and a graduate of the Learning, Design, and Technology program in the Graduate School of Education at Stanford University.

Katie Davis is an Assistant Professor at The University of Washington Information School. Davis is the co-author with Howard Gardner of

The App Generation: How Today's Youth Navigate Identity, Intimacy, and Imagination in a Digital World (2013, Yale University Press). She holds two Master's degrees and a doctorate in Human Development and Education from Harvard Graduate School of Education.

Anne Derryberry is a strategic advisor to learning institutions and learning technology providers. She is a founding member of the Badge Alliance and co-instructor of the MOOC, "Badges: New Currency for Professional Credentials."

Leanne Edwards is a Lead Ambassador for the Passport to Success digital badge initiative in the Corona-Norco Unified School District and 3D Modeling and Printing teacher at her intermediate school site. Ms. Edwards has experience in both elementary and secondary education and has been instrumental in researching intermediate student motivation in digital badging.

Jeffrey Evans is the Interim Director of Learning Innovation and Interim Associate Dean of Undergraduate Programs in the Polytechnic Institute at Purdue University. Dr. Evans teaches computer technology and competency-based learning experiences bridging technology and the humanities. His research focuses on combining computing with the fine arts.

Deborah Everhart is a strategist and innovator, analyzing trends in education and designing holistic solutions for learning and teaching. She is co-instructor of the MOOC, "Badges: New Currency for Professional Credentials."

Marisa Exter is an Assistant Professor of Learning Design and Technology in the College of Education at Purdue University (West Lafayette, IN). Dr. Exter's research aims to provide recommendations to improve or enhance university-level design and technology programs. She teaches courses related to evaluation and assessment, human performance technology, educational multimedia and software development, and instructional design research methods. She also leads the evaluation team for the Transdisciplinary Experience.

Joseph R. Fanfarelli is an Assistant Professor of Digital Media at the University of Central Florida. Dr. Fanfarelli's research focuses on video games for teaching and learning, digital badges, and research evaluation.

Jason Fish is the Director of Teaching and Learning Technologies at Purdue University, where he leads a team of innovators in creating groundbreaking tools that empower instructors and students in their teaching and learning missions. His organization has been recognized nationally and internationally for its contributions in the field of educational technology.

Chris Gamrat is an instructional designer for the College of Information Sciences & Technology at Penn State University. He develops and supports the College's Masters of Professional Studies degree programs. Chris was the principal investigator and lead researcher in a Penn State-funded grant to build a university-wide badging system. Chris is also a doctoral candidate in the Learning, Design, & Technology program in Penn State University's College of Education. He is currently focusing his research on the use of digital badges to support personalization in learning.

David A. Goodrum is the Director of Teaching & Learning Technologies for University Information Technology Services at Indiana University. Mr. Goodrum serves as chair of both the Learning Technologies Support and Implementation Team and the Next.IU Strategy Team, which have conducted pilot evaluations and functional analysis of three learning management systems and related collaboration and media management tools. Mr. Goodrum is currently completing his doctorate of education in Instructional Systems Technology at Indiana University. For his dissertation, he is studying the models for user evaluation of learning management systems within a higher education institution decision context.

Sheryl L. Grant is Director of Badge Research for HASTAC at Duke University. Her research focuses on value sensitive design, reputation and badge systems, identity management, digital media and learning, and technology adoption. She is author of What Counts as Learning: Open Digital Badges for New Opportunities, based on lessons learned from the 30 Badges for Lifelong Learning projects during their first year of design.

Janet Gregory is currently the Deputy Vice-Chancellor and Chief Executive Officer of Swinburne University of Technology Sarawak Campus in Malaysia, having commenced in this role in July 2015. Prior to taking on her position in Sarawak, Professor Gregory was the Professor of Learning Innovations in the Learning Transformations Unit at Swinburne, where she led initiatives for changing practices in the design and delivery of courses to enhance quality through the provision of more innovative and engaging learning experiences for students.

Daniel Hickey is Professor and Program Coordinator for the Learning Sciences program in the School of Education at Indiana University.

Pamela M. Karagory is a clinical assistant professor in Purdue University's School of Nursing. Also serving as director of Undergraduate Program and Director of Continuing Education at the Purdue University School of Nursing, Professor Karagory helped incorporate digital badges into the university's undergraduate nursing curriculum.

Julie Keane leads research and evaluation for all VIF programs, contributes to professional development curriculum design, and is a key contributor to the development of VIF's digital badging system. She holds a PhD in education from the University of North Carolina at Chapel Hill, and a Master's in political science from the Graduate Center of the City University of New York.

Kristen Kirby is a clinical assistant professor at Purdue University's School of Nursing, a board certified family nurse practitioner, and a certified nurse educator. Professor Kirby has spent her time at Purdue integrating Lean quality improvement and implementing a digital badge platform in Purdue's School of Nursing undergraduate curriculum.

Eve Klein is Portal to the Public Manager at Pacific Science Center in Seattle, Washington, and holds a Master's of Education degree from the State University of New York at Buffalo.

Erin Knight currently runs Badge Labs, a firm focused on catalyzing a new culture of learning, identity, and hiring. Formerly, she spearheaded the development of Open Badges through the Mozilla Foundation and the Badge Alliance. Erin is co-instructor of the MOOC, "Badges: New Currency for Professional Credentials."

Leslie Lipscomb works in collaboration with the product development team to design and develop VIF's online learning platform and has been integral to building VIF's digital badging system. She primarily focuses on developing an information architecture to support digital badging, user interactivity, database reporting, e-commerce, communications, systems integration, and interoperability with learning management systems. Leslie holds both an MAEd in instructional technologies and curriculum design and a BS in psychology from Virginia Polytechnic Institute.

Kulari Lokuge Dona is the Associate Director of eLearning at Monash College. Dr. Lokuge Dona was one of the lead designers and moderators of the Carpe Diem MOOC that was delivered by Swinburne University of Technology. She has been involved in learning technology since 2001 as a senior lecturer, instructional designer, assessment developer, and electronic learning facilitator.

Michael Paul Macklin is the Director of New Product Development at Colorado State University (CSU) (Fort Collins, CO), CSU's division of continuing education. Mr. Macklin directs digital badge initiatives and programming at CSU. His primary focuses are professional development, non-credit programming, and digital badge software development and management. Through Mr. Macklin's work with digital badges, he is leveraging the power of outreach extension education—the core of the land-grant university model.

He understands that digital badges are key in sustaining and expanding the land-grant system as this initiative allows for unprecedented access to affordable and credible information.

Sorin Adam Matei is an Associate Professor in the Brian Lamb School of Communication, Director of Research for Computational Social Science in the Cyber Center, and Discovery Park fellow at Purdue University (West Lafayette, IN). His area of research focuses on knowledge communities in a variety of settings.

Ştefania Matei is a PhD student in Sociology at the Faculty of Sociology and Social Work, University of Bucharest. She is collaborating as a researcher in the projects "Sociological Imagination and Disciplinary Orientation in Applied Social Research" and "Human-Computer Interaction in Collaborative Learning." Her research interests focus on technological mediation and digital cultures. She aims to contribute, in the long run, with postphenomenological insights into the role of technology, temporality, and social organization in situations of collective remembrance and knowledge-making.

Rudy McDaniel is Associate Professor of Digital Media and Assistant Dean of Research and Technology at the University of Central Florida. Dr. McDaniel's research focuses on narrative media and video games for teaching and learning, digital badges, and organizational knowledge management.

April M. Moore is the Director of Educational Technology at Corona-Norco Unified School District (Norco, CA). Dr. Moore oversees educational technology and programs promoting college and career readiness for all students. She led the development and implementation of digital badging in CNUSD.

Anastasia S. Morrone is Professor of Educational Psychology at Indiana University School of Education and Associate Vice President for Learning Technologies in the Office of the Vice President for Information Technology. Dr. Morrone provides leadership for several important university-wide initiatives designed to create rich learning environments that promote increased student learning and engagement. Her current research interests focus on technology-rich, active learning environments. Dr. Morrone received her PhD in educational psychology from the University of Texas at Austin.

Lin Y. Muilenburg, PhD, is an Associate Professor of Educational Studies at St. Mary's College of Maryland, teaching graduate courses in educational technology, instructional design, and teaching methods. Her research interests include blended and mobile learning, digital badges, educational uses of Web 2.0 tools, and K12 technology integration. Dr. Muilenburg was a 2014–2015 Fulbright Scholar in Slovenia.

Jamie Oberdick is an associate editor, publications, with Teaching and Learning with Technology at Penn State. He has 17 years' experience writing about technology, including the last ten years involving technology's profound impact on higher education. He has worked with leaders and innovators in educational technology fields, such as digital badging, multimedia development, course management systems, and online learning.

Mark Otter leads strategic and operational processes at VIF International Education. He is responsible for facilitating growth, sales, and marketing strategy and for turning broad ideas into innovative market-ready products, platforms, and programs. Mark holds a BS in biology and a BEd in secondary math and science from Acadia University, and an MAEd in education leadership from Concordia University.

Tamara Oxley manages marketing initiatives and operations and supports brand strategy for VIF International Education. Tamara holds a Master's degree in media and cultural studies from The University of Texas at Austin, and a BA in communications from the University of North Carolina at Chapel Hill.

Denise Paster, an Assistant Professor of English in Composition and Rhetoric, directs the First-Year Composition Program at Coastal Carolina University, where she also teaches writing courses, from first-year composition to graduate seminars in comp theory. Her scholarly interests include writing program administration and digital literacies; she is currently writing an inquiry-based composition textbook that invites students to investigate the intersections of college writing, new literacies, and the discourses of Web 2.0 in systematic ways.

Ekaterina Pechenkina is Researcher at the Learning Transformations Unit and Affiliate Researcher with Swinburne Institute for Social Research, Swinburne University of Technology. Dr. Pechenkina's current research interests focus on identity, education, and technology. Dr. Pechenkina received her PhD in cultural anthropology from the University of Melbourne.

Kyle Peck is Professor of Education and Co-director of the Center for Online Innovation in Learning (COIL) at Penn State University. His research and teaching focus on emerging technologies and their impact on learning and teaching.

Sam Piha is the founder and principal of Temescal Associates, a consulting group dedicated to building the capacity of leaders and organizations in education and youth development who are serious about improving the lives of young people.

Jan L. Plass, PhD, Paulette Goddard Professor of Digital Media and Learning Sciences in the Steinhardt School of Culture, Education, and Human Development at New York University, co-directs the Games for Learning Institute. He is the founding director of the CREATE Consortium for Research and Evaluation of Advanced Technology in Education, and directs the programs in Educational Communication and Technology at NYU MAGNET. Dr. Plass' research is at the intersection of cognitive science, learning sciences, and design, and seeks to enhance the effectiveness of interactive visual environments for learning. His current focus is on cognitive and emotional design patterns for simulations and games for math and science education and cognitive skills development.

Stella C. S. Porto is a Learning & Knowledge Management Specialist at the Inter-American Development Bank and an adjunct faculty in the Masters of Distance Education and E-Learning at University of Maryland University College, where she was the former director until 2014. Porto holds a doctorate in Computer Science and master's degree in Computer Science and Distance Education. Dr. Porto's professional activities involve e-learning projects for both adult education and professional training, with a focus in technology and management (http://sporto.wordpress.com).

Barton K. Pursel is the Faculty Programs Coordinator for Teaching and Learning with Technology at the Pennsylvania State University, where he works to align educational technology initiatives with faculty collaborators. Pursel is also the Co-Director of the Center for Online Innovation and Learning. His research focuses on the intersection of pedagogy and technology, specifically analytics, gaming, and Massive Open Online Courses (MOOCs).

Victoria Raish is the Online Learning Librarian at Pennsylvania State University. She is also a PhD candidate in the field of Learning, Design, and Technology. She has designed and implemented digital badges in a variety of contexts. Her research interests focus on online learning, the systemic perspectives on online learning, learning technologies for distance education students, and the experience of distance education students. Most recently, she was on a team developing information literacy digital badges for library instruction. In addition, she is interested in using digital badges as a supplement to virtual experiences for students in online learning environments.

Daniel L. Randall is a doctoral candidate in Instructional Psychology and Technology. His research interests include online learning in higher education, competency-based learning, and collaborative innovation. He is co-designer of the EdTec Badges (http://iptedtec.org). His research is available on his website, http://DanRandall.com.

Alan J. Reid is Assistant Professor of First-Year Writing and Instructional Technologies at Coastal Carolina University. In addition to teaching English courses in Composition and New Media, he is an Assessment & Evaluation Analyst in the Center for Research and Reform in Education at Johns Hopkins University and teaches Instructional Design & Technology courses in the ID&T doctoral program at Old Dominion University. His research focuses on metacognition, self-regulation, and uses and gratifications in new media.

Emily Rimland is the Sally W. Kalin Librarian for Learning Innovations at Penn State. She enjoys providing instruction, reference, and outreach services to undergraduate students. Her research interests include the following: pedagogical innovation and effective learning methodologies; the application of emerging technologies to library services; and instructional technologies. She was recently selected to be a Teaching and Learning with Technology Faculty Fellow at Penn State where her fellowship focused on digital badges.

Răzvan Rughiniş is a Professor at the Department of Computer Science, University Politehnica of Bucharest. His research focuses on human–computer interaction, security issues in computer networks, and the Internet of Things. He is also a co-founder of Tech Lounge Association, supporting the entrepreneurship culture in the ICT community, and a co-founder of Korect, an educational software company.

Chris Stubbs is the Manager of Emerging Technology and Media within the Pennsylvania State University Teaching and Learning with Technology group (TLT). Chris is responsible for strategically exploring and evaluating emerging technologies and trends to assess their potential to improve teaching and learning. In addition, he also oversees Penn State's Educational Gaming Commons (EGC), a group dedicated to the development and support of educational games and related tools and technologies, including Penn State's Digital Badging Platform.

Andrea Thomas is a technology writer at Purdue University (West Lafayette, IN), where she has been researching and documenting the university's success with its homegrown digital badge platform, Passport, as well as other innovative teaching and learning technologies.

Jacklyn J. Thompson is an e-learning professional with interests ranging from student success and wellness in distance learning to CBE and alternative and creative credentialing methods. She works as a virtual writing tutor for The Graduate School at UMUC as well as Pearson Smarthinking.

Phil Tietjen is a doctoral student in the Learning, Design, and Technology program at Penn State University. His general research areas include Computer-Supported Collaborative Learning (CSCL), the Learning Sciences, and research methods for studying online communities. Currently, he is finishing work on a dissertation that investigates knowledge building in open source software communities.

Peter Wardrip is a learning scientist at the Children's Museum of Pittsburgh and a visiting researcher at the University of Pittsburgh. Dr. Wardrip designs and studies ambitious learning experiences in and out of school. He has also through-hiked the Appalachian Trail.

Richard E. West is an Associate Professor in Instructional Psychology and Technology at Brigham Young University. He researches learning environments to support collaborative innovation, online social learning and presence, and effective strategies for K-16 technology integration. He is co-designer of the EdTec Badges (http://iptedtec.org).

James E. Willis III is a Research Associate in the Center for Research on Learning and Technology at Indiana University.

Heather Toomey Zimmerman is an Associate Professor in the Learning, Design, and Technology Program at Penn State University. Her research interests include culturally responsive learning environments for youth, mobile comput-ers, informal learning, and designing for learning across settings. She co-leads the Mobile and Augmented Learning Research Group: http://sites.psu.edu/augmentedlearning/ and http://sites.psu.edu/heatherzimmerman/.

INDEX